*Year of the Lord*

# Year of the Lord

*by Charles W. Meister*

‡ *A.D. Eighteen Forty-Four* ‡

*McFarland & Company, Inc., Publishers*
*Jefferson, North Carolina, & London*
*1983*

2/95

**Library of Congress Cataloging in Publication Data**

Meister, Charles W., 1917–
  *Year of the Lord.*

  Bibliography: p.
  Includes index.
  1. Religions – History – 19th century. 2. History,
Modern – 19th century. 3. Eighteen forty-four, A.D.
I. Title.
BL98.M44 1983      280'.09'034      82-23976

ISBN 0-89950-037-4

Manufactured in the United States of America

*gift*

To Ellie, my wife
who exemplifies the fruit of the Spirit
love, joy, peace
gentleness, goodness, faith

# Contents

# 1
## The Year 1844

The resumption of the cold war between the United States and the Soviet Union has caused the editors of the *Bulletin of the Atomic Scientists* to move the hands on the doomsday clock to two minutes before midnight. Midnight on the doomsday clock is the predicted period of the start of an ultimate nuclear war.

Dr. George Wald, Harvard University biologist who won the Nobel Prize in 1967, says, "I think human life is threatened as never before on this planet. Many perils are coming to a head at about the same time. I am one of those scientists who finds it hard to see how the human race is to bring itself much past the year 2000."

Dr. Norman Borlaug, who spearheaded "the Green Revolution," in which agricultural technology produced grain super-strains to help bolster food production to meet growing population needs, now admits that the increased oil prices will defeat the revolutionary effort to avoid famine, since cheap petroleum is needed for fertilizers and insecticides, as well as oil and gas for farm machinery. Hal Lindsey, in *The 1980's: Countdown to Armageddon*, quotes Dr. Borlaug as saying that he believes the hunger and misery of millions of people will provoke "a great global holocaust."

Not all prophets of doom are scientists. Millions of religious believers are becoming increasingly convinced that the signs of the times indicate that the world, as we know it, will soon end. Countless Christians expect Christ to return soon, as the beginning of the times of the end. A feeling of expectant millennialism is in the air. This is not the first time that the world has been deeply stirred by such feelings. This book will describe a previous period when many people had apocalyptic expectations.

Inflation, economic recession, high unemployment, disgust with the two major political parties, the feeling that the end of the world is coming, waves of religious fervor, the rise of far-out cults, fear of loss of family values, concern for the loss of individual liberty, a protest against the spread of materialism, a fervent plea for women's rights — the concerns of Americans in the year 1844 sound suspiciously similar to the concerns of modern Americans. Since so many modern problems have been met before, in one form or another, it is worthwhile to take a look at how our forebears reacted to these problems.

1

What is so significant about the year 1844? Particularly, what were the religious events that led some people to call it the "Year of the Lord"?

First of all, thousands of devout Christians eagerly expected Christ to return that year. So deep was the advent feeling that a major denomination, the Seventh-day Adventists, was born out of the ashes of the Great Disappointment when Christ did not appear.

Next, Joseph and Hyrum Smith were murdered in the Carthage, Illinois, jail that year. Mormonism, which had been nearly fatally split over the polygamy issue, rallied to become one of America's fastest growing religious movements.

Samuel F. B. Morse, in demonstrating to members of Congress that their $30,000 appropriation for his telegraph was a good investment, used the biblical message, "What hath God wrought." Little wonder—Morse was a born-again Christian, a Bible fundamentalist, whose deep faith in God kept him going when it seemed that all the world had turned against him.

Margaret Fuller, Emerson's transcendentalist friend who later took an active part in the Italian republican movement, wrote in 1844 the first great statement for women's equal rights in America. She pinned her argument on one significant belief—women, as well as men, are the works of One Creator, and a Heavenly Father of love and justice would not show partiality among His children.

In England, John Henry Newman brought to a head his intellectual struggle over whether his Anglican Church or the Roman Catholic Church was God's true church. His book on the development of church doctrine, which he wrote that year and which brought him into the Roman fold, is a landmark in modern theology, a work that had a significant influence upon the ideas of the Vatican II Council of 1962.

Russia's leading writer, Nikolai Gogol, in 1844 took a drastic step. Caught up in a wave of Orthodox fanaticism, he repudiated his great masterpieces, *The Inspector General* and *Dead Souls,* and he vowed henceforth to spend his time on two projects: purification of his soul before the Almighty and persuasion of his family and friends to do likewise. Great literary creativity was lost as Gogol sought an ever purer spiritual life.

In China a young teacher who had been converted to Christianity, Hung Hsiu-ch'üan, started on his quest to overthrow the corrupt Manchu dynasty. He nearly succeeded. Had he, it is quite possible that modern China would be Christian instead of communist. In his wake, his movement, the Taiping rebellion, left twenty million Chinese dead.

In Iran a young man, Mirza Ali Muhammad, afterward called the Bab, reported having a visitation from God, telling him that a new prophet was about to appear, one who would usher in a new era of world peace. Thus was born a new world religion, the Baha'i faith, which synthesizes all of the major world religions into a united faith for a world brotherhood of man under the Fatherhood of God.

Was it a coincidence that there were world-wide religious revelations in 1844? Carl Jung, the Swiss psychoanalyst, would answer "No!" Jung believed in the concept of synchronicity, which implies that there is a deep but hidden significance to the simultaneous occurrence of seemingly unrelated events. The will of God, working through the universal collective unconscious, brings about happenings, the meanings of which our conscious minds can but dimly perceive.

What were some of the specific religious events of 1844? Foremost was the preparation for the second coming of Christ, for many thousands of people believed that the "times of the end" had arrived.

Millennial thinking had long been in the air. The great scientist Isaac Newton had stated a commonly held belief that most modern Christian churches were no longer practicing New Testament Christianity. Newton believed that God was preparing the final times, getting ready to establish His millennial kingdom. Newton felt that God would send a new prophet to help mankind interpret the signs of the times.

Since the Great Awakening under Jonathan Edwards in New England, there had been an expectancy of Christ's second coming. Edwards interpreted the wholesale conversion at his revivals as signs of the end of time. People like Thomas Prince saw the French and Indian wars as "opening a way to enlighten the utmost regions of America" in preparation for the millennial reign. There was a widespread belief among American clergy of the millennial role to be played by the United States. Swarms of new immigrants each year arrived in a land which gave not only material satisfaction but perhaps more important the vague promise of becoming the long-awaited Kingdom of God upon earth.

In the year 1844, after the Great Disappointment, two persons reported millennial visions that became foundation pillars of the Seventh-day Adventist Church. In October Hiram Edson reported a vision in which Christ had entered the Most Holy Place in the heavenly sanctuary, thus initiating the beginning stages of the last judgment. In December Ellen Harmon reported having had two visions concerning the times of the end, and the necessity of having to confess Christ as savior before He came as the Heavenly Bridegroom to claim His bride, the church members.

The Second Great Awakening of the 1820's brought millennial thinking to a high peak. Charles Finney, a New England lawyer, reported having a Saul-like conversion experience. A changed man, he moved to western New York and became a great preacher. His combination of logic with vivid scenes of hell led thousands into conversion statements. One of his key phrases at the huge revivals was "Behold, I come quickly" (Revelation 22:7). In the mid-1830's Finney said, "If the church will do her duty, the millennium may come to this country in three years."

The churches that participated most vigorously in the great revivals of the period were the ones that grew fastest. By 1855 two revivalist churches, the Methodists and the Baptists, constituted about 70% of the Protestant membership in the United States.

The evangelical fervor fit right in with the revolution that Jacksonian democracy was accomplishing in American political life. Revivalism brought religion to the common people in a language they understood. It brushed aside denominational differences. It permitted women to pray as equals with men, and it lifted the laity to the level of the clergy. Above all, it stressed the importance of the individual soul in the sight of God. Just as Emerson was saying that every person could connect his soul directly with the Over-Soul (his name for God), the convert at the camp meeting felt tremendous inner joy and peace as the Holy Spirit seized possession of his heart.

John L. O'Sullivan, the Jacksonian editor, said that the United States was "destined to manifest to mankind the excellence of divine principles; to establish on earth the noblest temple ever dedicated to the worship of the Most High, governed by God's moral law of equality, the law of brotherhood." Hundreds of editors, orators, and citizens made similar statements throughout the 1840's.

When he published his popular *History of the United States* in 1834, George Bancroft drove home two major themes: liberty, and the United States as God's specially chosen nation. One reviewer said in jest that Bancroft wrote his country's history as if it were the story of God's Kingdom on earth.

"We are all a little mad here," wrote Emerson to Thomas Carlyle in 1840. "Not a reading man but has the draft of a new community in his pocket." The majority of the nearly fifty Utopian communities founded from 1830 to 1850 were based on deeply-felt religious principles.

For example, when the German immigrant William Keil founded the Bethel community in Shelby County, Missouri, in 1844, he alleged to be God's special messenger, one of the two witnesses mentioned in Revelation 11:3. The Amana community, established by Christian Metz near Buffalo between 1842 and 1844, was a German pietistic group, who moved to Iowa in 1855. Even the Skaneateles community in Onondaga County, New York, which professed disbelief in all religions, followed the precepts of Jesus because "they are true in themselves, and best adapted to promote the happiness of the race."

The year 1844 marked the high point of the Fourierist movement in the United States. That year Albert Brisbane and Horace Greeley persuaded George Ripley to convert Brook Farm into a Fourier-type phalanx, a self-contained economic unit that would endeavor to meet all its needs from within the community. Also that year Ripley was elected national president of Fourierist associations. Emerson, of course, remained unimpressed by collectives. "Fourier," he said, "had skipped no fact but one, namely, Life. Life scorns systems."

Several existing perfectionist communities hit crises in 1844. The Harmony community, which George Rapp had organized in 1805 on the basis of biblical passages, was so sure of Christ's imminent second coming that sexual virginity was required for membership, on the ground that the 144,000 persons mentioned as saved in Revelation 7:4 were expected to be virgins. As the religious excitement peaked in 1844, "Father" Rapp and his followers prepared to travel to Jerusalem to be ready to live and reign with Christ for a thousand years.

The Shakers were known as the Millennial Church, since their proper title was the United Society of Believers in Christ's Second Coming. Ann Lee, their chief prophet, taught that God is both male and female — that Christ came in man's form in Jesus and in woman's form in herself. Her important role was described in an anonymous work published in 1808, *The Testimony of Christ's Second Appearing*. The Shakers considered themselves to be "the Church of the Last Dispensation," since they believed that judgment day, and the beginning of Christ's kingdom on earth, dated from the establishment of their church. They believed they could communicate with the spirits of the dead. Like some other groups, they had holy hills, and secret stones with mystical inscriptions on them. "The Midnight Cry" was a ritual they used in which members went through buildings singing and calling fellow members to midnight services.

In 1843 a Shaker, Philemon Stuart, published a book called *The Holy, Sacred, and Divine Roll and Book, from the Lord God of Heaven to the Inhabitants of the Earth*. Stuart reported that an angel had appeared to him, warning humans to obey the commands of "the Blessed Son, either in his first or second coming." Although Stuart had scant education, the style is that of the King James Bible. One part of the book contained believers' testimony as to the divine origin of the book.

In 1844 Shaker seances were at a peak. It was alleged that Shakers met the spirits of Bible characters, including four mysterious angels. By the end of the year, when spirit manifestations seemed to decline, it was explained that Mother Ann Lee had left them temporarily, in order to re-enter the outside world in an effort to help redeem it.

Spiritualism was in high gear. Its chief proponent at the time was "the Poughkeepsie seer," Andrew Jackson Davis. Davis reported having a trance in March 1844 in which he had encountered the spirits of the Greek physician Galen and the Swedish mystic Emanuel Swedenborg. The spirits, he said, had commissioned him to "help Christ to regulate mankind." He stated that while in a trance he dictated an 800-page book on revelation. A professor of Hebrew at the University of New York, George Rush, endorsed the book, giving it semi-official acceptance. The book went through 34 editions in less than thirty years, a tribute to the credulity of the people of the period.

Reform societies multiplied like land-office sales. William Lloyd Garrison was active in six reform groups, Theodore Parker in seven, and Horace Greeley in eleven. Dorothea Dix, a Boston school teacher, began her career as a social reformer as a result of a Sunday School class taught in a prison. Her surveys of conditions in jails and mental institutions led to rapid improvements in both kinds of facilities. The Association of Medical Superintendents of American Institutions for the Insane was founded in 1844. Influenced by Dix, Warden Edmonds of Sing Sing prison initiated a series of reforms that year. He also helped organize the New York Prison Association in New York City in 1844.

While preparing a lecture on geology that year "the Learned Blacksmith," Elihu Burritt, was suddenly struck by the unity of the earth and the interdependency of its parts. So he turned his talk into a peace lecture, and he became the leading pacifist of the period. His linguistic expertise led him to postulate a family of man, based on similarities he found in seemingly dissimilar languages. War to him was utter folly, for it shattered the needed interrelationships among the members of the family of mankind.

Temperance societies flourished in the 1840's. On May 30, 1844, the Washington Temperance Society, an organization of reformed drunkards, staged a huge parade in downtown Boston. Over 12,000 members, accompanied by their children (called the Cold-Water Army) marched in sections headed by brass bands. This society alone claimed to have converted 500,000 drunkards—although their permanent conversions were probably closer to 100,000 persons.

The first American play to run 100 consecutive performances appeared in 1844. It was William H. Smith's *The Drunkard, or the Fallen Saved.* This play became a permanent feature of temperance programs for many years.

Abolition of slavery became an ever growing concern. On August 1, 1844, Emerson spoke on "Emancipation in the British West Indies" in Concord, and from then on Concord was a center for abolitionists. Emerson, Bronson Alcott, and Thoreau's mother all had special rooms in their homes for runaway slaves. The American Anti-Slavery Society, at its annual meeting in May 1844, adopted this resolution by an overwhelming vote: "Secession from the present United States government is the duty of every abolitionist." Since the federal Constitution condoned slavery, it too came under attack.

Churches were now splitting over slavery. In 1844 the Methodist Church split into two general conferences—one North, one South. The two parts did not re-merge until 1939. In 1845 the Baptist Church split over slavery. The division continues—there are now about 50 Baptist churches in the United States. The Presbyterian Church had divided over the slavery issue in 1838. There are now 10 Presbyterian church bodies in America.

In December 1844, after a period of eight years, Congress revoked the "gag rule," which stated that all congressional petitions mentioning slavery would automatically be tabled, since "agitation of the subject is disquieting and objectionable." A grateful John Quincy Adams wrote in his diary: "Blessed, forever blessed, be the name of God!"

The rapid influx of Catholic immigrants into the United States led to waves of rabid anti-Catholic feeling. Riots instigated by "nativists," those who disliked the newcomers, broke out in Philadelphia in 1844. Fundamentalist Protestants assumed that Catholics, by being loyal to their pope, were really un-American, for they should show all their loyalty to their new country.

Paralleling the shift towards the Roman Catholic Church being made by Newman in 1844 was the similar apostasy of the ardent transcendentalist Orestes Brownson to the Roman church that year. Brownson argued that the current philosophy of skepticism mistakenly built upon scientific method first, then sought for principles. But method, he argued, is "cold, lifeless, and offers only dead forms." Principles must come first, not method. And principles are discovered through revelation and faith. Man, he said, cannot be understood simply as a part of nature, but can only be fully understood as living in two orders, the supernatural as well as the natural. "All dependent life," he said, "is life by communion of the subject with the object," and thus the enigma of evil existing in a world made by a benevolent Creator can only be understood by reference to the values of the supernatural order.

As Brownson indicated, scientific thought and rationalism were advancing in this milieu of religious enthusiasm. The National Institute for the Promotion of Science sponsored the first national scientific congress in the United States in 1844. James Smithson's will in 1829 had left a fortune "for the increase and diffusion of knowledge"; Congress chartered the Smithsonian Institution in 1846. The switch of Samuel F. B. Morse from painting to invention helps depict America's hierarchy of values during this period.

England in early 1844 was still buzzing over the widespread acclaim given Charles Dickens' *A Christmas Carol*, which had appeared during the previous Christmas season. The prolific pen of Dickens produced two more works in 1844, *The Chimes* and *Martin Chuzzlewit*. A poem by the relatively obscure Elizabeth Barrett in 1844 was "The Dead Pan," which recounted the folk tale that when Christ hung from the cross, a cry "Great Pan is dead!" swept across the oceans, and from then on the oracles ceased to prophesy.

Julia Ward Howe described the visit she and her husband made to Florence Nightingale's home at Embley in 1844. "If I should devote my life to the nursing profession," Florence asked Dr. Samuel Gridley Howe, the philanthropist, "do you think it would be a dreadful thing?"

"Not a dreadful thing at all," he replied prophetically. "I think it would be a very good thing." Florence began to visit hospitals at home and abroad, and a revolution in nursing care and in hospital administration was in embryo.

Ever since his voyage on the *Beagle*, which began in 1831, Charles Darwin had been working on a new scientific theory. On January 11, 1844, he wrote to J. D. Hooker: "I think I have found a simple way by which species become exquisitely adapted to various ends." When Robert Chambers anonymously published *The Vestiges of a Natural History of Creation* that year, Darwin praised the book for its description of "the principle of progressive development." But Darwin disliked a work on fossil fishes published by Louis Agassiz, later to become professor of natural history at Harvard, since Agassiz took a stand in opposition to evolution. "It is impossible," said Agassiz, "to refer the first inhabitants of the earth to a few stocks, subsequently differentiated under the influence of external conditions of existence."

Darwin told his wife on July 5, 1844: "I have just finished my sketch of my species theory. If, as I believe, my theory will in time be accepted even by one competent judge, it will be a considerable step in science."

While he was expanding his earlier essay on evolution into a major work in 1858, Darwin received a manuscript from A. R. Wallace of Australia. Wallace's work repeated Darwin's, although in briefer form. There had been no previous contact between the two men. In each case a scientist had initially conceived of a hypothesis in an intuitive flash, and had later worked out the documentary evidence. One might say that the state of the science was such that the next logical hypothesis was probable. Carl Jung prefers to believe that archetypes from the collective unconscious act as agents of a continuing Creator, producing such "meaningful coincidences" as these events.

Although Darwin had been reticent about publishing his theory, lest he offend religious sensitivities, he now hastened to proceed with his proofs in an effort to make his work public. In time most scientists agreed with Darwin's original statement, when he published his *Origin of Species* in the following year.

Some religionists interpret the theory of evolution quite differently from Jung. Most fundamentalist churches feel that it is more likely the work of the Devil than of God. Jerome Clark says that Seventh-day Adventists believe that "Satan feared the Advent Movement and did not want its truths to be taught. While the Sabbath, the sanctuary, and the Spirit of Prophecy were being developed as distinctly Seventh-day Adventist doctrines and teachings, the theory of evolution was arising to destroy these very truths in the minds of scientists, theologians, and laymen. The real and the counterfeit were developed at the same time!"

In April 1844 Constantin Tischendorf made a great discovery in the library of the monastery of St. Catherine at the foot of Mount Sinai. In a wastebasket, destined for the furnace, Tischendorf found 129 sheets of a Greek copy of the Old Testament. Called Codex Sinaiticus, this is one of the two oldest parchment codices of the Old Testament. Later he found the entire Codex Sinaiticus, including the complete New Testament. Bible fundamentalists, who stress the literal truth of each word in the Bible, owe much to Tischendorf for his help in securing as authentic a text as possible.

In the year 1844 the Danish philosopher Sören Kierkegaard wrote one of his most important works, *The Concept of Dread*. To Kierkegaard dread was a sort of cosmic anxiety, a painful but necessary educational process leading toward religious faith. Without dread there could be no faith. There could also be no freedom from the tyranny of finite fears which plague us in our everyday lives. By dealing with the enormity of anticipated pains, dread prepares us to live in a real world somewhat less dreadful than we anticipated in our imagination.

Dread, in Kierkegaard's view, enables us to face death heroically, provided we have religious faith. Dread without faith leads to self-destruction in one form or another. Dread with faith encourages us to approach death in pleasant anticipation, like Socrates with his cup of hemlock.

Once having experienced, and overcome, the ultimate fear of personal extinction, all other finite fears seem harmless. Dread thus is seen as a spiritual cathartic, cleansing us from finite fears and petty concerns, preparing us for eternal life in union with God.

On October 15, 1844, a boy was born into the family of a Lutheran minister at Röcken, Prussia. Since it was the king's birthday, the lad was named after the king — Frederick William Nietzsche. But "the little minister," as he was called in his youth, grew to be an "Antichrist" in the eyes of many orthodox Christians. After a lifetime of ridicule of Christianity's alleged weakness and sentimentality, after attacking the "slave mentality" of democracy and postulating humanity's salvation in the evolving race of supermen, Nietzsche spent his final years alternating between deep depression and insanity.

Modern literature is full of scary warnings about imminent doom. In 1898 H. G. Wells described inter-planetary destruction in *The War of the Worlds*. T. S. Eliot in 1925 wrote about "the hollow men" of the present, saying

> This is the way the world ends
> Not with a bang but a whimper.

Winston Churchill was more fearful of the bang. In an article in *Hearst's International* in 1924 called "Shall We All Commit Suicide?" Churchill said that mankind was now faced with a last chance to avert the general doom of a world war. "This is the point in human destinies to which all the glories and toils of men have at last led them," he said. "The prevention of the supreme catastrophe ought to be the paramount object of all endeavor."

The perfection of nuclear weapons has accelerated the general feeling of hopelessness. Building upon Alfred Jarry's "pataphysics," which employed strict logic to arrive at senseless conclusions, a whole school of drama, the Theater of the Absurd, has arisen. Its goal is to shock mankind into the realization that modern life is patently absurd, concentrating on mass destruction in preference to mass preservation. If, as Nietzsche said, God is dead, then modern life is meaningless. Jean-Paul Sartre sees "no exit" from life's frustrations. Samuel Beckett sees mankind at "endgame" time.

The poet Allen Ginsberg sees doom and destruction coming in an inevitable nuclear war among the great powers in the coming decade.

Contemporary music reflects the apocalyptical feeling. Herman's Hermits, a rock group, had a best-selling hit in the 1960's called "The End of the World." French composer Olivier Messaien wrote a "Quartet for the End of Time." Many rock-and-roll lyrics suggest an ultimate war or Christ's second coming.

Before his assassination in 1968, Robert Kennedy revealed the stark facts underlying the Cuban missile crisis of 1962. He says that President Kennedy and his top advisers expected the Soviet Union not to obey the ultimatum to remove Soviet missile bases in Cuba, and that they then would initiate bombing of those bases which would precipitate World War III as a nuclear conflict. President Kennedy seemed to be most disturbed about the death of innocent children all over the world as a result of the atomic war. He was willing to risk an unprecedented holocaust rather than consider removing United States missile sites in Turkey, on the border of the Soviet Union, as Soviet leaders requested.

More recently President Jimmy Carter, in a speech to the United Nations on October 4, 1977, said that American nuclear forces would be used only in self-defense, that is, in case of an attack, nuclear or conventional, on the United States, its bases, or its allies. Thus, in the event of any kind of attack upon any of our 400 foreign bases or 60 treaty allies, President Carter announced the possibility of being the first to use nuclear weapons.

If the existing stockpile of over 60,000 nuclear weapons is ever detonated, the result may well resemble the Battle of Armageddon described in Revelation 16:16. Lacking world law, we live in a lawless world. International criminals armed with nuclear warheads are loose to commit blackmail, terrorism, and widespread destruction. The growing millennialism in the world will not subside as long as we live in a lawless world, a world in which massive destructive capacity grows each year while our ability to control this destruction remains stagnant.

The continued growth of Soviet nuclear power drives the United States to build larger nuclear stockpiles. Thus it is that, in the absence of international law, national security automatically means international insecurity. Our destructive cunning has tragically outrun our ability to build not only effective control systems but even the climate of opinion necessary to sustain such systems.

Biblical believers that the world shall soon end point to such signs as widespread crime and immorality, the spread of atheism and materialism, the growth of esoteric religious cults, and the rapid increase in uncoordinated knowledge.

Great fear and confusion, unprecedented warfare preparation, and the return of the Jews to the Holy Land all point to Christ's soon return, they feel. The growth of modern Israel they equate with Christ's parable of the blooming fig tree (Matthew 24:32). First the gospel must be preached in all the world (Matthew 24:14), and thus there is a command for widespread evangelism. The powers of heaven shall be shaken (Luke 21:26), perhaps by a nuclear holocaust. "All Israel shall be saved," said Paul in Romans 11:26. "And there shall be one fold and one shepherd," added John in John 10:16.

Some Bible prognosticators say that the valley of dry bones described in Ezekiel 37 represents the conversion of the Jews to Christianity, and that Ezekiel 38 describes Gog, meaning the Soviet Union and its allies (a land north of Israel) as attacking Israel to begin the final war. The army of 200 million godless soldiers attacking from the east (Revelation 9:16) is equated with the commitment of China's armies into the war.

Looking at the 1844 experience, and adding the modern potential for mass destruction, we can reasonably expect to see these trends: a growing adventist fervor, with ever more converts to the cause; scoffers who ridicule the adventists and opportunists who devise schemes to make money off of last-minute adventist desperation; the majority, neutral bystanders, who will probably not commit themselves to take a forthright stand but who will hesitate to make fun of adventists, since after all they may be right.

Denominationalism has long been one of Christianity's chief problems. Not long ago a perplexed Navajo Indian asked a missionary, "Please tell me which is the correct Jesus — the Baptist Jesus or the Presbyterian Jesus?" Like the Hindu parable of the six blind men and the elephant, each person believes that the part of the reality of God that he has hold of constitutes the entire reality.

Sectarianism also underlay many of the religious problems of early 19th century America. As a young man, Joseph Smith was as confused as the Navajo Indian. William Miller, who led the Adventist movement, believed that there were already far too many denominations; it hurt him to realize that as an outgrowth of his movement, there was to be yet another church.

Each reformer, including John Henry Newman, endeavored to restore the original New Testament church. Because they had different backgrounds and beliefs, the reformers ended up miles apart, even though each sincerely felt he had restored the primitive church.

Alexander Campbell, for example, who played a leading role in establishing the Disciples of Christ, attacked councils, creeds, religious hierarchy, and other denominational requirements, seeing how they generally led to division and disunity among Christians. The need for him to clarify his own beliefs to his followers, however, led him in 1846 to publish a statement of his ten fundamental religious beliefs. The moment he published his credo he cut himself off from many other Christians. So does every religious leader. How is one to determine which is the "true" approach? Is there no one "true" approach? This book will shed light on how one can seek answers to these perplexing questions.

Every year in the Christian Era is anno Domini, "in the year of the Lord." Recognizing the fact that all of time is God's, Christians feel the need to redeem the time, to make good use of each year of their lives in order to bear good witness to their faith.

Religion, which can be one of mankind's greatest sources of good, has often proved to be one of the greatest sources of evil. What goes wrong? Is there some way that religion can continue as an unquestioned asset to man, without all the hatred, wars, and alienation that have accompanied religion in mankind's history?

Can the major religions of the world live together in harmony and peace, or must they attack one another? Can religion serve as a cause of peace and unity rather than war and discord? Is there a religious solution to the troubles of the Holy Land?

To the individual, what can religion accomplish that nothing else can? How can religion be an anchor of faith in the stormy days ahead? How can we grow in our personal faith without suffering alienation from others who are also growing?

Why did so many earth-shaking events occur in the year 1844? Did Christ really return then? Is He coming soon?

Readers of this book will not find answers to all of the above questions. What they will find is a series of experiences to a number of people in different lands, all of which shed light on those questions from different perspectives. What can be promised is that the reader will be more knowledgeable about events of the past century that still have an important bearing on our time.

It might be hoped that an outcome of reading the book would be to help the reader gain greater self-insight, and come to love God and His creation, including fellow human beings, even greater. To achieve even a small percentage of these goals would be to make this book worthwhile.

# 2

# *The Second Coming of Christ*

October 1 began the last month in the history of the world. The many months, the many years of warning people to leave their sinful ways were now over. Many had heeded the warning, and would greet their Lord as He descended from a cloud in all His glory. Thanks be to God, that some souls had been saved in time!

But far more people had refused to listen, too absorbed in their daily ruts, too eager to make money or to try to win their neighbors' favor. The Bible had warned that "the world" would not know the Lord, nor seek to discover the signs of His immediate return. These, the majority, would be adjudged goats, and their wicked souls would burn in eternal fire.

So reasoned the followers of William Miller in October 1844. Miller, a farmer from upstate New York, had galvanized the world with his shocking prediction that in 1844 the age would come to an end, as Christ came to reward believers, reign justly for a thousand years, and condemn unbelievers to eternal torment. Miller's source was the Bible. An unschooled but a self-educated man, Miller found reason to believe that the Bible pointed toward 1843 or 1844 as the time of the end. His proofs were many, and they stood the tests of Bible scholars quite well.

Originally Miller believed that the world would end by March 21, 1844. Every biblical sign seemed to him to point toward that terminal date. But now friends of his presented convincing logic that Christ's second advent would occur on October 22. It seemed to him and his 50,000 followers in America and many more abroad that surely the Lord was about to return and judge all people.

What does one do when the world is about to end? A number of ardent believers in northern New England had felt it was futile to plant crops that year. Some merchants sold their wares at special low prices, so that they could pay all their debts by the 22nd. A few gave away merchandise, demonstrating their charity. Crimes were freely confessed. One man sent five dollars to the U. S. Treasury. Another sent $120 to a New York insurance company with the note: "The Lord is at hand. This was unlawfully taken from you, and I ask forgiveness, for the Lord has forgiven me much." A conscience-stricken woman confessed having committed a murder in England several years previously, and wanted to return there for a trial.

13

William Miller and the Second Coming — drawing of "Judgment Day" by a follower. (Religious News Service Photo.)

Some shopkeepers closed their stores. They felt they had to prepare themselves to meet the Lord, and they wanted to devote the last few days to efforts to persuade others to get ready. Some people sold all their possessions, feeling the money could be used to help publicize the need for personal preparation for the Great Event. They also wanted to be debt-free by October 22, and they hoped to have funds left for the poor.

A Philadelphia tailor hung this sign in his window:

> This shop is closed in honor of the King of Kings
> Who will appear about the 22nd of October.
> Get ready, friends, to crown Him Lord of all.

Miller himself was slow to accept October 22 as the crucial date. Too often had his hopes been high, only to be dashed when nothing would happen. But the mounting fervor proved to be too much. On October 6 he and his companion Joshua Himes finally accepted the date of October 22. On October 14 they were temporarily saddened at the death of another Millerite leader, Charles Fitch, but they were confident that in about a week they would be reunited. Fitch had died from a cold he contracted while baptizing some last-minute converts in the chilly autumn weather.

Miller's followers had a dilemma: if their behavior was odd while expecting the Lord, they would be called queer; if their behavior was routine, it would be a sign that they did not really expect Him. On the whole, their conduct at the critical hour was more acceptable than that of their critics. Broadsides lampooning Millerites appeared, showing them clad in ascension robes, rising on a cloud. One broadside depicted the entire Boston tabernacle mounted heavenward, leaving behind Himes who was weighed down with money he had made from publishing Millerite tracts. The devil, holding Himes' coattails, was saying, "Joshua, you must stay with me."

Newspapers in three states told of the death of John Shortridge of Portsmouth, New Hampshire, saying he climbed a tree, clad in a white robe, preparing to meet Christ but instead fell to the earth, dead from a broken neck. Mr. Shortridge, quite alive, wrote letters of protest to the editors.

Unruly mobs of non-believers interrupted services in the Boston tabernacle so that the meetings had to be canceled. Papers in Portland and Baltimore mistakenly reported that police closed the meetings due to the behavior of the adventists. When the same thing happened in Philadelphia, a New Hampshire newspaper finally came to the Millerites' defense. Closing Millerite meetings, it reported, was like telling a homeowner: "You must not presume to have glass windows in your house, because many unruly boys are disposed to break them."

Miller said that October 13 would be the last Sunday sinners would have on probation, for in a few days they would have to confront Him whom they hated, Christ. On October 16 the editors of the *Advent Herald* announced: "Our work is now finished. All we have to do is to go out to meet the Bridegroom. Our controversies are all over, the battle has been fought, and our warfare ended." The editors stated that this was the last issue that would be published, since there would be no more Wednesdays (their day of publication) on this earth.

There is no evidence to support the widespread notion that Millerites went to mountain tops or graveyards during the last days. A group of about 150 adventists gathered in a field outside Philadelphia on October 21 to await the coming of the lord. Rumors later spread that two of their children died unattended in a hurricane. But the hurricane had occurred on October 19, before the people left the city. The rumors, as usual, were false.

On October 22 Millerites went to meeting houses and churches to prepare for Christ's return. Where meeting places were closed by police order, as in New York City, they gathered in private homes for prayer meetings. In Cincinnati, a Millerite center, a group of 1500 people gathered in their tabernacle. A newspaper reporter who attended said that they were calm and orderly, despite several efforts made by a gang of rowdies outside to disturb their meeting. At about 9 P.M. the benediction was pronounced, and they went home to await the Lord's coming. They maintained a hopeful vigil until midnight.

How can we account for the widespread conviction that the world was about to end and that Christ was about to return? Where did Miller and his followers get their information? Are there those who still believe that Christ's return is imminent?

The main source of Miller's prediction was the Bible, particularly the prophetic books of Daniel and Revelation. Christ often mentions His return in the New Testament, and later His disciples frequently refer to it. A number of Bible passages refer to Christ's return at the last judgment.

Psalm 50 speaks of a destructive fire "devouring before God," as He prepares to judge His people. In His parable of the tares, Christ describes the harvest, when the tares are burned and the wheat stored in the master's barn. Paul speaks of everlasting destruction of non-believers, when Christ comes to be "glorified in His saints" (II Thessalonians 1:8–10). And Jude recalls Enoch's prophecy, when "the Lord cometh with ten thousands of his saints to execute judgment upon all."

Historic church creeds refer to Christ's role on judgment day. The Apostles' Creed, the Nicene Creed, and the Athanasian Creed all mention this, as do the Lutheran Augsburg Confession, the Anglican Thirty-Nine Articles, and the Presbyterian Westminster Confession. Other Christian churches generally include a statement of Christ's return to judge humans at the end of the world.

Most Puritans also spoke of Christ's second coming. Such men as John Cotton, Roger Williams, Cotton and Increase Mather, John Eliot, and Samuel Sewall all believed strongly in it. So did their spiritual descendants:

Jonathan Edwards, Samuel Hopkins, Timothy Dwight, and Elias Boudinot, who founded the American Bible Society in 1816. President of Yale in 1812, Dwight thought he could perceive the dawn of the millennium that year. President Eliphalet Nott of Union College, in a Presbyterian sermon in 1806, said the millennium was "at the door," and would be "introduced by human exertions." In 1810 Reverend William Davis of South Carolina published a pamphlet stating that Christ would return in 1844.

Sir Isaac Newton wrote a book, *Observations Upon the Prophecies of Daniel, and the Apocalypse of St. John,* in which he expressed the belief that Bible prophecies remain veiled until their time of near fulfillment, and then God raises up a prophet to interpret their meaning. Newton felt that the world was now approaching the last age, and therefore humans should try to interpret the apocalyptical prophecies of Daniel and John. He noted that many Bible prophecies had already been realized. Newton felt that most churches had corrupted New Testament Christianity, but that the many clear biblical prophecies concerning Christ's second coming would help moderns restore primitive Christianity, and set up "a kingdom wherein dwells righteousness." He added: "I seem to gather that God is about opening these mysteries."

Radical social change brings fear and chaos to people's minds. The  Industrial Revolution severely altered most people's life patterns. The American Revolution brought promise and portent to an awakening world. The French Revolution kindled terror and utopianism in human hearts. And the specter of world conquest, made real by a small Corsican named Napoleon, further ignited the fires of fear and confusion.

In 1812 a Catholic priest born in Chile, Manuel de Lacunza, published a book called *The Coming of Messiah in Majesty and Glory.* By 1820 about 300 Anglican and 600 Nonconformist clergymen in England were preaching Christ's early return. A Jewish convert, Joseph Wolff, spread the advent doctrine to more than twenty countries in the Middle East and Asia between 1831 and 1845. In 1820 Archibald Mason in Scotland predicted that 1844 would be the year of Christ's return. Alexander Cambell, in a famous debate with Robert Owen in 1829, also selected 1844 as the year. Tennyson, writing "In Memoriam" at this time, perceives

> One God, one law, one element
> And one far-off divine event
> To which the whole creation moves.

The climate of early nineteenth century America was conducive to the growth of new religious outlooks. Liberalism had weakened the traditionally strong Anglican and Congregational churches. Vigorous new Baptist and Methodist churches, through revivals and camp meetings, spread an evangelical fervor through the western frontier. The rising number of Catholic Americans revived Protestant prejudice, and provided a rallying point for Protestant ecumenism. The constitutional guarantee of free worship, plus the traditional separation of church and state, gave newly transplanted Europeans wide latitude to embrace new religious viewpoints.

Charles Finney, who later became president of Oberlin College, began a series of revivals that led to the Second Great Awakening in America. Just as Jonathan Edwards had fanned a similar fervor a century before, Finney got people to seriously consider the state of their souls. One result was an unprecedented stress on social reforms, to hasten the coming of God's kingdom on earth. Witness the spontaneous outburst of organizations that were started: American Education Society – 1815; American Sunday School Union – 1824; American Tract Society – 1825; American Temperance Society – 1826; American Peace Society – 1828; American Anti-Slavery Society – 1833.

Another result was the stress on millennialism. John Humphrey Noyes brought millennial views to his Oneida community. The Shakers, also known as The Millennial Church, reached their highest point of development at this time. Western New York State was called "the Burned-over District," because the fires of revivalism had so often swept through the area. Within two decades this region saw the rise of Mormonism, Adventism, and spiritualism.

Whittier, the poet, asked: "Is the idea itself a vain one? Is there no hope that this world-wide prophecy of the human soul, uttered in all climes, in all times, shall yet be fulfilled? Is not its truth proved by its universality?"

Certain celestial happenings seemed to be signs. The famous "Dark Day," May 19, 1780, in New England was seen as fulfillment of the Biblical description of darkness as the end nears. The spectucular shower of meteorites in 1833 and the brilliant comet in 1843 were felt to be the "falling stars" predicted in Matthew 24:29 and Revelation 6:13.

In 1842 William Foy, a Baptist preacher, told of two visions he had of Christ's second coming. In 1844 he reported a third vision of three mysterious platforms. Hazen Foss in the fall of 1844 told of a vision he had of the second coming, in which three steps were depicted. Twice more he reported receiving this vision. Seventh-day Adventists interpret these visions as referring to the messages concerning the last days as told by the three angels in Revelation 14.

The person who did the most to focus attention on Christ's second coming was William Miller. The eldest of sixteen children, Miller was born in Pittsfield, Massachusetts, on February 15, 1782. His father had been a captain in Washington's army. His mother, reared in a parsonage, made sure there were daily religious observances in the family.

When he was a small child the family moved to Low Hampton in eastern New York. Here he grew up on a farm. Each winter he had three months of schooling, but in addition he read many books. Soon his fame as a gifted writer spread. If anyone wanted verses composed, or an important letter written, Miller was the one to do it.

After he married Lucy Smith in 1803, they moved to her home town, Poultney, Vermont. He joined the Masons, and soon became a high officer. Besides farming, he served as a peace officer: constable, sheriff, and justice of the peace. Reading such men as Voltaire and Paine, Miller became a deist and made fun of such orthodox Christians as his grandfather, Elnathan Phelps, a respected Baptist preacher.

The War of 1812 changed Miller. A lieutenant in the state militia, he felt the need to serve his country, and so he became a lieutenant in the U. S. Army. Since there was no draft, officers had to enlist their own men. He enlisted 47 volunteers, and served until 1815. In 1814 he was promoted to captain. The American victory at the Battle of Plattsburg, where 5,000 troops overcame the 15,000 British, Miller attributed to God's intervention. Deistic assumptions about man's innate goodness also were shelved by Miller, who saw evil to be a widespread reality in wartime.

He now sought for a deeper religious faith. In September 1816 he had a profound religious experience. He suddenly felt the nearness of Christ as Savior, "a Being so good and compassionate as to Himself atone for our transgressions. I found the Lord God to be a Rock in the midst of the ocean of life." His life changed. He joined a Baptist church, erected a family altar, and made his home a center for Bible study and prayer meetings. Now his skeptical friends threw the same questions at him that he had formerly asked: "How do you know about Christ? How do you know the Bible is true?"

To answer such questions he began a two-year intensive study of the Bible. He came to believe that the Bible is its own interpreter — commentaries are not needed. He believed in following the Bible literally. When common sense prevented a literal interpretation, he sought for a figurative meaning. He noticed that although biblical prophecies are usually given in figurative language, they are fulfilled literally. His comparison of historical events with biblical predictions seemed to confirm this belief. Since prophecies have been fulfilled in the past, he felt they would also be fulfilled in the future.

A key belief of Miller's was that the Bible teaches a pre-millennial advent. He countered the post-millennialists, who believed it necessary to establish God's kingdom on earth through right faith and righteous acts, and then Christ would come. Miller said God's kingdom will not come on earth until after Christ returns to judge the world, claiming the righteous and casting out the wicked. The earth will be consumed by fire and become a new world where the righteous will dwell with Christ forever. The bodies of the wicked will be destroyed, and God's kingdom will have come, when His will will be done on earth as it is done in heaven. The only millennium is the 1000-year interval of Revelation 20 between the first resurrection of the saved and the second resurrection of the wicked. "There can be no conversion of the world before the advent," Miller said.

Miller found that all events predicted in the Bible as occurring before the advent had now been accomplished. He was aware that "no man knoweth of that day and that hour" (Mark 13:32), but he responded with the fact that the Bible informs us of the signs of when the advent is near. True, the Jews had not yet returned to Palestine, but Paul had said, "There is no difference between the Jew and the Greek" (Romans 10:12). Miller had two other answers to this objection: first, the Jews *had* returned from Babylonian captivity, and second, the Jews referred to here are "spiritual Jews," that is, persons who have accepted Christ.

As he looked for biblical prophecy concerning Christ's second coming, a key text for Miller became Daniel 8:14: "Unto 2300 days; then shall the sanctuary be cleansed." Many students of prophecy equated a prophetic day with a solar (or calendar) year, as described in Numbers 14:34 and Ezekiel 4:6. So Miller also equated a prophetic day with a calendar year.

The beginning year in Miller's calculations was 457 B.C., the year that Artaxerxes Longimanus, King of Persia, decreed the rebuilding of Jerusalem (Ezra 7:12–26). Since Daniel's vision had concerned the end of the world, Miller assumed that the cleansing of the sanctuary referred to the purification of the earth by fire at Christ's second coming. The prophecy in Daniel 9:25 that the rebuilding would be completed in seven weeks (49 years) had been accomplished in 408 B.C. The seventy weeks (490 years) of Daniel 9:24 from the rebuilding to the anointment of the Most Holy One had been achieved at Christ's resurrection in A.D. 33. Since Daniel had said that the seventy weeks are "determined upon thy people" in Daniel 9:24, Miller subtracted the seventy weeks (490 years) from the 2300 days (2300 years) and got 1810 years. This added to A.D. 33 gave Miller the date for the end of the world — 1843.

Other prophetic figures seemed to corroborate these calculations. For example, Daniel 12:11 stated that there would be 1290 days (that is, years) from the taking away of the daily sacrifice to the setting up of the abomination of desolation. Miller dated the taking away of the daily sacrifice at A.D. 508, when papal supremacy was established. Adding the 1290 years gave Miller 1798, the year that the French deposed the Pope. Daniel 12:12 mentioned the bliss in 1335 days (years), which was 45 years later than the 1290 years. And 45 years beyond 1798 was 1843.

Thus, by the year 1818 Miller had come to believe that the advent year would be 1843. But it was thirteen more years before he felt sure enough of his calculations to share them with the public.

On November 4, 1826, he had a very forceful dream. He felt he saw the blood of Jesus running from a rail-fence. He saw the cross, with garments drenched in blood. He received a book, which he was told would direct him. When he opened it, his eyes came to Isaiah 48:17: "I lead thee by the way thou shouldst go." He then had a vision of a paradise beyond description, and then he awoke. He began to feel that God could use even a humble farmer to awaken the world to biblical prophecy.

Like Joseph Smith, Miller felt that sectarian rivalry was badly weakening Christianity. "I believe that before Christ comes in His glory," he wrote, "all sectarian principles will be shaken, and the votaries of the several sects scattered to the four winds; and that none will be able to stand but those who are built on the word of God."

One Saturday morning in August 1831 Miller felt the call to tell the world about Christ's imminent return. Still somewhat reticent, he made an apparently safe bargain with God: he promised God that if he was ever called upon to preach, he would preach Christ's second coming. Since he had never had such an invitation, the bargain seemed safe enough. But that very day a young man arrived from nearby Dresden, inviting him to preach the following day. Angry, Miller refused. But his conscience bothered him. His six-year-old daughter Lucy told her mother: "Something's the matter with Daddy." Miller had gone into a grove to pray about the invitation to preach. As Francis Nichol summarized: "He went into the grove a farmer, and came out a preacher." He could not go back on his word to God. So he hitched up his horse, and traveled the sixteen miles to Dresden.

His sermon told listeners to prepare for Christ's soon return. He listed his proofs. The sermon was an immediate hit. He was asked to remain a week to discuss various aspects of the advent doctrine. People drove from nearby towns to hear of the biblical prophecy concerning the coming end of the world.

When he got home he found another invitation to speak on the topic, this time from the church in Poultney. Again the people received him warmly, and Elder Fuller of the Poultney church became the first of many ministers to accept the accuracy of Miller's dates.

Suddenly, "churches were thrown open everywhere," said Miller. "I lectured to crowded houses through the western part of Vermont, the nothern part of New York, and in Canada East; and powerful reformations were the results of my labors." The enthusiastic welcome he received indicates the widespread interest that already existed even before he began preaching.

In 1832 he wrote sixteen articles on the advent for the *Vermont Telegraph*. The articles attracted attention, not all of it favorable. The term "Millerite" began to be used to describe a somewhat unbalanced person. The articles were gathered into a 64-page pamphlet published in 1833 called *Evidences from Scripture and History of the Second Coming of Christ about the Year A.D. 1843*. He received a Baptist license to preach in 1833, by which time at least eight ministers were confirmed believers in his dates. Miller disliked being called "Reverend," since the title is not used in the New Testament, he said.

Aboard a steamboat in 1833, a fellow traveler commented that there were so many remarkable inventions recently that the pace of progress could not possibly continue, "or man will attain to something more than human." Miller replied by quoting Daniel 12:4: "At the time of the end, many shall run to and fro, and knowledge shall be increased." The crowd, interested, asked more questions. Miller discussed several chapters of Daniel with them. The passengers asked Miller for copies of his pamphlet.

In August 1834 Miller preached 32 sermons on the advent in 28 days. He said: "The evidence is so clear, the testimony is so strong, that we live on the eve of the present dispensation, towards the dawn of the Glorious Day, that I wonder why ministers and people do not wake up and trim their lamps." His chief adversaries were the Universalists, who taught that an all-loving God would ultimately forgive all sinners. To them Miller replied: "Read the Bible. The wicked shall be punished. It would be unjust for God to reward wicked and good alike."

A doctor called him a "monomaniac" on the subject of the advent, so Miller went to his office to have his disease treated. Miller rehearsed his numbers: 2300 − 490 = 1810; 1810 + 33 = 1843. The doctor, angry, ended the appointment. The next day he told Miller: "You are right about A.D. 1843. I am unprepared and must go to hell." Miller calmly reassured him that Christ died for sinners like him, and he could be saved. Converted, the doctor soon became a "monomaniac" on the advent issue.

Miller continued to find biblical confirmation of the accuracy of his date calculations. History, he felt, had revealed the four kingdoms of Daniel 2 (as well as the four great beasts of Daniel 7) to be the Chaldean, Persian, Greek, and Roman. The ten horns of the fourth beast were the ten kingdoms into which the former Roman Empire was divided by its conquerors in A.D. 476. The little horn of Daniel 8 Miller identified with the Roman Empire, as Sir Isaac Newton had done. The little horn of Daniel 7 Miller felt was the papacy; many Protestants had given this interpretation before Miller. The destruction of the little horn, given in Daniel 7:25 as "a time and times and the dividing of times," Miller interpreted thusly: a time equals one prophetic year (360 prophetic days or 360 solar years). Times equals twice that amount, and dividing equals half that amount. So the total is 360 + 720 + 180, or 1260 years. Since the Eastern empire had recognized papal supremacy in A.D. 538, Miller started from that date, added 1260 years, and arrived at 1798, the year that the French army deposed the Pope. Also, in Chapters 11, 12, and 13 of Revelation he found the mention of 1260 years, each time marking the coming of the time of the end. Miller came to believe that "the time of the end" was not a single point in time, but rather the period extending from 1798 until the very final end.

In some cases Miller interpreted a prophetical day as 1000 years. For example, when Hosea says, "In the third day he will raise us up" (Hosea 6:2), Miller saw the application as beginning in 158 B.C., and thus two millennia ended in 1842, and the beginning of the third millennium in 1843 would be the time for the raising up.

Similarly, when Christ says, "I do cures today and tomorrow, and the third day I shall be perfected" (Luke 13:32), Miller felt that the beginning of the third millennium would be the time for Christ's return in glory.

By the end of 1834 Miller was devoting virtually full time to preaching his advent message. He traveled extensively in 1835, generally paying his own expenses as he went. His dress was common, more like a farmer's than a preacher's. He was about five feet, seven inches tall. He had broad shoulders, light brown hair, and shrewd twinkling blue eyes. Listeners were impressed by his strong mellow voice and earnest manner. Sophisticates objected to his homely phraseology and his frequently ungrammatical sentences.

His pamphlet was reprinted in 1835, and an unauthorized reprinting occurred in 1836, when a printer could not resist the temptation to make money on an item that was so much in demand. In 1836 Miller published a book containing many of the lectures that were making him such a popular public figure. The book sold well.

His health was never good. His travels aggravated a chronic bilious condition. In later years he had erysipelas, and boils developed all over his body. Friends mentioned that his head shook, as if from a slight attack of palsy.

It bothered him that he was so often gone from his family at Low Hampton. He had eight children (two others died in infancy), and the older children, helped by good neighbors, ran the farm during his absence. His wife dutifully supported him in all of his work. His mother never accepted his views on the coming advent, but she encouraged him to continue to preach the Bible as God inspired him.

The Panic of 1837 brought political disillusionment, and at the same time encouraged interest in religious matters. If Jacksonian democracy was not going to be an earthly utopia, maybe that utopia was nevertheless coming soon, ushered in by the Prince of Peace Himself.

An important convert to Millerism in 1838 was the Methodist preacher Josiah Litch. That year Litch published two advent works: a pamphlet summarizing Miller's views and a book of his own called *The Probability of the Second Coming of Christ About 1843*. Litch interpreted the trumpet sounds of the seven angels mentioned in Revelation 8 and 9. The first four announced the fall of the western Roman empire, and the next two of the eastern Roman empire. Then Litch predicted that on August 11, 1840, the seventh trumpet would announce the fall of the great "Babylonian" empire, Ottoman Turkey. Basing his prediction on the duration of "an hour, a day, a month, and a year" of Revelation 9:15, Litch looked two years ahead to Turkey's downfall. At war with Egypt, the sultan of Turkey on August 11, 1840, wrote to representatives of England, Russia, Austria, and Prussia for assurance of their help, in case he turned down an ultimatum from the pasha of Egypt. Litch accepted this concession as evidence that Turkey could no longer defend itself without help from abroad, and thus that the great Ottoman Empire was at an end. Another biblical prophecy concerning the coming of the end had been fulfilled, in the eyes of many. This seemingly successful prediction not only reassured adventists; Litch stated that within a few months many freethinkers and agnostics had written to him stating that they now accepted the Bible as God's word.

Miller's views frequently involved him in biblical controversy. On one occasion, when two elders had attacked Miller for his views on salvation, but from diametrically opposed positions, both based upon biblical texts, Miller finally decided: "I have finally come to this conclusion that I must read the Bible for myself, try all that in me lies to divest myself of prejudice, judge with candor, get rid of self, preach what I believe to be truth, try to please God more than man, and then leave all in the hand of my divine Master."

In 1839 Miller spoke at the Chardon Street Christian Church in Boston at the invitation of its pastor, Joshua Himes. Himes adopted Miller's adventist views, and became one of Miller's leading supporters. Himes in turn helped convert Joseph Bates, a sea-captain, to the advent cause. A reformed alcoholic, Bates used to read rules to his sailors before starting a trip: no liquor, no swearing, no mending clothes on Sunday! Like Himes, Bates was a strong abolitionist. He bravely preached abolition and Millerism in Maryland, where mobs several times tried to beat him because of his views.

The church of Himes was noted as a rallying place for reform movements. Besides supporting adventism and the abolition of slavery, Himes was a devoted pacifist. With great faith in the power of the written word, Himes published the first adventist paper, *Signs of the Times*, on February 28, 1840. Confident of the rightness of their cause, Himes even printed attacks on Miller. In the first issue of his paper Himes said: "Rev. Parsons Cook of Lynn asserts in the *Puritan* that Mr. Miller's lectures are more demoralizing than the theater!"

In response to the growing demand, B. B. Mussey, a Boston publisher, printed 5,000 copies of Miller's *Lectures* in 1840. Maine proved to be a hotbed of Millerism. In Portland a young man entered a rum-shop where a dozen of his friends were playing cards, and invited them to Miller's lecture. They went, were convinced, and all became adventists. A Portland minister said: "The good work is spreading all over the city. Such a time was never known here. A number of grogshops have been broken up and converted into little meeting-houses. Prayer meetings have been set up in almost every part of the city." Similar results were reported in Portsmouth, Rye, Exeter, and other Maine towns. Sales of Bibles mounted rapidly throughout New England.

In 1840 Miller spoke for the first time in New York City. On October 13, 1840, the first general conference on "The Second Coming of the Lord Jesus Christ" began in Boston. Presiding was Henry Dana Ward of New York, an Episcopal clergyman who had graduated from Harvard. The conference type of organization was borrowed from the Methodists, and was later used by Seventh-day Adventists.

Despite recurrent illness, Miller continued to travel and preach. He estimated that from October 1, 1839, to April 15, 1841, he traveled 4560 miles, preached 627 lectures, and had 5,000 conversions.

On June 15, 1841, a second general conference was held in Lowell, Massachusetts. This conference placed great stress upon the need for dissemination of printed material. As one response, Himes printed thousands of stickers for sealing envelopes, on which were printed scripture verses about the second coming. Other conferences that year were held at Portland, New York City, Low Hampton, and Boston. The latter one, held at Chardon Street Chapel, raised $1000 for publications (at a time when an average workingman's daily wage was about 75¢).

More advent conferences were held in 1842, in Connecticut, New York, New Hampshire, and Vermont. Charles Stewart, postmaster in Morristown, Vermont, urged Miller to come to his town to lecture on "the great event about to transpire. Come down ere we die," Stewart pled.

In 1842 Himes converted *Signs of the Times* from a semi-monthly to a weekly paper. He also published volumes by many men in the Second Advent Library series. By now advent publications had been sent to missionary centers in North America, Europe, Asia, and Africa. A chart showing 1843 as the world's end was developed, showing the accomplishment of the various biblical prophecies concerning the end. Traveling Millerite preachers, of whom there were now 200 ordained clergy and 500 lay lecturers, often hung up "The '43 Chart" in railroad cars or on station walls, in order to answer the questions of the curious who wondered about the meaning of the strange animals depicted on the chart.

Since it was often hard to get churches for meetings, it was decided to try the Methodists' successful route—camp meetings. The time was growing short. It was necessary now to spread "the midnight cry" from the parable of the ten virgins: "Behold, the Bridegroom cometh; go ye out to meet him."

A camp meeting at East Kingston, New Hampshire, from June 28 to July 5, 1842, had about 10,000 persons present. Large tents were provided, to give shelter for groups from each church or town represented. Sometimes non-believers, who attended to scoff, were converted. A collection of $1,000 was raised, to buy a huge tent, so that many camp meetings could be held. Special advent hymns were composed and sung at each meeting. John Greenleaf Whittier described the East Kingston meeting, which he attended:

"There were about a thousand people present. A hymn kindled to higher intensity their already excited enthusiasm. The preachers were placed in a rude pulpit of rough boards, tasseled not with silk and velvet but with the green boughs of the sombre hemlocks around it. The main preacher's description of the last day had all the terrible distinctness of Anelli's painting of the 'End of the World.' Suspended from the front of the rude pulpit were two broad sheets of canvas, upon one of which was the figure of a man—the head of gold, the breast and arms of silver, the belly of brass, the legs of iron, and the feet of clay — the dream of Nebuchadnezzar! On the other were depicted the wonders of the Apocalyptic vision — the beasts — the dragons — the scarlet woman seen by the seer of Patmos — oriental types and figures and mystic symbols translated into staring Yankee realities."

The great tent was first raised in Concord, New Hampshire, in early August of 1842. It was 120 feet in diameter and 50 feet high at the center, and could accommodate 3,000 people. The *New York Herald*, reporting on a camp meeting in Newark, New Jersey, in early November 1842 said that there were no disorderly people present, despite the fact that over 6,000 persons attended. When rains came, the program was moved to a sympathetic church. Once rain drove the group into an iron foundry large enough to handle the crowd of 5,000 persons. The *Herald* reporter was "completely fagged out" by the end of the week. He wrote: "I thought the Methodists were pretty indefatigable at camp meetings, but these people can beat them hollow."

The approach of 1843 spurred Millerites into hastened action. Within four months thirty camp meetings were held. In the three years of 1842 through 1844 the Millerites held 125 camp meetings attended by an estimated 500,000 persons. As the year 1843 approached, crowds grew larger. Even deists, Universalists, and scoffers began to feel uneasy — what if Father Miller should prove right? Are we ready to face judgment?

Phrenology was a fad at the time. A phrenologist examined Miller's head, not knowing who he was. Impressed by Miller's well developed and well balanced head, the phrenologist commented: "*This* man would not easily be converted to William Miller's hare-brained theory!" He was embarrassed to hear his subject's name: "William Miller, the Adventist."

In November 1842 Himes started another adventist paper, *The Midnight Cry*. A daily, 10,000 copies of each issue were printed and distributed free. Now everything was of secondary importance, compared to Christ's imminent return. Copies of the two adventist papers, plus tracts and pamphlets and sometimes books, were taken to docks for free distribution to sailors. Since one of the biblical pre-conditions was the preaching of the gospel throughout the world, every effort was made to spread the teachings of the Bible to many foreign countries. By now the predicted second coming was a topic of current discussion in such places as Norway, Chile, and the Sandwich Islands (Hawaii).

The long-awaited year of 1843 finally arrived. Miller greeted it with a 14-point summary of his views, followed by fifteen Bible passages supporting his position that Christ would return sometime between March 21, 1843, and March 21, 1844. His dates were chosen to coincide with the Jewish calendar. He said to his followers: "This year is the last year that Satan will reign in our earth. Jesus Christ will come, and bruise his head. Christ will come and bring all His saints with Him, and then He will reward every man as his work shall be. Let every one of us try by persuasion to get at least one of our friends to come to Christ, in this last year of redemption. Yes, the glorious work of salvation within a few short months will be finished forever."

In Miller's view these events would occur: Christ would return. There would be resurrection of the righteous dead and translation of the living righteous. The saints would be judged, and marriage consummated between Christ and His church. The wicked would be destroyed, and their souls, along with the devil and all evil spirits, would be banished. The earth would be cleansed by fire, after which Christ and His saints would return to the earth for a thousand years of righteous rule.

The thousand-year reign would terminate as follows: The saints would gather into a holy city on earth, and the wicked would be resurrected. The devil, unloosed, would deceive the wicked and prepare them to battle the saints. The wicked would be judged by the saints and cast into a lake of perpetual fire. Then the saints would possess the earth with Christ forever.

Scoffers had a field day. Some of them falsely claimed that Miller had set a specific day for Christ's return. Sometimes pranksters would shout "Fire!" to disrupt his meetings, and the building owner would cancel the meeting, for fear of a panic which might destroy his property. There were many hoaxes. At one of them in Washington, D.C., a false statement had been issued that Miller would speak in front of the Patent Office, and a crowd of 7,500 appeared only to be disappointed as Miller did not arrive.

False advertisements appeared in newspapers and magazines, ridiculing Miller and other adventist leaders. A heading in large print would state "END OF THE WORLD!" and then the seller of some lozenges or cigars would say, "Enjoy these before the world ends." Newspapers printed many cartoons and caricatures which lampooned Miller. For the more scholarly, geologists spoke on the rock evidence that the world was a long time in the making and would probably be a long time in the dissolution.

In Philadelphia a comedy called "Miller, or the End of the World" was staged shortly after Miller spoke there. The press in many cities called him a fool, a liar, and a fat illiterate, and charged that his talks had driven a number of people insane. Sometimes there were threats of violence being used against him, but he remained quite calm, interpreting the threats as evidence of the righteousness of his cause. He often compared himself to Noah. "People made fun of the ark," he would say. "Just wait and see who is right!"

Some of Miller's opposition came from those who believed in the advent but felt the timing was inaccurate or the type of expected event would be quite different. A Baptist minister, John Dowling, said that the beginning of the new age would not be 1843 or 1844, but 1866, 1987, or 2015 (probably the latter). He described the millennium as "a time when true religion shall prevail in all the world, and the Church of Christ shall be raised to a state of prosperity far greater than has ever yet been enjoyed."

A Presbyterian minister, Dr. William Brownlee, said that in 1843–44 the big event would be the restoration of the Jews to the Holy Land, and that by 2016 all events leading up to the millennium would have been accomplished. Brownlee did predict, however, that in 1843 the greatest moral change the earth had ever seen would take place.

George Bush, professor of Hebrew and Oriental literature at New York City University, supported Miller in most of his calculations but felt that his chief error was to expect a sudden physical event rather than gradual moral regeneration. Bush predicted that "1843 would mark the beginning of an earthly millennium, with righteousness gaining domination of the world by gradual steps."

Summing up their position, Millerite leaders said: "That we are on the brink of some mighty and wonderful event, all are ready to admit. What is the nature of these events? is the great question at issue."

When the most brilliant comet of the century appeared for the whole month of March, 1843, it seemed to many that the heavens themselves were in readiness to announce the second coming of Christ.

When the *New York Herald* mistakenly announced that Miller had set the advent date for April 3, some wag suggested that a more likely date would be two days sooner. Despite pressure for commitment to a specific date, Miller stuck with the predicted range of one year following March 21.

Up to 1843, Miller and his fellow leaders recommended that advent believers stay in their own churches and try to convince members of the coming great event. But increasing numbers of churches closed their doors to Millerite speakers, and even started to excommunicate members who preached an imminent advent. As many adventists were disfellowshiped from their churches, the conviction grew that Protestant churches had joined the Catholic Church as a part of the Babylon and Antichrist described in Revelation 18.

The constant proliferation of Protestant sects and churches were to Millerites a sign of the babble and confusion epitomized in the story of the tower of Babel as told in Genesis 11. George Storrs, a Methodist adventist, said: "Instead of the Church of God, a loving, united, brotherly body, you now have Baptists, Methodists, Presbyterians, et cetera; and the so-called churches are each making war on the other, because their creeds differ. Hence 'confusion' or 'Babylon' is truly their name." Storrs by no means recommended starting another church. "No church can be organized by man's invention," he stated, "but what it becomes Babylon the moment it is organized. The Lord organizes His own church by the strong bonds of love."

Henry Jones, a Congregational minister who had written books on prophecy and Bible interpretation, had suggested to Miller as early as 1834 that perhaps Protestant churches were a part of Babylon for condoning gambling, lewdness, covetousness, slavery, and war. By 1834 Jones, one of the first clergy to take Miller seriously, had committed to memory the entire book of Revelation. A fervent believer in the advent, Jones was one of the few Millerite leaders who did not accept Miller's date calculations.

Difficulties adventists experienced in their churches led another Congregational adventist minister, Charles Fitch, to preach an influential sermon in July 1843 called "Come Out of Her, My People!" Based upon the passage in Revelation 18:4 in which John calls upon believers to leave corrupt Babylon, Fitch said that adventists should leave both Catholic and Protestant churches. He called the Catholic Church Antichrist for installing a mere man, the pope, to reign on earth, whereas Christ should personally reign on earth. Protestant churches, for likewise rejecting Christ's personal reign, also became in his view a part of Babylon and Antichrist. The implication was that unless one separated oneself from these anti-Christian organizations, one would be found lacking at the imminent final judgment.

Although Fitch's views were not held by all Millerite leaders and were never considered official doctrine, they were influential in causing thousands of Protestants to leave their churches over the advent issue. Miller himself reluctantly adopted the views in January 1844, although he later deplored them for having opened up unnecessary chasms between adventist and non-adventist Christians. Miller seemed to be particularly grieved that his own Baptist denomination had been called "Babylon."

Opponents of Miller charged his movement with inconsistency when the adventists dedicated a tabernacle holding 3500 people in Boston on May 4, 1843. "Why build a building if the end is nearly here?" they asked. Millerites replied that since their movement was interdenominational, there was no meeting place they could count on, especially in inclement weather. The building burned down in 1846.

Despite the high excitement of the religious fervor at adventist meetings, there was relatively little fanaticism. Exceptions to this occurred at three camp meetings in Connecticut in the summer of 1843. One group felt it had acquired the gift of discerning spirits. They felt that just by touching a person's forehead they could tell whether the person was saved or lost. One woman was convinced she could walk on water, and insisted on trying it out on the nearby Connecticut River (but was fortunately restrained). Josiah Litch, who was present at the meeting, attacked the fanaticism in the next issue of *The Midnight Cry*. Miller and Himes also publicly discouraged fanaticism.

Miller complained of noisy excesses, whenever they occurred at adventist meetings. He said such meetings started to sound to him like Babel. He said he preferred "a kindly eye, a wet cheek, or a choked utterance as evidence of inward piety."

It should be remembered that public meetings in early nineteenth century America were frequently noisy and sometimes rowdy. Political campaigns were often extravaganzas. At the huge temperance convention in Boston in 1844, railroads transported whaleboats and harpoons to accompany a boatload of whalers, as part of a gala parade attended by thousands.

At some camp meetings run by Methodists and Presbyterians, as many as 20,000 persons attended. James Buckley, in *A History of Methodists in the United States*, says: "So many were struck to the ground at one meeting that, to prevent their being trodden underfoot by the multitude, they were laid out in order on two squares of the central meeting house." Thus it would be unusual if Millerite meetings did not also contain some unrestrained exuberance, in view of the magnitude of the expected event.

Illness kept Miller from being very active in the summer of 1843. Other leaders, however, maintained an active pace. Himes continued his speaking and publishing. He reported that in 1843 3500 letters were written to him, as editor of *The Midnight Cry*. He changed the name of *Signs of the Times* to *The Advent Herald*, reasoning "the advent of the Lord being 'at the door,' we 'herald' its approach with joy." By May 1844 Himes announced that 5,000,000 copies of adventist publications had been distributed.

As the months of 1843 passed without any apparent advent, several reactions took place within the movement. On the one hand, there was an increase in missionary activity, since surely now time was running out. It was necessary to reach as many people as possible in the few remaining months. On the other hand, there was continued search of the scriptures to see whether there were further helpful signs of the time of Christ's return.

Miller himself noted the important Jewish feasts and ceremonies which occurred during the seventh Jewish month (September 24 – October 24), and he began to feel that the great event would occur shortly after the autumnal equinox. Other adventists began to shift away from the Rabbinical chronology of Jewish dates and began to use the Karaite reckoning. The Karaites, following Leviticus 23:10-11, computed the new year as beginning one month later than the Rabbinical calculation, and thus discarded A.D. 33 as the year of Christ's crucifixion and shifted to A.D. 34.

Dr. William Hales, an Irish clergyman and chronologist, placed the crucifixion (in the middle of the seventieth week, per Daniel 9:27) at A.D. 31, making the end of the week at A.D. 34, and thus the end of the world for 1844.

Samuel S. Snow, a Congregational adventist, during the winter of 1843-44 also introduced a correction favorable to 1844 as the final year. He felt that the order to rebuild Jerusalem (Daniel 9:25) had been issued toward the end of 457 B.C., and that the 69th week (also Daniel 9:25) had ended in the autumn of A.D. 27 when Christ began His ministry. Subtracting 483 days (69 weeks) from 2300 gave Snow 1817, and 1817 plus 27 gave 1844.

Advent scholars found still another reason to correct their prediction from 1843 to 1844. Since there was no Year Zero (the time from 1 B.C. to A.D. 1 being only one year, not two), their calculations based on Year Zero had to be corrected by adding one more year to Christ's projected return. Thus, as the year 1843 passed with no advent, hopes were still high among most adventists that Christ would come in all His glory in 1844.

Adventists disappointed in 1843 found comfort in Habakkuk 2:3:

"For the vision is yet for an appointed time, but at the end it shall speak and not lie; though it tarry, wait for it, because it will surely come, it will not tarry." Faithful believers said that this period of waiting was for the purpose of purifying advent believers, to see whose faith was truly pure. The period after March 21, 1843, was called "the tarrying time, when the Bridegroom tarries" (Matthew 25:5). Other comforting biblical phrases were "the waiting time" (Hebrews 2:1, 4), the "day" (Hebrews 10:25), the "little while" (Hebrews 10:37), and "quickly" (Revelation 11:14).

At the beginning of 1844 Miller arrived back in Low Hampton after a lecture tour of 85 lectures in eight weeks. He was 62 and in poor health, but far from discouraged. "Already the world begins to shout victory over us," he warned his followers. "Does your heart begin to quail? Never has my faith been stronger than at this very moment." In the preceding twelve years he had given 4500 advent lectures to over 500,000 different people, and he was not about to give up on the eve of his triumph.

On January 28 he began a week of lectures at the Boston tabernacle. Crowds had to be turned away, for the building was filled to overflowing. Meetings followed in New York City, Philadelphia, and Washington. Everywhere the crowds were huge. Ministers, expelled from their churches for preaching adventism, supported him from every denomination. In February *The Midnight Cry* repeated Fitch's message: "Come out of her, my people!" Maybe Fitch was right after all — the Protestant churches too were Babylon, many adventists felt.

Fitch had solved his transportation problem that winter easily. A young businessman from Cleveland, who had bought a horse and buggy for the purpose of traveling all winter on an extended vacation, attended an advent lecture by Fitch, decided the end was near, and drove Fitch from one meeting place to another throughout the winter.

There was difficulty finding enough meeting houses that winter, since many churches were now boycotting the Millerites. The solution to the problem was to build a number of tabernacles quickly. In Toronto, Canada, for instance, a structure measuring thirty feet by ninety feet was erected in eight days. Similar structures were raised in a number of cities and towns. By the spring of 1844, the editors of *The Advent Herald* were proud to call themselves and other Millerite leaders "Adventists," since it aptly described their consuming concern.

American folklore likes to recall the weird antics of the adventists in what they felt were their final months. But scholars refute the popular notion that large numbers of these people engaged in fanatical behavior. Whitney Cross, in *The Burned-over District*, denies the antics commonly ascribed to them. During the first three months of 1844 (which led to Miller's terminal date of March 21), Cross says that "none seems to have quit earning daily bread, prepared ascension robes, or gathered on hills or in cemeteries the better to swing aloft with the heavenly chariot." After a careful study of contemporary sources, Francis Nichol completely buries the fiction about ascension robes. He also refutes the charge that adventists gathered on high places to be nearer the Lord upon His arrival.

March 21, the long-awaited day, finally arrived. Adventists gathered in meeting halls or private homes for prayer and preparation. Surely, this time their Lord would come. This time the Bridegroom would not tarry!

Alas! the long-expected One did not arrive. The day came, endured briefly, and passed away, just as every day passes into time's oblivion. The hardship was almost more than one could bear. Even in England and other far-off places adventists wept in bitter disappointment.

Eliphalet Nott, president of Union College, quoted a number of Bible passages purporting to show Miller's error in reckoning the advent date. At a talk on "Origin, Duration, and End of the World" in Washington on April 4, Nott gave geological evidence to show that the most likely way that the world might end would be if the internal fires and volcanoes on earth were dammed up, creating unbearable pressure upon the earth's crust.

Miller was still awaiting his Lord. Along with others, he began to feel that perhaps the Karaite Jewish calendar was correct, and that the advent would be one lunar month later than he had calculated. But April 21 like-wise brought no advent. On May 2 he confessed his error and his disap-pointment to his chief followers. Later in May, at a large conference in the Boston tabernacle, he publicly confessed his error. "I'm willing to confess that Christ did not come," he admitted, "but I can't see where I'm wrong." He and other leaders continued to believe that Christ was coming soon. They were buoyed by the revised calculations of Snow and others who had extended the advent prophecy to include the entire calendar year of 1844.

During the summer of 1844 Miller and Himes traveled on the western frontier, still preaching the advent doctrine. Everywhere large crowds greeted them. It was as if there was a mass guilt syndrome, in which total absolution for all sins could be granted in one encounter. Himes now sup-ported the doctrine of "Come out of her, my people." Miller, more cautious, was reluctant to do so. He continued to say that his mission was to revive the true biblical teaching concerning Christ's second coming without dis-turbing existing churches or creating a new one.

In August Samuel Snow issued a new periodical, *The True Midnight Cry*, setting a new date for Christ's return: October 22. Following reasoning used the previous year by Miller, Snow decided that the advent would oc-cur on the Karaite Day of Atonement, Yom Kippur (the day when the high priest, whom Snow identified with Christ, went into the Most Holy Place of the tabernacle, representing heaven). The return out of the holy place Snow felt would coincide with Christ's return. Examining the parable of the ten virgins (Matthew 25:1–13), Snow found that the tardy bridegroom did not arrive at midday but at midnight. One-half of a prophetic day equals one-half of a calendar year, and six months from March 21 led to October 22. Here was a final half-year of grace. God was giving further opportunity for those who had not yet turned to Him to now see the light.

In Matthew 25:6 one reads: "Behold, the bridegroom cometh; go ye out to meet him." Snow said that the five wise virgins were those who accepted Christ; the five foolish virgins were unbelievers; the lamp was the Bible; the bridegroom was Christ. The "midnight cry" was the voice of the angel in Revelation 14:7 who was announcing the approach of judgment day. All the missionary work, the tracts, even religious events like the growing Sunday School movement were the wise virgins trimming their lamps in time, by spreading the good news of the gospel.

A camp meeting held at Exeter, Massachusetts, from August 12–17 raised the new enthusiasm to a high pitch. Once again Millerites had great expectations of their Lord's imminent return. The movement came to be known as the Seventh Month movement, because that would be the month in which Christ would re-appear. The new battle-cry was, "Behold, the bridegroom cometh." George Storrs said, "When this cry gets hold of the heart, farmers leave their farms to go out and sound the alarm, and mechanics their shops." Storrs believed that the chief stress in these last days should be to arouse the "sleeping virgins" — those who had fallen from the faith since 1843. Tobacco and "other idle habits" were to be abandoned, since they benefited neither oneself nor God. Announcements concerning adventist meetings often carried the phrase "Providence permitting" or "if time continue."

Nevertheless, the behavior of the Millerites continued to be reasonable even in the last days. Whittier, describing a camp meeting he attended in mid-September at Derry, New Hampshire, found them to be "sober, intelligent men" and "gentle and pious women." He did object somewhat to the literal description of the saints' heavenly abode in Millerite hymns. A Louisville paper said that a camp meeting there observed "perfect decorum and the absence of everything like selfishness and folly." The leader of the Disciples of Christ, Alexander Campbell, writing in his periodical *The Millennial Harbinger*, said previously that although he could not accept their calculations, Millerite leaders were "sincere, noble, and pure Christians," whose virtues were the main reason for the comparative success of their movement.

And so, with countless last-minute chores to attend to, the Millerites faced the final month of the world's history. They were dedicated, faithful, and utterly convinced of the rightness of their cause, to the bitter end.

Hiram Edson described reaction to what came to be known as the Great Disappointment: "We looked for our coming Lord until the clock tolled 12 at midnight. Then our fondest hopes and expectations were blasted, and such a spirit of weeping came over us as I have never experienbefore. The loss of all earthly friends could have been no comparison. We wept and wept till the day dawn. If this, the richest and brightest of all my Christian experiences, had proved a failure, what was the rest of my Christian experience worth? Has the Bible proved a failure? Is there no God, no heaven, no paradise? Is all this but a cunningly devised fable?"

Joshua Himes summarized the feeling of abandonment: "We had to say, as Mary Magdalen had once said, 'They have carried away my Lord, and I cannot tell where they have taken Him.' " Some adventists said they felt the way the disciples did after Christ's crucifixion. One of them lay prostrate for two days without pain, sick with disappointment. Then suddenly his strength returned, and he went back to his usual life. One group of seventy believers decided to stay together "until the Lord comes." They put all of their money in a milk pan, and anyone who needed money took it from the pan. Finally, acting upon outside advice, they returned to their normal life routines.

Adding to their pain was the ridicule of scoffers. "Millerite! Millerite! When are you going up?" they often heard. Their children were ostracized from their playmates, as if unsafe or contaminated. Doubly hard to bear was the defection within their own ranks. They discovered that many of their number had apparently joined the cause simply out of fear, not on the basis of deep faith.

Most Millerites had left their jobs during the last few days—some during the past few weeks. They needed help getting back to work. Those who had sold their possessions and were now destitute also needed help. Himes, in the first issue of *The Midnight Cry* after the Great Disappointment (October 31), appealed to all adventists to take care of their own, rather than to let the outside scoffing world pick up the tab.

Within a month after the Great Disappointment, articles appeared in the two leading Millerite papers "confessing the errors" of the two big disappointments. But the leaders had not relinquished all hopes. They said that perhaps they had been led to predict an exact date in order to reveal those who truly loved the Lord and awaited His return. They remembered Jonah, who had said Ninevah would be overthrown in forty days unless it repented. It was not destroyed then, but was destroyed later. They likewise remembered Abraham, willing to slay his own son Isaac to show his faith in God. Having thus tested Abraham's faith, God stayed his hand. So too God had now offered them a modern test of faith.

They remained unshaken. They said: "It will be our purpose the little while we may continue here to present the doctrine of the advent in all its purity." In reply to charges that they had encouraged idleness during the last days (by recommending that persons leave their work to prepare to meet the Lord), they quoted a Whig newspaper in Boston which had recommended that persons leave their jobs to campaign for Whig candidates. They also pointed to the disciples, who had left their jobs in order to follow Jesus. They now recommended a middle course between idleness and constant pursuit of goods and money. Although they still chided churches for being too lax concerning biblical prophecy, they admitted they had been "in danger of fixing upon exact times with too great positiveness, and of finding signs where God has not given them."

Still finding no error in his calculations, Miller continued to believe that Christ would come soon. He regretted the hard feeling that had developed between adventists and orthodox churches. He found that much had been learned during the adventist crusade. Adventists had learned humility, and others had learned much about the Bible. Even though much had been learned, he did not feel that an exact date for Christ's second coming should ever again be set. Searching himself and other leaders for weaknesses, he said there had been too much pride, fanaticism, and sectarianism in their movement. On December 3 he confessed: "We are responsible for the creation of a new schismatic church. May God forgive us."

An advent conference was held at Low Hampton on December 28–29, 1844. The leaders met to strengthen each other's faith and to clarify their thinking about their present position. Miller told the group that perhaps chronologists had made an error of four or five years, and perhaps the advent was still imminent. Himes concluded the meeting with a request for funds, for coffers were low.

In a letter to a Boston newspaper in January 1845 Miller defined his position: "Millerism is to believe, try to understand, love, and proclaim to others the good news contained in the Bible." Nevertheless that month he and his chief followers were excommunicated from the Baptist church.

Miller drew up a constitution for a conference of adventists who met in Albany in April 1845. The meeting framed a series of resolutions of belief. Their goal was to preach the gospel to all, but to avoid fanaticism. They proceeded testily, fearful that possibly another denomination, and thus further Babylon, might be born.

In August 1845 Miller published a pamphlet *Apology and Defense* which recounted his religious growth. He refused to accept any new theories that had developed to explain the Great Disappointment. He still believed that the cleansing of the sanctuary described by Daniel would be accomplished physically on earth soon. His final admonition was: "Avoid everything that shall cause offenses. Let your lives be models of goodness and propriety. Avoid unnecessary controversy. God will raise up those to whom He will commit the direction of His cause."

In 1848 Miller's sight failed and his health declined. Still expecting Christ's imminent return, he died on December 20, 1849, at the age of 68. On his gravestone one-half mile from his home the inscription reads: "At the time appointed the end shall be."

One of the charges against Millerism (and other religious revivals) was that it led unstable people into insanity, suicide, or murder. No traceable murder or suicide was ever committed out of "advent enthusiasm or fear," Nichol concluded after a careful study. He checked the records of New England mental institutions for the key years of 1842, 1843, and 1844. Medical superintendents for that period warned that when family members or friends commit a patient and list the malady, they are frequently in error. Also, what seems to be a cause may really be a result. Thus, a person might turn to religion after a mental illness rather than have the mental illness because of religion. Although some of the cases of insanity in 1842–44 were attributed to "Millerism," Nichol quotes a group of modern medical superintendents (plus a psychiatrist and a professor of neurology) to the effect that the charges that Millerite preaching filled the asylums are due to "religious prejudice, psychiatric ignorance, or the native ability of some people to invent a sensational story."

In sum, the predictions of Miller obviously led to extravagant claims and to unnecessary disappointment. Hoping to unite Protestant Christianity, he further fractured it. But he can scarcely be charged with blame for all of the hectic religious enthusiasm of the period. He and fellow leaders seem to have been sincere and respectable persons. Like Sir Isaac Newton, Miller felt his generation was in the last days. His reading of the Bible led him to make advent predictions which were unrealized. Later generations can learn at least two things from his experience: Avoid dogmatic calculations about a specific date for Christ's return, and as one tries sincerely to ascertain what God's will is for one's life, one should be wary of projecting one's personal resolution as a general panacea.

Some of Miller's influence is still felt. The Advent Christian Church, which believed that there was a ten-year error in Miller's calculations and looked in vain for Christ's return in 1853–54, is the largest body of First-day Adventists today, with about 31,000 members. But the largest inheritors of the Millerite tradition is the Seventh-day Adventist Church, which can be said to have been born out of the ashes of the Great Disappointment.

On October 23, 1844, the day after Christ failed to appear, Hiram Edson, a Methodist Millerite, reported having a vision in a field near Canandaiga, New York. In his vision Edson saw Christ, as High Priest, going from the holy place of the heavenly sanctuary into the Most Holy Place. Christ had gone to the wedding the previous night, and had received from God a kingdom, dominion, and glory. Edson said, "I saw that He had a work to perform in the most holy before coming to earth." So for Seventh-day Adventists, "the 1844 message was a judgment-hour message. The judgment work had begun, but it was in the heavenly sanctuary." They feel that the Millerites had been correct in predicting the date but wrong in interpreting the event to take place. Christ had begun His work as High Priest, as mediator between God and man. Indeed it was late in human history; now all mankind must do is await Christ's return from the wedding.

Edson told several friends about his vision, and together they found several biblical passages seeming to explain its meaning (Hebrews 9:11, 24 and Leviticus 16:29–34 and 23:26–32). Edson wrote about his vision in a paper he helped publish, *The Day Dawn.* Several of the founders of the Seventh-day Adventist movement read his story and were influenced by it.

The mocking and scorn they had received after the Great Disappointment convinced one group of adventists that the door had indeed been shut against any further salvation (Matthew 25:10–12). This "shut-door" belief made missionary activity virtually stop among them for several years.

Miller believed there was still time to awaken the "sleeping virgins," Christian non-adventists, but these people, followers of the Seventh Month doctrine, felt that no new converts could be made.

In December 1844 a 17-year-old girl in Portland, Ellen Gould Harmon, reported having a vision of the heavenly sanctuary, which she described in the context of Hebrews 9:3–5 and the marriage supper of the Lamb of God. The vision confirmed the validity of the Midnight Cry of the Seventh Month movement — the door had been shut in 1844. As an immediate result of her vision, she and sixty of her followers acknowledged their Seventh Month experience to be the work of God.

A week later she told of a second vision. She was informed of the trials she would have to go through, but that she should tell others about her visions. In spiritual torment, she felt too weak to witness. She had been a semi-invalid since being struck by a rock thrown by a playmate when she was nine years old. She longed for death as a release from her responsibility. Then one day, at a prayer session, "a sudden light came upon me," she said. "Something that seemed to me like a ball of fire struck me right over the heart." An angel spoke to her: "Make known to others what I have revealed to you." An elderly man, Father Pearson, who was present, said that he saw "a ball of fire came down from heaven, and struck sister Ellen Harmon right on the heart. I saw it!"

From then on, Ellen told others about visions she received. For members of the Seventh-day Adventist Church, her messages constitute the Spirit of Prophecy, a part of the Third Angel's message (Revelation 14:12, 17), which figures importantly in that church's doctrine. Ellen received visionary messages for seventy years, until her death in 1915.

In February 1845 Ellen Harmon reported a third vision. In it Christ as the Bridegroom was given the kingdom of this world from God. As soon as He returned from the wedding He would claim this world. The Midnight Cry was depicted as a great light emanating from Christ. Two groups were before the heavenly throne: a bowed group, representing the adventists, and an uninterested, carefree group, representing the church and the world. A great light passed from God to Christ, and hovered over both groups. Most in the second group ran away from it, but a few accepted the light and joined the praying adventists. Christ then entered into the Most Holy Place, where he officiated as High Priest. In this role He accepted those who believed in Him, but the remainder were lost to Satan's influence.

In 1845 Ellen met James White, a penniless schoolteacher who had become a Millerite preacher in Maine. He described the suffering he had gone through for his advent preaching: "We have been brought before magistrates — publicly whipped — put in jail — workhouse, and families torn asunder — all to prevent us from following the Lamb: but to no effect." When asked satirically, "Mr. White, are you yet in the land of the living?" he would reply, "No, sir, I am in the land of the dying, but at the coming of the Lord I expect to go to the land of the living."

In 1846 Ellen married James White. That year they heard Joseph Bates, the Millerite sea-captain, preach on observing the true Sabbath. Bates had preached on observing the Sabbath on the seventh day, rather than on the first day, ever since reading about it in an adventist paper, *The Hope of Israel*, in February 1845. Ellen and James did not accept the seventh-day Sabbath until Ellen reported having an unusual vision, in which she saw Christ raise the cover of the Ark of the Covenant, revealing the Ten Commandments. In the very center she saw the Fourth Commandment: "Remember the Sabbath day to keep it holy. Six days you shall labor, but the seventh day is a Sabbath to the Lord your God. In it you shall not do any work" (Exodus 20:8–10). This commandment was bathed in a halo of light. An angel told her: "It is the only one of the ten which defines the living God Who created the heavens and the earth." Ellen felt that if the true Sabbath had been kept, there never would have been an atheist: "The observance of the Sabbath would have preserved the world from idolatry." She now believed that, just prior to Christ's return, mankind is being warned to return to true allegiance in God. She now realized the importance of the Third Angel's message: "Keep the commandments of God, and the faith of Jesus" (Revelation 14:12).

The Seventh-day Adventist movement resulted from a merger of adventist thought with Seventh-day Baptist sabbatarian views. During the winter of 1843, Mrs. Rachel Oakes, a Seventh-day Baptist, convinced Reverend Frederick Wheeler, a Methodist Millerite, that the true Sabbath should be observed on Saturday (the seventh day). Mrs. Oakes' followers in Washington, New Hampshire, became the first Seventh-day Adventists, although the name was not officially adopted until 1860, by which time the Whites and others had made major contributions to the development of church doctrine.

Ellen reported having a vision on April 3, 1847, which told her that since Christ's mission was now in the Most Holy Place, human attention should be directed there. When she focused on the Most Holy Place, she found the Ten Commandments. She now realized that the only commandment implicit from the creation was observance of the Sabbath. She concluded that the function of this vision was to inform her of the overwhelming significance of the true observation of the Fourth Commandment. This is all that remained for Christ to return, and He would not return until the Sabbath is properly observed. Since the Sabbath is a sign between God and His people, the human breaking of this covenant is indeed a serious transgression. Ellen called the Sabbath "the seal of the living God" (Revelation 7:2) and said it was God's "greatest and last truth," which continues forever. She said, "The holy Sabbath is the separating wall between the true Israel of God and unbelievers." But she held out hope that all Christians would someday observe what she felt was the true Sabbath.

At a conference of sabbatarian adventists in November 1848 Ellen reported receiving a vision which stated that the proper observation of the

Sabbath was a "sealing sign" for Christians. Her followers assumed this meant that she wanted the sabbatarian adventist doctrine proclaimed throughout the world. But was it not true that the door had been shut for new believers since 1844?

In March 1849 Ellen reported a vision which answered this question. Although Christ had shut the door in the holy place in 1844, at the same time He had opened the door in the Most Holy Place, and no mere mortal can shut it. Thus there were now two great emphases: observe all Commandments, especially the Fourth, and tell the needy world about the urgency of this condition.

An immediate great change took place. With the door no longer shut to new believers, there was an urgent need to proclaim the message, while time remains. The 100 sabbatarian adventists in 1849 felt called upon to try to achieve the 144,000 saved souls (of Revelation 7:4) as soon as possible. Then Christ would surely return in person to this earth.

In 1850 Ellen told her followers that the burden of their missionary thrust should be the messages of the three angels mentioned in Revelation 14. The First Angel had announced the final judgment. The Second Angel condemned Babylon because of its fornication. The message of the Third Angel, she felt, explained the Great Disappointment of 1844 and made its experience meaningful to all who would see. The Third Angel made clear that worshippers of the beast of Babylon receive hellfire, but those who keep God's commandments and the faith of Jesus are saved.

The sabbatarian adventists began to think of themselves as "the saving remnant" mentioned in Revelation 12:17. They felt that perhaps their biggest influence in these final days would be the testimony of their daily lives. Discouraged by what she thought was a lack of faith, Ellen exhorted them to live more pure lives, if they were indeed the true remnant. One result of her efforts was a still greater missionary thrust. If believers wanted to see their Lord, it would take a supreme effort on their parts. She compared them to Elijah and to John the Baptist — their function was to prepare the way for the coming of the Lord. And they must be patient. Just as Moses had to condition the Jews to forty years of wandering in the Sinai wilderness before entering the Promised Land, so the sabbatarian adventists would have their waiting period between 1844 and Christ's second coming.

Ellen's husband, James White, pioneered in editing publications containing their views. The first sabbatarian adventist journal, *The Present Truth*, appeared in 1849. It merged with *Advent Review* in 1850, and as *Advent Review and Sabbath Herald* it became a leading organ of opinion.

There was controversy over whether to accept Ellen's visions, and if they were accepted, what importance to attach to them. By summer 1851 it was decided not to publish any more of her visions in *Advent Review and Sabbath Herald*, for too many readers refused to accept them as authentic visitations from God. To accommodate those who did accept the visions as valid, a book was published in 1851, *A Sketch of the Christian Experience and Views of Ellen G. White.* The book eliminated several references to the shut door and included revised versions of several previously printed visions. In his writings at this time, James White quoted open-door passages such as Isaiah 22:22 and Revelation 3:7-8.

The great rise of spiritualism after 1844 confirmed sabbatarian adventists that Babylon indeed had fallen, and spiritualism was evidence of its moral decay. Other things that sabbatarian adventists objected to were gambling, festivals, fairs, and plays put on to raise funds for churches. White noted that these worldly things were even more abundant following the widespread religious revivals of 1858. Ellen attacked these revivals as "false reformations." Satan was using them to deceive naive people into thinking that God still worked through the churches, she said. Instead, they would "leave the world and the church in a worse condition than before."

A big problem facing sabbatarian adventists throughout the 1850's was their lack of organization. Their adversaries were the first to call them "Seventh-day Adventists," and eventually they adopted the name. Initially they were opposed to having an organization and a name, the latter implying some type of structure. There were already too many sects — that was part of Babylon's problem.

In order to codify doctrine, to prevent chaotic individualism, and to organize an effective missionary program, some type of structure was inevitable. The name was agreed upon in 1860. Finally in 1863 the Seventh-day Adventist church organized itself legally, with only two types of church officers: deacons, to manage the temporal affairs, and elders, who were the spiritual overseers. James White, who had been very active in drawing viewpoints together, served as president of the general conference of the church for many years.

Early missionary work concentrated in the United States, since there was a feeling that this country occupied a providential place in world history. But particularly as ever more immigrants came to America, SDA publications began to appear in German, French, and Dutch. The first attempt to reach American Indians came in 1857. By 1859 people in Iceland, Norway, and France were receiving SDA publications from America.

In 1858 Ellen explained Christ's ministry of atonement. In 1844, she said, He had entered the Most Holy Place in the heavenly sanctuary to make a special atonement for Israel. Since 1844, however, He was engaged in a final atonement for all who could benefit from His mediation — for example, for those, living and dead, who through ignorance have broken God's laws. Increasingly the SDA outreach, through both conversion efforts and charity work, became world-wide.

Ellen said that the best SDA missionary was one who led a Christlike life. Christ's unselfishness was used as a model to motivate missionaries. The goal was to be that described in 1 Peter 2:9: "a chosen generation, a royal priesthood, a holy nation, a peculiar people." But clannishness was to be avoided at all costs. "How can you be the light of the world and the salt of the earth if you huddle together only with those of like faith?" asked James White. Ellen criticized the SDA tendency to gather into homogeneous communities in Battle Creek, Michigan, and Bordoville, Vermont.

Thus the SDA movement adopted an ecumenical outlook. Ellen spoke of Christian virtues like meekness, purity, and justice as characterizing the "oneness of Christ's followers the world over." Thinking of individuals rather than churches, she said, "The children of God, the world over, are one great brotherhood." As early as July 1850 she reported a vision stating that disobedient SDA's would be purged from the ranks of believers, their places taken by non-SDA's who would "embrace the truth" and be saved.

The SDA's do not consider themselves to be the only true Christians. Ellen said, "There are true Christians in every church, not excepting the Roman Catholic communion," although she did believe that the greater part of Christianity were Protestants.

Her advice to SDA ministers was: "Seek to come near to the ministers of other denominations. Pray for and with these men, for whom Christ is interceding." She felt that SDA's should try to agree with others "on every point we can conscientiously," and to come as near as possible to other people, "and then the light and truth we have may benefit them."

Quoting Revelation 19:10, "The testimony of Jesus is the spirit of prophecy," SDA's felt that Ellen's visions had been sent from God, and thus should be heeded. In 1862 a book was published by SDA's, showing the continuity of New Testament gifts of the Holy Spirit throughout the history of Christianity, including Ellen's gifts. James White wrote the introduction to the book.

Ellen's standards were high, and not many SDA's lived up to them. In 1867 she said that it looked as if only a remnant of the remnant would be saved. In 1868 she stated that not one in twenty SDA's "is living out the self-sacrificing principles of the word of God." In fact, she felt that the failure of SDA's to live up to their principles could well be one of the prime reasons for the postponement of Christ's second coming.

Interesting enough, she who had pioneered in opposing church structures came to defend them when her views became a new orthodoxy. After the General Conference of the SDA church was organized in 1863, she said: "God has bestowed power on the church and the ministers of the church, and it is not a light matter to resist the authority of God's ministers." She felt that the only legitimate channel for new views was the General Conference of the church.

Their sabbatarian position has made the SDA church a pioneer for religious liberty. Through their periodical, *Religious Liberty*, which deals not only with SDA issues but with the broad field of religious liberty, they have consistently opposed Sunday legislation as a violation of the constitutional guarantee of separation of church and state. To them Sunday, as the first day of the week, is a work day, and they oppose state laws outlawing Sunday work. They feel that in times past, when the Sabbath issue had not been raised, it was no sin to observe the wrong day for the Sabbath. But now, when attention has been called to the proper day for Sabbath observance, they feel it is a grievous sin to observe the Sabbath on any day except Saturday.

A leading characteristic of the SDA movement is its stress on health reform. Joseph Bates not only had been an adventist, abolitionist, and temperance leader, but by 1844 he had abandoned all forms of alcohol, tea, coffee, tobacco, meat, and "greasy and rich foods." Jerome Clark, a SDA historian, says that "subsequently, Seventh-day Adventists accepted every one of the health principles Joseph Bates had adopted."

In 1848 Ellen reported having a vision warning of the injurious effects of tobacco, tea, and coffee. Later she called these things "idols," because people were so attracted to them. She found many reasons why people should abstain from substances harmful to the body: First, to have good spiritual health, one needed good physical health, and so one should refrain from impairing one's body; next, in the light of the imminent second coming of Christ, one should keep one's holy temple clean; and last, money saved from buying these harmful products could be used in missionary work.

As a result of a vision that Ellen reported in 1863, her followers were encouraged to adopt a vegetarian diet. She said that temperance was not only a dietary principle—people needed to be temperate in exercising emotions and even in their work habits. She quoted biblical authority to confirm that health is God's special gift to humanity.

In 1864 Ellen published her first extensive treatise on health, in which she advocated a holistic approach, seeing health as a correct bodily-mental-spiritual relationship. Wine's deleterious effect on the body led to impairment of the mind, which in turn negatively affected one's spirit.

In 1865 Ellen visited her husband James in a hydrotherapy clinic in Dansville, New York. He had been stricken with paralysis, perhaps as a result of overwork. The beneficial treatment he received strengthened her belief in vegetarianism and hydrotherapy. That year she reported a vision she had on Christmas Day, which affirmed that God wanted humans to reform their living habits. As a direct result of this vision, the Western Health Reform Institute was established in Battle Creek in 1866. Its functions were the treatment of disease and the teaching of the principles of healthful living. Ellen said: "This institution is designed of God to be one of the greatest aids in preparing a people to be perfect before God." It was also seen as an important missionary vehicle. Ellen said that physicians should administer not only to the body but to sin-sick souls and to diseased minds, pointing them to "the never-failing remedy, the Savior who died for them." She even went so far as to say that "it is a sin to be sick, for all sickness is the result of transgression."

In response to those who said it was contradictory to build large hospitals when the second coming was so imminent, she said that the Institute would hasten Christ's return because it would put people in a state of readiness for Him. In 1866 the periodical *Health Reformer* was begun, spreading SDA views on health. The stress on health reform led ultimately to a world-wide system of sanitariums and hospitals, powerful missionary tools in helping spread the message of the Third Angel to mankind: Obey God's commandments and keep the faith of Jesus, for the end is near.

In 1879 the SDA church formed the American Health and Temperance Association, with Dr. John Harvey Kellogg as president. The Association merged in 1893 with the SDA Medical Missionary and Benevolent Association. Dr. Kellogg pioneered in introducing health foods, especially breakfast cereals, to the American public. Nowadays all SDA high schools and colleges have chapters of the American Temperance Society.

As non-combatants, SDA's do not bear arms in wartime but they do volunteer to do Medical Corps work. To prepare for such work SDA youth attend medical cadet corps training academies at their own expense. Tens of thousands of SDA youth have been so trained, and many have served in American armed forces.

Although the SDA church grew slowly at first, it has always been an unusually active church. By 1875 this group of 8,000 believers was already supporting two publishing houses, a college, a medical institution, and a rapidly growing missionary program. A hundred years later the church has 3,000,000 members and operates 142 hospitals and sanitariums and 251 dispensaries and clinics. In addition it operates a school system, including colleges and a medical school, which enrolls half a million students. Its publishing houses now print material in 203 languages and dialects. Extending aid to non-SDA's as well as to their own members, they help nearly ten million people annually through charity. Needless to say, they tithe. As Monsignor Algermissen of the Catholic seminary at Hildesheim, Germany, says: "Truth demands the honest recognition of their readiness for sacrifice."

Nevertheless, this doughty group of believers keep their eyes set steadfastly upon the imminent return of their Lord. Seeing our enslavement to technology, the increasing frequency of world crises, and the production of ever more destructive military weapons, they feel that the day of His return is indeed near. Unlike many modern adventists, they feel that the faithful will live and reign with Christ for 1,000 years in heaven, not on earth. Earth will remain a "desolate, depopulated wilderness" throughout the millennium. After that, there will be the resurrection and punishment of the unbelievers and the setting up of the New Jerusalem on earth. After the earth is purified by fire, it will be "re-created at the command of Christ into the eternal home of His redeemed."

It is interesting that all three facets of this vigorous faith had their origins in 1844: the sanctuary doctrine of the advent, as seen in visions by Hiram Edson and Ellen Harmon; the seventh-day Sabbath, as promulgated by Rachel Oakes and Joseph Bates; and the Spirit of Prophecy, as embodied in the visions of Ellen Harmon.

Another adventist group still active began in England during the

1820's. Edward Irving, a London preacher, predicted that Christ would return in 1864, and that about a generation before this time Christ would revive in His church the offices of the New Testament church. It was stated that miraculous medical cures occurred during Irving's sermons. Henry Drummond, a banker who supported Irving, announced that the Holy Spirit had visited him, appointing new apostles chosen by Christ for the new age. The church has thus been called the Catholic Apostolic Church. Over half of its 60,000 members now live in Germany.

A smaller adventist sect in Germany, called "The Association in Jesus Christ" believe that the world will end at Christ's return to earth in the year 2000.

Charles Taze Russell, a Presbyterian from Pittsburgh, founded Jehovah's Witnesses in 1874 out of a Bible-study group which had been discussing adventist predictions in Revelation. Russell said Christ had returned invisibly in 1874, and that the millennium, with Christ as ruler, would begin in 1914. Joseph Franklin Rutherford, a Baptist lawyer who took over the leadership of Jehovah's Witnesses upon Russell's death in 1918, explained that in 1914 Christ had ascended His heavenly throne to lead the final struggle against Satan and his followers. In 1918 Satan, defeated in heaven, returned to earth and is hard at work here, but soon Armageddon will take place, and Satan's final overthrow will occur, Rutherford said.

Many Pentecostal groups believe in an imminent return of Christ, and cite what they feel is the presence of the Holy Spirit as precursor of the advent. Speaking in tongues and seemingly miraculous cures are evidence of the work of the Holy Spirit, they aver. These groups are in revolt against what they call "rationalized, superficial, sophisticated" Christianity.

In the Soviet Union recently a university lecturer was declared to be a schizophrenic and was put into a psychiatric hospital for distributing leaflets announcing Christ's second coming. The lecturer, Vyacheslav Zaitsev, a member of the Russian Orthodox Church, has had two doctoral dissertations turned down because they state that "religion is a determining factor in the history of mankind."

The leading non-fiction best-selling book in the United States in the 1970's was *The Late Great Planet Earth*, in which author Hal Lindsey argued that Christ's second coming was fast approaching. The unsettled conditions in the modern world and the near approach of the year 2000 will undoubtedly fan the fire of advent enthusiasts ever more greatly in the immediate years ahead.

# 3
## The Genesis of Mormonism

The morning of June 27, 1844, Dan Jones, a Mormon convert from Wales, spoke to Frank Worrell, an officer of the Carthage Greys, a military unit charged with local law enforcement. Worrell said to Jones: "We have had too much trouble to bring Old Joe here to let him escape alive. Unless you want to die with him you had better leave before sundown. You'll see that I can prophesy better than Old Joe, for neither he nor his brother, nor anyone who will remain with them, will see the sun set today."

Jones hurried to the Carthage jail and told Joseph Smith what Worrell had said. Smith told Jones to report the conversation to Governor Ford of Illinois, who had come to Carthage to try to keep order.

Feelings were running high between the Mormons and their adversaries. When the first issue of *The Nauvoo Expositor* had attacked Joseph Smith and other Mormon leaders on June 7, Smith had ordered the press destroyed. "Could we suffer a set of worthless vagabonds to come into our city and vilify not only ourselves but the character of our wives and daughters?" Smith asked Governor Ford.

Aroused Illinoisans were concerned not only about freedom of the press. They felt that there was undesirable fusion of church and state in Nauvoo, the Mormon settlement on the Mississippi which was the largest city in Illinois. Many believed that the Nauvoo charter, granted by the state legislature, was being abused and that legal due process was no longer being observed there. Rumors ran underground about Joseph Smith and other Mormon leaders living in polygamy, and that the Sons of Dan, a Mormon protective association, had been guilty of several "holy murders."

Governor Ford's reply to Jones was, "You are unnecessarily alarmed for the safety of your friends. The people are not that cruel."

Unconvinced, Jones started back toward the jail. He heard an officer of the militia from Warsaw, a nearby town, tell his men: "Our troops will be discharged this morning in obedience to orders, but when the governor and the McDonough troops have left for Nauvoo this afternoon, we will return and kill these men, if we have to tear the jail down."

Jones was unable to get into the jail that afternoon. Joseph Smith sent word by Willard Richards that Jonathan Dunham should immediately bring the Nauvoo Legion to Carthage. But instead, Governor Ford

Joseph Smith as pictured in contemporary prints, preaching to the Indians and being murdered. (Religious News Service Photo.)

persuaded Dunham to have the Legion, a branch of the state militia, disarmed.

Joseph Smith and his brother, Hyrum, spent the day writing letters. Joseph asked John Taylor, the Canadian convert who had established the mission station in Liverpool, to sing the hymn, "A Poor Wayfaring Man of Grief." Taylor complied.

At four that afternoon the prison guard was changed. At about five o'clock a mob of about one hundred men assembled at the prison. Some had blackened faces. One group rushed the prison door. At twenty feet the guards fired over their heads.

In a moment the mob was mounting the stairway to the second floor room in which the two Smiths, Taylor, and Richards were being detained. Taylor and Richards, armed with canes, tried to parry rifle barrels and keep out the intruders. Several musket shots were fired, some through the door.

Joseph Smith emptied his six-shot pistol into the coming mob. His brother Hyrum, shot in the nose, neck, and legs, said, "I am a dead man," and fell. Taylor was shot five times; a heavy watch deflected what otherwise would have been a fatal bullet. Richards escaped miraculously with only a grazed left ear.

His gun empty, Joseph ran for the window. Bullets hit him from both front and back. Shouting, "O Lord, my God!" he fell from the window. To ensure his death, four men fired bullets into his body, where it lay propped against a well.

The mob cheered and dispersed. The whole affair lasted only three minutes. Members of the Carthage Greys arrived late, and made no attempt to pursue the attackers. Later, Richards retrieved Joseph's body and put it beside his brother's. Artois Hamilton then took the bodies to his hotel, to await the construction of coffins.

When they had fled across the river to Iowa, Hyrum had persuaded Joseph to go back to face trial. "If you go back," Joseph had told Hyrum, "I will go with you, but we shall be butchered." In Wallace Stegner's words, "Whatever else Joseph Smith was, he was at the end neither a scoundrel nor a coward."

What prompted such high feeling against this man and his religious movement? Did his martyrdom keep his movement from serious internal split and possible dissolution? What are some of the unique beliefs of these "peculiar people, zealous of good works"?

Shortly after the American Revolution, many Americans felt that the biblical prophecy of Daniel was about to be fulfilled—the millennium was at hand, and Christ's kingdom was coming on earth. One who believed this was Asael Smith, Joseph's grandfather, as outlined in a letter he wrote in 1796. Asael's son Joseph Smith, senior, was often preoccupied with religious thoughts and frequently had dreams involving visions of God. He and his wife Lucy reared their children in a highly religious atmosphere.

Their fourth child, Joseph Smith, junior, was born in Sharon,

Vermont, on December 23, 1805. The family moved often. In 1816 the Smiths moved to the village of Palmyra, New York, and then in 1820 to Manchester in the Finger Lake district.

As a young man Joseph was a treasure seeker. Guided by his seer stone, a piece of native crystal, Joseph would lead friends to alleged treasure sites. Since they usually found nothing, Joseph explained the failure as due to the influence of evil spirits. Sometimes an effort would be made to placate the evil spirits by sprinkling the blood of a dead animal on the excavation site.

The use of seer stones was widespread in this area. There had been exploration of Indian burial sites nearby, and sometimes artifacts or relics were exhumed that were of some value.

Some diggers were religious mystics who were not primarily seeking monetary treasure. One religious cult in Wells, Vermont, claimed to be descendants of the lost tribes of Israel. They, like many others, preached that Christ's second coming was imminent. They wanted to restore primitive Christianity with its attendant gifts of healing. They also had a practice of using what they called "miraculous rods" to help them find buried treasure. Oliver Cowdery, one of Joseph's first converts, possessed such a rod, his father having been a member of that sect.

In later years Brigham Young said that Joseph had told him: "Every man who lived on the earth is entitled to a seer stone, but they are kept from them in consequence of their wickedness." Joseph's mother and some of his closest friends, such as David Whitmer and Martin Harris, said that Joseph used a seer stone in translating much of the *Book of Mormon* and in giving many of his early revelations.

Joseph's world was one of a Protestant civil war. Each church tended to proclaim itself the unique repository of true Christianity. Especially active at this time were Presbyterians, Methodists, and Baptists. Joseph, like his father, was Presbyterian, but he was confused by the Babel of rival claims. Seeking help in scripture, he read James 1:5: "If any of you lack wisdom, let him ask of God, and it shall be given him." So Joseph asked God for wisdom, on a spring day in 1820. He describes the response: "I had scarcely done so, when immediately I was seized upon by some power which entirely overcame me, and had such an astonishing influence over me as to bind my tongue so that I could not speak. Thick darkness gathered around me, and it seemed to me for a time as if I were doomed to sudden destruction. I saw a pillar of light exactly over my head, above the bright-ness of the sun, which descended gradually until it fell upon me. It no sooner appeared than I found myself delivered from the enemy which held me bound. I saw two Personages standing above me. One of them spake unto me, calling me by name, and said, pointing to the other — 'This is My Beloved Son. Hear Him!' I asked the Personages who stood above me which of all the sects was right. I was answered that I must join none of them, for they were all wrong."

Joseph said that he was instructed that at some future time he would be given further information. When he told others about his vision, he was roundly attacked. As might be expected, ministers particularly objected to being told that God did not support their churches.

Joseph told of another supernatural visitation that occurred to him on the night of September 21, 1823. While praying, he was visited by the angel Moroni, who told him that God had work for him to do, and that his name would be "both good and evil spoken of among all people." Moroni told of a buried book, written upon gold plates, telling of early inhabitants of America. He said there were two stones in silver bows, fastened to a breastplate. These things, called the Urim and Thummim, were the signs of seers in former days, and would assist in the translation of the book. Moroni said that many Bible prophecies were about to be fulfilled, such as those contained in Isaiah 11, Joel 2, Malachi 3 and 4, and Acts 3. Moroni, who repeated his message three times that night, said that great judgments were coming to the earth — great desolation by famine, sword, and pestilence. He said, however, that America was "a land which is choice above all other lands," and the site of the New Jerusalem foretold by prophets.

The next day, while working with his father, Joseph fell helpless to the ground. He says he saw Moroni standing over him. Moroni told Joseph to relate his experience to his father. When he did, his father declared the vision to be sent by God and told Joseph to obey Moroni. Joseph found the plates and the Urim and Thummim in a stone box. When he began to examine them he was stopped by Moroni, who told him to come back to the spot each year on September 21. Joseph swore his family to secrecy about the visits of Moroni.

His mother described a weird family scene — all family members seated in a circle around Joseph, an 18-year-old lad who had never read the Bible through in his life, a boy who did not read as much as the other children but who often seemed to be absorbed in deep meditation. Each year Joseph returned to the burial site on Hill Cumorah outside Palmyra, but each time Moroni told him, "No, not yet."

The background was one of religious enthusiasm. The Second Great Awakening was on. Fiery Protestant preachers like Charles Finney warned of impending doom unless the word of God were heeded. Camp meetings spread throughout the area.

The inhabitants of western New York, many of them originally from New England, had consciences quick to respond to the warnings of revivalists. Many were ultraists, people who became single-minded in espousing a particular panacea. Temperance meant total abstinence. Abolition meant immediate freeing of the slaves. People left traditional churches to experiment with new faiths. The followers of Emanuel Swedenborg, the mystic, and Franz Mesmer, the hypnotist, flourished. Spiritualism became popular. Utopian socialism, especially the phalanx system of Charles Fourier, was spreading.

Religious extremism moved in two directions: some believers became hard-shell fundamentalists, and others became extremely liberal and open to new insights. All sorts of religious groups sprang up: Bible, tract, missionary, and temperance societies. The Disciples of Christ, led by Alexander Campbell, were claiming to restore primitive Christianity, as were the Millerites, the Shakers, and other Protestant groups. Each group considered itself unique in re-establishing the true church of Christ.

In September 1826 William Morgan of Batavia, New York, a former Mason who threatened to reveal Masonic secrets, mysteriously disappeared. Masons were accused of murdering him. Joseph Smith attended some anti-Masonic meetings, and seemed to be influenced by them. He was already paying a price for his religious views. On March 20, 1826, he had been brought before a justice of the peace in Bainbridge, New York, on charges of being a disorderly person and an impostor, but the charges had been dropped. In January 1827 he married Emma Hale of Harmony, Pennsylvania.

In 1827, at his annual visit to Hill Cumorah, Joseph said that Moroni indicated that the time was now appropriate for disclosing the plates. Accordingly, on September 22, 1827, Joseph said that he received them, along with the Urim and Thummim.

Joseph's brother, William, said that Joseph brought the gold plates home wrapped in an old frock. He allowed family members to handle them behind a sheet but not see them, at first. William said they seemed to be sheets of metal, like pages in a book. He said they were a mixture of copper and gold, and weighed about sixty pounds.

Joseph's mother described the Urim and Thummim as "two smooth, three-cornered diamonds set in glass and the glasses set in silver bows, like old-fashioned spectacles." The breastplate, she said, was "concave-convex, with metal straps for fastening to hips and shoulders, made for a man of extraordinary size."

Many people wanted to see the plates, but Joseph showed them to only eleven trusted persons, whose affidavits appear at the beginning of the *Book of Mormon*. Three of these people were his father and two of his brothers, and five others were members of the Whitmer family, early followers of Joseph. The other three witnesses were Oliver Cowdery, Martin Harris, and Hiram Page. None of the eleven ever recanted their testimony, although Cowdery, Harris, and David Whitmer later left the church.

To escape harassment, Joseph moved to Susquehanna County in Pennsylvania, where he copied much of the material from the plates. He then translated the material, aided by the Urim and Thummim. His method of translation was to sit behind a curtain and dictate slowly and distinctly to a scribe. Scribes he used included his wife, Oliver Cowdery, and Martin Harris.

Harris took a manuscript of 116 pages of the translation to Palmyra to convince some friends of its value, but lost the manuscript. Possibly his wife destroyed it, for she suspected that Joseph would take their property away from them. This part of the *Book of Mormon* has never been recovered. Joseph said he had had a revelation telling him it had fallen into Satan's hands and had been altered. He said that he was not to retranslate the lost section, but to rely on other sections of the book that related the same events.

Three witnesses, Harris, Cowdery, and David Whitmer, testified that in June 1829 they had had a revelation in which the voice of God told them that the *Book of Mormon* was true and that the translation was correct.

During the previous month Cowdery and Joseph said that John the Baptist had appeared to them in a vision, ordaining them to the Aaronic priesthood, which holds the keys of the ministering of angels, the gospel of repentance, and baptism by immersion for remission of sins. This priesthood is divided into deacons, teachers, priests, and bishops.

Shortly thereafter Cowdery and Joseph reported that Peter, James, and John had appeared to them, ordaining them into the Melchizedek priesthood, which gave them the authority to organize God's kingdom on earth in these latter days. This priesthood is divided into elders, seventies, high priests, patriarchs (or evangelists), apostles, and prophets.

Ideas contained in the *Book of Mormon* were by no means unfamiliar to Joseph's contemporaries. Many passages paraphrase the King James version of the Bible. Seven of the fifteen books in the *Book of Mormon* contain material parallel to that found in Masonic sources. A backwoods preacher named James Adair had published a history of American Indians in 1735 in which he had stated that they were descendants of the lost tribes of Israel. Solomon Spaulding, in a work written in a biblical style called *The Manuscript Found*, had recently made a similar assertion. Spaulding said that his work was a translation of an ancient manuscript found in an Indian burial mound in western New York State. Ethan Smith, a Congregational minister from Vermont unrelated to Joseph, in 1823 published *View of the Hebrews*, in which the Indian origins were traced to Israel. In his analysis of the *Book of Mormon* in 1832 in a book called *Delusions*, Alexander Campbell showed that Joseph's book contained material on virtually every religious doctrine which had been discussed in New York State's fervent "Burned-over District" in the preceding decade.

Joseph said that Moroni retained the plates after the translation had been made. Martin Harris sold part of his farm to help pay publishing costs of the *Book of Mormon*, printed by a small shop in Palmyra in March 1830. Joseph's father and brothers immediately embarked on a campaign to sell the book to farmers throughout the area.

The *Book of Mormon* tells the story of Lehi, who had left Jerusalem with his family about 600 B.C. A godly man, Lehi had been warned of the destruction to come during the reign of Zedekiah. So he and his family built a ship, sailed westward, and landed on the American continent. Two sons, Laman and Lemuel, sinned, and their skins were turned dark as a punishment. Their descendants, the Lamanites, had some good qualities, but were often savage, idolatrous, and quarrelsome. The Nephites, God's chosen people, were descendants of the youngest son, Nephi. The Nephites prospered, maintaining their Old Testament heritage, to which was added their own record of prophecy and history.

When Jesus was crucified in Palestine, cataclysmic events occurred in America. Some cities sank into the sea, some were swallowed up by the earth, and some were destroyed by heavenly fire. Total darkness covered the earth for three days. Then the resurrected Christ appeared and established His church among the Nephites. He ordained leaders and taught as He had in Palestine.

For a while, the Nephites prospered. But in time they grew indifferent to their religious teachings, and they were destroyed by the warlike Lamanites. One of their chief prophets, Mormon, tried to exhort them to adhere to their faith. He also kept a record of his people. He gave an abridgement of this record, on golden plates, to his son Moroni. The Nephites were destroyed in A.D. 385, and Moroni buried the plates on Hill Cumorah in A.D. 421.

Joseph stated that he was told that he had been chosen to restore the true church of Christ, which had existed on earth from the time of Adam. There had been restorations by Abraham and Moses in previous dispensations, but that now mankind was entering "the dispensation of the fullness of times" mentioned in Ephesians 1:10. Since the Catholic Church had suffered great apostasy, he said, even its Protestant branches were corrupt. Mankind's only hope was to restore the original church of Christ.

Inherent in this faith is belief in progressive revelation. Why would God confine His revelation to one people at one time and place, Joseph asked. No, said Joseph, God has revealed, is revealing, and will reveal important matters pertaining to His Kingdom through all of time.

In September 1830 Joseph reported a revelation in which the Lord explained that He had sent Peter, James, and John to ordain Joseph and Cowdery as apostles and special witnesses, to give them the keys of His Kingdom in this dispensation, in which the Lord shall "gather together in one all things in Christ, both which are in heaven, and which are on earth" (Ephesians 1:10). The gospel, Joseph was told, should be preached to the dead: "The dead shall hear the voice of the Son of God" (John 5:25).

One month after the *Book of Mormon* had been published, the church, called The Church of Christ, had been organized, with six members. Within weeks, it had hundreds of members. By the end of the year there were over a thousand members. It certainly seemed as if a religious thirst was being quenched.

When a friend, Newel Knight, suffered a seizure which distorted his face and limbs, Joseph took his hand and commanded the devil to leave his body, in the name of Jesus Christ. Newel claimed that he saw the devil depart, and he was cured. Joseph said that he had done no miracle—it had been done by the Lord. But the news spread quickly about this strange new prophet.

In 1830 he was twice charged with disorderly conduct for preaching from the *Book of Mormon*, but each time he was acquitted. Emma, Joseph's wife, suffered much. She had seen her husband harassed, she had missed him in his frequent absence on religious business, and she had lost her first child. In July 1830 Joseph said he received a revelation for her, which recognized her unhappiness but ordered her to support his work. She was told to comfort "my servant, Joseph, in the spirit of meekness." She was pronounced an "elect lady," and was appointed to select hymns for church meetings. The news of the revelation seemed to placate her.

Hiram Page, who had married a Whitmer girl, began to announce that he was receiving revelations about church organization and government. Several days later Joseph reported a revelation stating that no one was to receive divine revelations except him. It seemed in those days that as soon as his followers were beyond his sight and influence they began to lose their common spirit. Already in 1830 Cowdery and David Whitmer were beginning to grow discontented with Joseph's leadership.

President Andrew Jackson was determined to move Indian tribes west of the Mississippi River. Between 1829 and 1837 the federal government negotiated 94 treaties with Indians, mostly involving their resettlement westward. Joseph interpreted this action as the beginning of the gathering of the Israelites, which was to precede the millennium. As a result of a revelation, Joseph sent missionaries to these Lamanite descendants, but few Indians were converted at the time.

A group of four missionaries, including Parley P. Pratt, a former follower of Alexander Campbell, traveled westward in 1830 to Kirtland, Ohio, where Sidney Rigdon led a Campbellite community. Upon Rigdon's conversion to Mormonism he brought 127 members of his group into the Mormon fellowship. Shortly after this, Joseph reported a revelation, telling him to move the church to Kirtland. This Joseph did in January 1831, against the desires of many of his followers, including his wife Emma.

The four missionaries pushed on to Independence, Missouri, where they found friendly Indians and good soil, and thus a good site for a colony of believers. By July 1831 Joseph and twenty-eight other church members went to Missouri and helped establish a community there. For the next seven years the two main church centers were separated by the 1000 miles between Kirtland and Independence.

One of Joseph's perennial battles was with poverty. In February 1831, however, he reported a revelation stating the the Kirtland Saints should build a house for their prophet. Accordingly, Isaac Morley put up a cabin for the Smiths on his own land.

When Mrs. Johnson, a farmer's wife, was partially paralyzed from rheumatism, Joseph took her hand and commanded, in the name of Jesus Christ, that she be made whole. When her paralysis seemed to disappear instantly, the word spread, and more converts were made.

In 1831 James Gordon Bennett published a series of articles in the *Morning Courier and New York Enquirer* attacking the Mormon movement. Thus began a newspaper trend of sensational and frequently misinformed stories about Joseph and his church.

Joseph was impressed with the possibilities of the Independence area as a future site for the whole church. In fact, he reported having a revelation in 1831 telling him that the Independence region would be the site of the New Jerusalem after the millennium. A Mormon community, transplanted from Colesville, New York, expressed disappointment with the relatively barren land they found in Missouri when they dutifully followed their prophet's advice to move west.

Some Mormon leaders expressed displeasure with the rapid rise of Sidney Rigdon in the church. Joseph, a relatively unschooled man, leaned heavily upon the well-educated Rigdon for advice. On February 16, 1832, Joseph and Rigdon reported receiving a vision at Hiram, Ohio. They said they saw angels and saints worshipping God and Christ, and a voice declaring Christ as the "only begotten Lamb of the Father."

On March 24, 1832, Joseph and Rigdon were tarred and feathered in Hiram. The mob apparently had been stirred up by Simonds Ryder, an apostate Mormon, who told the people that the church would take their property away from them. Joseph was also accused of having had sex relations with Nancy Johnson. Years later, after Joseph's death, he was sealed in eternal marriage to Nancy with the consent of her husband, Orson Hyde.

The day after having been tarred and feathered Joseph preached an effective sermon in the Hiram church. Townspeople admired the rapid recuperative powers of the tall, handsome prophet.

On Christmas Day, 1832, Joseph reported one of his most noted revelations. Joseph forecast the future: the South Carolina insurrection would ultimately lead to a great war which would cause many deaths. The Southern states would call upon other nations, including Great Britain, to help them in their war to preserve slavery. Ultimately, the strife would lead to "a full end of all nations," and the day of the Lord would come. Joseph felt that the end of the world was imminent. "Fifty-six years," he said, "should wind up the scene."

During his first two years in Ohio, Joseph reported having had 49 revelations. Some of the chief topics of his revelations were the appointment of leaders, the repudiation of false spirits, warning concerning Christ's second coming, selection of the temple site and the seat of Zion, and the dispatch of missionaries.

When persons criticized the grammar of his revelations, which were generally dictated by Joseph to a scribe, he replied that "every word of the revelation had been dictated by Jesus Christ." Before publication, however, the revelations were revised by a committee consisting of Joseph, Rigdon, and Cowdery. Some Mormons resented this editorial work, wondering whether any accuracy had been lost.

Rigdon and Orson Pratt compiled the *Book of Doctrines and Covenants* from the *Book of Mormon* and Joseph's other revelations. *The Pearl of Great Price*, which Joseph said he translated in 1835, purports to be a lost scripture written by Jacob's son, Joseph, when he was in Egypt.

The Mormon Church, called The Church of Christ from its inception in 1830 until 1834, then was renamed The Church of the Latter-day Saints. In 1838 as a result of one of Joseph's revelations the church received its current name: The Church of Jesus Christ of Latter-day Saints. The very name of the church reflects the belief that "the times of the end" are near.

Largely because of the Mormon influx, Kirtland grew from 1,000 to 5,000 within five years. Beneath the surface problems were brewing, but outwardly the church seemed to flourish. However, there were open problems in Missouri.

From the beginning the Missourians disliked the Mormons. The Mormon teaching that the Indians would regain lost power and prestige was viewed as an incitement to the Indians to rebel. Since practically all Mormons were Northerners, who disavowed slavery, it was feared that they would sow dissension among the slaves. Also, the Mormon tradition of self-sufficiency was interpreted as a threat to all neighboring land-owners.

Several free black Mormons tried to move to Independence, but a Missouri law required one to have a certificate of citizenship from another state. William Phelps, editor of the Mormon paper, *The Evening and the Morning Star*, in July 1833 encouraged blacks to move to Missouri. Missourians objected, saying that they would "corrupt our blacks and instigate them to bloodshed." In a clumsy effort to calm a growing tempest, Phelps published a new version: "Our intention was not only to prevent free people of color from emigrating to this state, but to prevent them from being admitted as members of the Church." This was not church policy – as a matter of fact, many Mormons had befriended blacks in Missouri and elsewhere.

Unconvinced, a mob of 300 white men destroyed Phelps' press. They also tarred and feathered Mormon leaders Edward Partridge and Charles Allen. Reacting to this pressure, the Mormons promised to leave Jackson County. When they asked restitution for damage to their property, however, mobs struck again, beating men and breaking windows and furniture. Persuaded by conciliators to surrender their arms, the Mormons did so in good faith. But the frontiersmen attacked again, burning or pillaging over 200 homes and driving 1200 Mormons out into the cold November night.

Camped out on a riverbank during the early morning of November 13, 1833, the Saints witnessed one of the greatest meteorite displays of the century. Many Mormons, as well as other believers, felt that this was the beginning of the end, a preparation for Christ's return.

In court in February 1834 charges against the mob leaders were dismissed. One defendant, John Walker, said that in self-defense he did "necessarily a little beat, bruise, wound and ill treat said Edward Partridge," and "unavoidably did besmear the said Edward with a little pitch, tar, and feathers." Whenever the Mormons tried to return home, they met violence.

When the news reached Kirtland, Joseph was enraged. His petition for aid to President Jackson ignored, Joseph turned to prayer. God revealed to him, he said, that they would have to supply their own help to their beleagured comrades. Accordingly, Zion's Camp, a group of 200 armed men, made the grueling journey to Missouri. It took forty days. Samuel Baker, nearly 80, walked the whole way. Joseph's leadership was outstanding. He never seemed tired, he always encouraged the faint hearted, and he was the first to share meager rations with others.

In Missouri negotiations with the frontiersmen kept the discord from accelerating. Some Mormons criticized Joseph for not condoning the use of violence. They wanted revenge, and they wanted property restitution. Then a severe cholera attack killed fourteen of Joseph's army. On July 3, 1834, when Zion's Camp disbanded, having done very little for the Missouri Mormons, each person received payment of a sum of $1.14.

But as Wallace Stegner has observed, the effort was "one of those ludicrous but somehow constructive failures with which his whole career was marked." For what had happened was the adversity had welded together a faithful band of brethren, who now knew they could endure hardship for their cause. Great leaders were molded: Brigham Young, Heber Kimball, Orson Pratt, Parley P. Pratt, Orson Hyde, and others. A major church unit evolved, the Quorum of the Twelve Apostles, which held the Saints together after Joseph's death. And the skill in learning to move large numbers of people across barren land paid rich dividends later in the westward trek to Utah.

By 1835 the church had five governing bodies which revelation had supposedly declared to be equal: President, Twelve Apostles, The Seventies, and the High Councils of Kirtland and Zion (Independence). When the Apostles began to exert the most influence, Joseph reported a revelation which established the President as supreme over the church, as seer, revelator, translator, and prophet. Joseph's father was made patriarch of the church, Sidney Rigdon first counselor, brother Hyrum Smith second counselor, and youngest brother Don Carlos Smith president of the high priests.

Now Joseph's star was in apogee. Most of the restored scriptures were at hand. Loyal and capable supporters were in abundance. Converts continued to join the church in a steady stream. Indeed, the extension of the rights of priesthood to lay members carried out in religious terms the equalitarian promise of Jacksonian democracy.

But as with all great leaders Joseph had his fatal flaw, his Achilles heel. In Joseph's case it was polygamy.

Ever since 1831 it had been murmured that first Joseph, then his most trusted aides, had been practicing polygamy. In 1835 rumors began to spread about Joseph's relation to Fannie Alger, the 17-year-old girl who lived in the Smith home. One Saint, Benjamin Johnson, said that "without doubt, Fannie was the prophet's first plural wife." Oliver Cowdery called Joseph's relationship to Fannie a "dirty, nasty, filthy affair."

Although Mormons were forbidden to perform marriage ceremonies by Geauga County Court on the ground that they were not regularly ordained ministers, Joseph did perform marriage ceremonies. His first, on November 24, 1835, joined Newel Knight to a pretty convert, Lydia Goldthwait, whose husband would neither join the church nor divorce her. Mormon biographer Donna Hill says, "The prophet sympathized with the predicament of his faithful friend," and performed the ceremony. Knight said that Joseph mentioned that soon a number of disclosures about the ancient institution of marriage would be made.

To allay a growing criticism, the church announced its official opposition to polygamy, but church leaders close to Joseph began to lose respect for him when they noticed the disparity between his preaching and his practicing.

Joseph continued to report revelations. He said that on January 21, 1836, a vision appeared to him, his two counselors, and his father. He said they saw the heavens open, revealing God, Christ, Adam, and Abraham. They also saw Joseph's dead brother, Alvin. In the vision the voice of the Lord said: "All who have died without a knowledge of this gospel, who would have received it if they had been permitted to tarry, shall be heirs of the celestial kingdom of God; also all that shall die henceforth without a knowledge of it, who would have received it with all their hearts, shall be heirs of that kingdom, for I, the Lord, will judge all men according to their works, according to the desire of their hearts."

The first Mormon temple, the one in Kirtland, had been under construction since early 1833. Owing to the importance of the temple in sealing Mormon ceremonies, great stress was placed upon completing it. Finally the temple was dedicated for use on April 3, 1836, and then the long-awaited mystical rites of washing, anointing, and sealing began.

Joseph reported that on that day he and Cowdery had had a revelation involving Christ, Moses, and Elijah. In the vision Christ had accepted "this house," the temple. Malachi 4:5-6 had promised that God would send the prophet Elijah to earth before Christ's second coming, "to turn the heart of the fathers to the children, and the heart of the children to their fathers." Declaring the day of the Lord to be at hand, Elijah had turned over to Joseph and Cowdery the keys of the dispensation for turning the hearts of the fathers and children as prescribed by scripture. Joseph and Cowdery explained this teaching to mean not only should love cement all family relationships but also people should seek out their forefathers so that they can be baptized for the dead relatives.

In January 1837 Joseph set up the Kirtland Safety Society Bank, but when the Ohio legislature refused to charter it, Joseph operated it as the Kirtland Safety Society Anti-Banking Company. The plan was for the anti-bank to issue notes to landowners in return for mortgages which would become the basis for more notes, a common practice at the time.

President Jackson's adamant opposition to the U.S. Bank led to the growth of many wildcat banks, since there was a need for currency in the expanding economy. Most of the shareholders in the anti-bank were Mormon leaders, who paid about 26¢ per share for shares with a face value of $50.00. Many gullible shareholders thought that they were rich, and started a wave of big spending. Land values in Kirtland soared from an original $1.25 per acre to prices as high as $2000.00 per acre.

But the boom was short lived. By February the anti-bank had failed, and Joseph was charged with illegal banking. He was found guilty and fined $1000.00 plus costs. Throughout the United States 800 banks failed that month, causing financial panic. In June Rigdon was sued for making spurious money, and he resigned from the anti-bank. In August Joseph's paper carried a warning that the notes of the anti-bank were not valid in Kirtland.

Nor were Joseph's troubles at an end. Three times he was arrested for debt, but each time he was acquitted. Grandison Newel charged Joseph with conspiracy to take his life, but the case was dismissed. In all, a dozen lawsuits were filed against Joseph within a year.

Midst all the turmoil, Joseph made what proved to be a very far-sighted decision. In June he sent three of his most trusted aides as missionaries to England. This was the beginning of a movement which ultimately led to the migration of 100,000 converts to Utah, many of whom became church leaders. The same mill hands and farm workers who a century before had eagerly accepted Methodism now were ready to embrace a new religion from the New World, and emigrate to the Zion of their dreams.

Joseph's mounting problems were both external and internal. In Kirtland non-Mormons resented the material success the Saints had achieved by their hard work and single-mindedness. They also were jealous of people who sang and danced and seemed to enjoy life. They considered the temple, built of quarried stone and with much of the interior finished by that good carpenter Brigham Young, as being entirely too luxurious for saintly people to use their money to build. They of course disliked being thought of as unsaved, simply because they rejected this new version of Christianity. And always there were undercurrents about the many wives of Joseph and other Mormon leaders.

Also, by July there were serious internal splits in the church. The three original witnesses to the *Book of Mormon* — Cowdery, Harris, and David Whitmer — began to speak against Joseph. They met secretly with many other Mormons who were questioning Joseph's conduct and authority. Harris now said that the three men never saw the gold plates "with their natural eyes, only in vision or imagination." Cowdery opposed Joseph's polygamy, and also resented the church's tendency to involve itself in temporal affairs. David Whitmer felt that Joseph had lost his prophetic powers when he had stopped using his seer stone, and consequently he had led the church astray. By the time he left the church in 1838, Whitmer feared for his life because he felt that the Sons of Dan, a Mormon armed protective group, might kill him for having opposed Joseph. Although the three witnesses had left the church by 1838, all three, including Harris, said in later years that they had seen and handled the gold plates of the *Book of Mormon*.

So high ran the feeling against Joseph that on December 22, 1837, Brigham Young was forced out of Kirtland by a group of dissenters, "for declaring in public that Joseph was a prophet of the Most High God and was not in transgression."

Finally, when he heard that Grandison Newel had sworn out a warrant for his arrest on a charge of fraud, Joseph decided to leave Kirtland on January 12, 1838, "to escape mob violence," he said, "which was about to burst upon us under the color of legal process." He and Rigdon left for Missouri on the fastest horses they could find.

In March, when they reached Missouri, there were about 10,000 Mormons there. This number soon grew to 20,000 as emigrants arrived from Kirtland, New York, and England. At this time the Mormons were the largest organized minority group in Missouri.

The town of Far West, located about sixty miles northeast of Independence, had mostly Mormons in its population of 1500. Joseph said it was the exact spot where Cain had killed Abel, and that a neighboring Mormon town, called Adam-ondi-Ahman, was where Adam and Eve had lived after their expulsion from the Garden of Eden.

But Missouri proved to be no paradise for the Mormons. Surrounding Gentiles resented the Saints because of their peculiar religious beliefs, their success as farmers and businessmen, and the fact that they did not hold slaves. By now the Mormons were learning to live apart from others, to avoid ridicule and possible violence.

Rigdon gave a speech on July 4, in which he asserted that the Mormons were fully prepared to defend themselves, if need be by violent means, against any attack upon them. When Gentiles tried to keep Mormons from voting in Gallatin on August 6, a free-for-all fight ensued. On October 15 the Apostle David Patten led the Sons of Dan on a raid and pillage of Gallatin. In retaliation Gentiles attacked at Crooked River on October 24, killing Patten and several other Mormons.

Harassed Mormons fled to Far West, where the Saints were arming themselves in self-protection. Governor Lilburn Boggs issued an order to the state militia on October 27, accusing the Mormons of defiance of the laws. "The Mormons," he said, "must be treated as enemies and must be exterminated or driven from the state for the public good."

On October 30 a group of 240 raiders, led by Nehemia Comstock, attacked a small Mormon settlement at Haun's Mill. Of the 38 Saints living there, 17 were killed and 14 seriously wounded. In addition, there was great destruction of property.

Joseph sought an armistice. He sent an emissary to the commanding officer, Major General Samuel Lucas. The emissary betrayed Joseph, having told the general that the Mormon leaders were willing to stand trial for treason, and that the Mormons would surrender arms and property and leave the state. When Joseph and other Mormon leaders voluntarily surrendered on October 31, they were given a drumhead court-martial, found guilty, and sentenced to be executed the following day.

Brigadier General A. W. Doniphan refused to carry out the execution order, stating "It is cold-blooded murder. I will not obey your order. If you execute these men, I will hold you responsible before an earthly tribunal, so help me God!" Interestingly, Doniphan was never disciplined for refusing to obey the order.

After disarming the Mormons, militiamen ransacked Mormon homes and stores. Joseph and 50 other leaders were taken to Independence for trial, charged with treason, murder, arson, and other offenses. When Mormons gave lists of witnesses, the witnesses were jailed on the same charges as the defendants. Representative Scott of the Missouri legislature called Judge Austin King "the most unfit man I know" to preside in the case. Despite the questionable legal procedures, most of the prisoners were freed for lack of evidence.

On November 30 Joseph and five other Mormon leaders were imprisoned in Liberty awaiting trial for treason and murder. During their long stay in jail Joseph once again converted adversity into a positive force. He got Brigham Young to supervise the evacuation of the Mormons to Illinois. He wrote letters to many of the faithful, giving consolation, advice, and thanks. He re-affirmed his faith in the U.S. Constitution and in God's ultimate justice. Some of his most famous revelations came while he was in prison. His strength and courage were excellent models for all Mormons who had suffered persecution. By the time he left jail Joseph was clear in his own head about the proper organization, government, and financial structure of the church.

By April 1839 tempers had cooled. Taking a hint from a sympathetic judge, Joseph and his fellow prisoners were able to bribe their guards, secure horses, and flee to Quincy, Illinois, where many refugees from Missouri had gathered.

The experience in Missouri, coming on the heels of the Kirtland disaster, was a chastening one. Joseph's brother Hyrum said that over 300 Mormons had been killed, over 12,000 Saints driven from their homes, and much property taken from them. Joseph estimated total Mormon losses at $2,000,000. He said he had spent $50,000 on lawyers' fees, for which he had little to show.

Initially Illinois treated the Mormons better than Missouri had. Feeling they had been mistreated, Governor and Mrs. Thomas Carlin took a personal interest in their plight. People in Quincy took Mormons into their homes and helped them find jobs. It seemed that they were finally to be given decent treatment.

On the bank of the Mississippi River north of Quincy, Joseph and his followers built a new settlement alongside the village of Commerce. Joseph said the name of the new town, Nauvoo, meant "beautiful plantation," but it seemed a misnomer in 1839. The low, marshy land was an excellent breeding ground for swamp fever — a number of Mormons died of it. Joseph spent much time visiting the ill, and several Saints told of faith-healing miracles he performed among them. The settlers drained the swamps, built wide streets, and started to develop a town worthy of its name.

Joseph visited Washington in 1839, seeking compensation for losses his people had suffered. He showed President Van Buren affidavits verifying wrongdoings the Mormons had experienced, with supporting letters from the governors of Ohio, Illinois, and Iowa Territory. Van Buren showed sympathy, but said that the problem was one to be settled at the state level. Joseph's appeal to Congress likewise produced no tangible results.

Strained relations developed along the Mississippi in 1840. Some Mormons crossed the river, trying to recover their losses by making raids on Missouri property. Missourians retaliated, and once again the Mormons were surrounded by hostility. By a stroke of good luck, however, their request for a town charter was passed by the Illinois legislature in December 1840. The Mormons felt that the charter would give them the autonomy needed for a self-sustaining community. Although the Mormons had not supported him, an obscure Whig legislator named Abraham Lincoln had voted for the act, and had visited Nauvoo to offer his congratulations.

With all the problems of establishing a new settlement, Joseph sent the entire Council of Twelve Apostles abroad as missionaries in 1840. They lacked travel funds. "Go," said Joseph, "the Lord provides." And indeed He did, it seemed, for the missionary work produced immediate results, especially in England.

While preaching in Herefordshire, Wilford Woodruff was confronted by a constable with a warrant for his arrest as an unlicensed preacher. Woodruff asked the constable to listen to his message. When baptism time came, at the end of the sermon, the constable was baptized as a Mormon. In eight months Woodruff alone made 1800 converts. Among them were a number of ministers, many of whom took some of their flock with them into the new church. By 1842 there were 6,000 Mormons in Great Britain, in addition to the 2,750 who had migrated to Nauvoo. It is estimated that eventually these English converts and their descendants provided well over half of all church leaders.

In May 1841 Joseph was seized by sheriffs from Missouri, under extradition orders from Governor Boggs, the old Mormon enemy. Joseph was released on a writ of habeas corpus, which the charter empowered the Nauvoo City Council to issue. Judge Stephen A. Douglas quashed the Missouri warrant, and extradition was not carried out.

A Masonic lodge was installed in Nauvoo in March 1842. Joseph had long been interested in Masonic rituals, and many of his temple ordinances and endowments show a strong Masonic influence. He and other Mormon leaders became the head of the Nauvoo lodge, which was the largest one in Illinois at that time.

James Gordon Bennett, who had started *The New York Herald* as a penny sheet in 1835, had turned the paper rapidly into one of the nation's largest. In 1842 he ran a series of interpretative articles on the Mormons, stressing the idiosyncrasies of this "curious new sect." Other papers, particularly in Illinois, followed suit, and an image developed of a group of fanatics who were outside the mainstream of American society. The lack of sympathetic treatment in the press did much damage to the Mormon cause.

Joseph was the driving force behind the growth of Nauvoo, which was the largest city in Illinois by 1842. Businesses flourished, and a number of Mormons grew to be quite wealthy. Joseph himself was never a very successful businessman. He tried his hand at running such things as a bank, a general store, a sawmill, and a tannery, but they never seemed to work out. One reason could have been his generosity in mixing his religion into his business, for he was always helping some poor Mormon family.

In an effort to defend themselves from the persecution they were constantly experiencing, the Mormons developed their own militia, the Nauvoo Legion. By February 1842 they had 2,000 men in uniform. Governor Carlin gave Joseph an appointment as lieutenant-general, in command. A new convert who had made a meteoric rise in the Mormon hierarchy, Dr. John Cook Bennett, was made major-general, second in command. As quartermaster of the state militia, Dr. Bennett was able to arm the Legion with rifles, to the envy of state militia units that merely had muskets. In colorful costumes and band accompaniment, the Legion executed smooth and precise routines. Unfortunately, non-Mormons began to fear the Legion, overestimate its numbers, and ascribe aggressive goals to it. To worsen matters, Joseph was quoted as saying that if they continued to be molested, the Mormons would establish their religion by the sword, and he himself would have to become a second Mohammed.

Nearby Warsaw was jealous of Nauvoo's rapid economic and political growth. In the gubernatorial election of 1842 Joseph's support was eagerly sought by candidates, for the Mormons tended to vote as a bloc. Since the Democrats had helped Nauvoo secure its charter, Joseph announced his support of them. The Whig candidate for governor said that the Legion should have its rifles taken away and be made a regular part of the state militia.

A hectic political battle ensued. Enough anti-Mormon feeling surfaced to force the Democrats to disavow any direct connection to the Mormons. When their candidate suddenly died, the Democrats selected as a replacement state supreme court justice Thomas Ford, a man noted for his fairness but certainly having no ties to Mormonism, as his later performance as governor demonstrated.

The year 1842 marked a turning point in Joseph's fortunes. The first big problem was the apostasy of Dr. Bennett. Besides acting as First Counselor to Joseph during Rigdon's illness, Dr. Bennett also served as mayor of Nauvoo, chancellor of the new university, and president of the Nauvoo agricultural and manufacturing association. Although Joseph and several other high Mormon leaders were now practicing polygamy, no public statement on the topic had yet been made.

Dr. Bennett ardently endeavored to persuade a number of women that one-night "spiritual wifery" was condoned by the church. He assured them that if they became pregnant, he would get them medicine for abortions. Joseph told Dr. Bennett that he was misinterpreting Old Testament practice. Suspecting Bennett of trying to turn the Legion against him, Joseph withdrew Bennett's name from church membership on May 17.

Initially Bennett did not protest but later he attacked Joseph unmercifully. He accused Joseph of forcing a confession from him at gunpoint. He labeled Joseph a charlatan, practicing "lasciviousness under pretense of religion and instituting hierarchies of women prostitutes."

Bennett accused Joseph of fraud in connection with his bankruptcy declaration of April 18, 1842. On that day Joseph had recorded a transfer of 230 Nauvoo lots from his and his wife's name to himself as trustee for the church. Joseph said that the transfer had taken place on October 5, 1841. Later, after his death, the court ruled that Illinois law prevented a church from owning more than ten acres of property, and so the excess property was subject to a lien. Three foreclosure sales were held to satisfy creditors. The federal government satisfied its claims by seizing a steamboat owned by the church.

On May 6 ex-Governor Boggs of Missouri was seriously wounded by an assassin. Bennett took affidavits from enemies of Joseph in Nauvoo who implicated him as instigator of the attempted murder. Porter Rockwell, Joseph's bodyguard, was alleged to be the person who shot Boggs. On August 8 Joseph and Rockwell were arrested in Nauvoo. The municipal court released both men on a writ of habeas corpus. The two men disappeared, and rewards were offered for their capture. For four months Joseph lived underground in the Nauvoo area, moving from one home to another. On January 4, 1843, the judge dismissed the charge against Joseph, on the ground that the arrest warrant was improperly prepared. Rockwell was imprisoned in Missouri until December, 1843, when he was released for lack of evidence.

Bennett's attack continued. He went on a speaking tour selling copies of a book he had written, called *The History of the Saints; or an Exposé of Joe Smith and the Mormons.* Among other charges, the book gave lurid accounts of licentious behavior among the Nauvoo Mormons. Despite the fact that most of the book was untruthful or exaggerated, the press received it warmly. Many newspapers accepted Bennett's word at face value, eager to repudiate a movement they were hostile toward anyway. The image spreading from Illinois was that this sect, unlike others that had sprung up in America, somehow posed a seditious threat that should not be tolerated.

Joseph always liked to have a good time—he was gregarious by nature. He quoted scripture about making a joyful noise unto the Lord. Outsiders liked to visit Nauvoo because of its gaiety, especially on holidays. There would be plenty of music, dancing, parades, cornhusking parties, riverboat rides, games, and cotillion parties. Amateur dramatic groups and debating societies abounded. Everyone seemed to be doing something he liked to do. This was Joseph's idea of Zion.

But Nauvoo was not truly Zion. On June 21, 1843, Joseph was arrested on the old treason charge from Missouri. Joseph said he had been kidnapped by the arresting officers, who had disguised themselves as Mormon elders. He therefore felt that he had been deprived of due process. After a long hearing on July 1, the Lee County Court freed him. Back in Nauvoo he spoke heatedly to a group of 10,000 Saints: "Before I will bear this unhallowed persecution any longer, I will spill the last drop of blood in my veins, and will see all my enemies in hell."

In December the city council in Nauvoo passed an ordinance saying that any person who brought an arrest writ for Joseph based on the Missouri charge would be subject to a life sentence in the Nauvoo jail—a sentence not even the governor could commute, unless approved by the major of Nauvoo: Joseph.

Governor Ford protested that the court erred in allowing a city government to issue writs of habeas corpus on action against charges involving higher governmental bodies. Ford tried to persuade the Illinois legislature to revise Nauvoo's charter, but, with an eye on the Mormon vote, they refused. Fearing that Ford might have Joseph arrested, the Mormons supported Joseph Hoge, the Democratic candidate for Congress. Joseph personally supported the Whig candidate, who had befriended him. Saints were confused, since Hyrum Smith had had a revelation stating that Hoge should be supported. Paradoxically, Joseph said, "I'll vote Whig—you follow Hyrum's revelation," and the Democrats won the contest. But the Whigs always felt they had been betrayed.

Many challenges Joseph seemed able to parry successfully, but the allegation of polygamy had been with him for years. William Phelps said that Joseph had had a revelation in 1831 foretelling that white men would take polygamous Indian wives for a purpose: "Ye should take unto you wives of the Lamanites and Nephites, that their posterity may become white, delightsome and just."

Joseph realized that not all of his revelations could be made public at once. While in Kirtland he told Brigham Young: "If I were to reveal to this people what the Lord has revealed to me, there is not a man or woman that would stay with me." So in public Joseph continued to deny his plural marriages.

In 1841 Joseph started to send out feelers, suggesting that a restored church should consider restoring the marital practices of Abraham and Isaac. Hostility bristled. His younger brother, Don Carlos, said: "Any man who will teach and practice the doctrine of spiritual wifery will go to hell, I don't care if it is my brother Joseph." Seeing the continuing adverse reception this doctrine received, Joseph realized that the introduction of the new revelation was perhaps further off than he had first suspected. But he resolutely went forward to prepare his followers for the new doctrine. From January 1841 to July 1843 he told of nine revelations he had had on the subject. He was carefully laying a doctrinal foundation for the whole concept of celestial, or eternal, marriage. He said that power and authority in the after-life would be commensurate with the number of "wives, children and friends that we inherit here, and that our mission to the earth was to organize a nucleus of Heaven, to take with us." To him, the doctrine of sealing in eternal marriage became an important part of a person's salvation.

Finally, on August 12, 1843, came the long-awaited revelation on polygamy. On that date Joseph told the church's high council that polygamy was to be "a new and everlasting" covenant among the Saints. The immediate reaction was sensational, and the long-term effect was to produce a irremediable and permanent split in the church.

Joseph said that his revelation grew out of his question to God: Why did Abraham, Moses, David, and other Old Testament leaders have so many wives and concubines? The answer was that God had made a promise to Abraham concerning his posterity, of whom Joseph was one. Following God's order, Sarah had given her maidservant Hagar to Abraham as a wife. Now God was restoring all aspects of the old religion, through Joseph, and whatever Joseph "bound on earth in the name of the Lord was to be bound in heaven." Pertaining to priests, a man might wed ten virgins and not commit adultery. But if one of the ten virgins, after marriage, shall lie with another man, "she has committed adultery and shall be destroyed."

If a Mormon priest taught this law to his wife, she must "believe and administer unto him, or she shall be destroyed." The revelation told Emma to "receive all those that have been given unto my servant Joseph or she shall be destroyed." Unimpressed and angry, Emma first pleaded with Joseph to renounce the revelation and, failing, she burned it. Fortunate for Joseph, other copies existed.

Some of the highest Mormon leaders were shocked by Joseph's position on plural marriage. Brigham Young stated that when Joseph first told him of the doctrine of celestial marriage, his reaction was, "Let me have but one wife. It was the first time in my life that I desired the grave and I could hardly get over it for a long time." But in 1842 he had followed Joseph's injunction, marrying his first polygamous wife, 20-year old Lucy Ann Decker. In 1843 he married two more women, aged 19 and 41.

Austin Cowles, whose daughter Elvira Joseph had married in 1842, raised strenuous objection, as did such stalwarts as John Taylor and Heber Kimball. Sometimes it seemed as if Joseph was testing the loyalty of his followers by courting a girl through her father or brother. Helen Kimball, who was 15 in the summer of 1843, was shocked when approached by her father, Heber, but after being taught by Joseph that this act would insure her "eternal salvation and exaltation and that of your father's household and all of your kindred," she acquiesced, saying, "This promise was so great that I willingly gave myself to purchase so glorious a reward." Also, Benjamin Johnson taught the principles of celestial marriage to his sister Elmera, who married Joseph on April 5, 1843.

Sometimes insufficient groundwork had been laid. At the time that Joseph proposed marriage to Nancy, the 19-year-old daughter of Sidney Rigdon, Rigdon was unaware of the incipient doctrine of celestial marriage, and hard feelings resulted. Sarah, the wife of Apostle Orson Pratt, reported that during Orson's mission to England Joseph had made "propositions" to her that enraged her.

Some leaders reminded Joseph of the teaching against polygamy in the *Book of Mormon.* In 2 Jacob 2:24–27, it said, "David and Solomon truly had many wives and concubines, which thing was abominable before, saith the Lord. Wherefore, I the Lord God will not suffer that this people shall do like unto them of old. Hearken to the word of the Lord: For there shall not any man among you have save it be one wife, and concubines he shall have none."

Joseph replied that revelation is continuous — one generation's commandment did not necessarily bind another generation. After all, Christ was not bound by the dispensation of Moses. Joseph said that the dispensation of these latter days "differs from either yet includes both." The Lord would continue to reveal His will for modern times through his selected prophet, Joseph.

Receiving revelations is not easy, Joseph said, because some revelations come from God, some from Satan, and some from man. Only the prophet knows the difference, and sometimes mistakes are made which can be recognized only later. But Joseph told William Clayton that "the doctrine of plural and celestial marriage is the most holy and important doctrine ever revealed to man." He informed John Taylor that "the church could not go on until polygamy was established, and without it the highest glory could not be attained in heaven."

When people criticized his actions, Joseph replied, "A prophet is only a prophet when he is acting as such." In addition to an overactive libido, Joseph had an extraordinary capacity to love, as attested by many who knew him. He wished to bind his loved ones to himself through all time and eternity, and he envisioned God's plan as creating eternal family unions.

Emma was slow to accept the doctrine. Donna Hill says, "At times certain that her husband was a common philanderer, she raged at him, spied upon him, threw out the women whom she thought temptation had put in his way, railed behind his back and fought his efforts with every means she could command." But she fought a losing battle.

Despite the fact that at least six of his plural wives had lived with the Smiths for extended periods of time, Joseph seems to have shown a genuine affection for Emma. She finally agreed that he could take two more wives, provided she chose them. So she chose the sisters Emily and Eliza Partridge, not knowing that he had secretly wed them several months previously. Lucy Walker, who married Joseph in 1843 when she was 17, said she knew he had married the Partridge sisters, as well as the Lawrence sisters, Sarah and Maria, who came from Canada. "Instead of a feeling of jealousy, it was a source of comfort to us," she said. "We were as sisters to each other."

Since Joseph stressed the importance of a large family in the hereafter, it is striking that apparently he had no children from his polygamous marriages. Possibly he practiced birth control. Most of his wives seem to have been treated well by him. Nevertheless Emily Partridge, who had had polygamous marriages to both Joseph and Brigham Young, wrote in her journal in 1874: "Long live woman's suffrage and equal rights. No need for four-fifths of the inhabitants of the earth to grovel in the dust in order that the other fifth may stand a little higher."

Some Mormon women gladly accepted polygamy. Heber Kimball's wife urged her husband to marry a pretty young English girl who had traveled in his group from Liverpool to Nauvoo. The ostensible reason was to be sure that the young woman had a husband for eternity. If a man married a widow it was believed that the wife returned to her first husband in the next life, provided of course that the first marriage had been sealed in the temple for eternity. Since it was understood that the husband would provide for all wives and children, only the more affluent men could afford to have multiple wives. It is estimated that no more than twenty percent of all Mormon men ever practiced polygamy.

Believing that the Mormons were God's chosen people, "the seed of Abraham in the last dispensation," Joseph felt that it was their job to prepare for the millennium by beginning the establishment of God's kingdom on earth. He had reported a revelation on January 19, 1841, that all kings and earthly rulers were to receive an admonition from him to accept the gospel. He addressed a religious proclamation to the executives of all nations, calling upon them to repent of their sins, believe in Christ, and build fine temples in Zion. Nauvoo was to be the nucleus of the coming kingdom.

Frustrated by the persecution his followers suffered in New York, Ohio, Missouri, and now Illinois, Joseph contemplated setting up a separate autonomous Mormon state. He sent out feelers to Russia and to the Republic of Texas to see if he could get support for such a state. A council member, George Miller, said, "In this council we ordained Joseph Smith as King on earth." Governor Ford of Illinois felt that Joseph had monarchial ambitions. Ford stated, "The Mormons openly denounced the government of the United States as utterly corrupt, and as being about to pass away, and to be replaced by the government of God, to be administered by His servant Joseph."

Joseph spoke of finding a resting place in the mountains, "where we can enjoy the liberty of conscience guaranteed to us by the Constitution of our country, denied to us by the present authorities, who have smuggled themselves into power in the states and nation."

In January 1844 the council selected Joseph as a candidate for President of the United States. This was felt to be the first step in establishing God's kingdom on earth. In accepting, Joseph felt he need not campaign. "There is oratory enough in the church to carry me into the presidential chair the first slide," he said.

His platform had elements of broad appeal. Prisons should become learning institutions, felons should work on roads, slavery should be abolished with slaveholders reimbursed by income from sales of public lands, and a national bank should be established. He proposed that the country be expanded instantly from coast to coast, provided the Indians agreed, and that Texas, Canada, and Mexico be taken into the Union, at their request.

What was his attitude towards black people? In the Book of Mormon (2 Nephi 26:33) it says, "The Lord denieth none that come unto him, black and white, bond and free, male and female." The early church had black members, but several Mormons quoted Joseph as saying that blacks could not be priests. Initially Joseph felt that obdurate abolitionists might provoke violence and war but from 1842 on he persistently opposed slavery. He did not, like Jefferson, think blacks were congenitally inferior, but felt that their low status was due to lack of opportunity and education. Like most of his contemporaries, however, he opposed racial inter-marriage. As mayor of Nauvoo in 1844 he fined two black men for attempting to marry white women.

In March 1844 Joseph wrote letters to President Tyler and to Congress, suggesting that he be appointed an officer in the U.S. Army with power to raise 100,000 armed volunteers "to open unsettled regions and to protect the borders of the United States." He now realized Nauvoo could no longer be the seat of Zion. He looked longingly westward, considering California, Oregon, and Vancouver. But his final preference rested with a site somewhere in the Rocky Mountains.

Ever since his declaration of his revelation on celestial polygamy, Joseph's life had been in danger. Knowing this, Joseph had a secret escape route built into his Mansion House in Nauvoo. Joseph appointed forty Nauvoo policement to serve as his personal bodyguard, protecting him from "a Judas in our midst," said Joseph. Some Mormon leaders resented his armed guard. William Law, who was beginning to oppose Joseph, feared retribution from this police force. Joseph's obdurate stand on polygamy was beginning to mar his effectiveness as a leader.

In early 1844 Dr. Robert Foster, a contractor and church leader, stated that Joseph had tried to seduce his wife, under the guise of celestial marriage. Parley Pratt and Henry Jacobs had acquiesced to having Joseph wed their wives in this fashion, and Newel Whitney had given his daughter in wedlock to Joseph similarly. Hiram Kimball, like Foster, resented Joseph's effort to have his wife in celestial wedlock.

The alienation of William Law, Joseph's Second Counselor, had begun in 1843. Law accused Joseph of making personal profits from the Mormon inn, Nauvoo House, and of using church funds to engage in personal land speculation. Law also insisted that he and Foster had the right to be private building contractors, competing against the church monopoly in that regard. Unable to stop them, Joseph proposed "spiritual marriage" to Law's attractive wife, Jane. Incensed, she reported the incident to her husband.

Law was furious. He said that unless Joseph would confess and repent before the High Council, he would expose Joseph's sins to the world. Austin Cowles, whose wife also had resisted Joseph's amorous talk, joined Law and Foster in opposition to Joseph. Soon a number of prominent Mormon leaders were meeting secretly to discuss strategy.

On March 24, 1844, Joseph attacked the conspiracy against him, bringing charges against them in the High Council. While they were assembling their witnesses, Joseph announced the Council's decision: excommunication for "unchristianlike conduct." On April 17 Joseph published accounts of the secret meetings, including mention of his alleged attempt to seduce Mrs. Foster. A trial against Foster was set up in the High Council.

When Joseph heard that Foster planned to call over forty witnesses, the trial was cancelled. Foster, Law, Jane Law, and Law's brother Wilson were expelled from the church.

Law, now considering Joseph not a false but a fallen prophet, set up his own church with himself as president. He also filed a suit against Joseph, charging him with adultery and bigamy. Foster and Joseph Jackson sued Joseph for false swearing. Francis Higbee, in a third suit, asked for damages because of Joseph's malicious slander.

Joseph, in turn, accused Higbee of perjury, seduction, and adultery. Defending Joseph, Brigham Young said that Higbee had contracted venereal disease from prostitutes. In a sermon on May 26 Joseph savagely lashed back at his enemies.

Law and others supplied funds to buy a press to expose Joseph. Calling their paper *The Nauvoo Expositor*, they published their first and only issue on June 7. The paper carried a story of how Joseph initiated an innocent English girl into the mysteries of plural marriage. Affidavits testified that the Laws and Austin Cowles had seen or heard read the revelation of a man's right to marry ten virgins. The paper attacked Joseph's grasping for political power, and his financial manipulation and land speculation. It accused him of misuse of the Nauvoo charter and of allying church and state.

The paper caused fear among Mormon leaders practicing polygamy, and created distrust among church members whose image of their leaders, particularly Joseph, was shattered. Joseph knew he faced the biggest challenge of his life. He told his old friend William Marks that he had been mistaken: polygamy is a curse to mankind, and the church would have to put a stop to it. He now understood that his 1843 revelation had referred to Old Testament times, and had no relevance for the present. He said that unless stopped, polygamy would destroy the church. He instructed Marks to bring all polygamists to trial before the High Council, offering to prefer charges himself. He promised Marks he would preach against the doctrine in church.

But Joseph also felt he had to quash the opposition. So he got the city council to pass an ordinance declaring the new paper a public nuisance, authorizing him as mayor to remove it as he saw fit. He ordered the city marshall to destroy the press, and it was done on the evening of June 10.

Fearful of their lives, Joseph's foes fled to the nearby towns of Warsaw and Carthage. Foster and Law swore out warrants for Joseph's arrest on charges of riot. Through use of habeas corpus in the Nauvoo municipal court, Joseph evaded these charges. He wrote a long letter to Governor Thomas Ford, explaining why he had destroyed the press.

Foster described the attack on the newspaper, plus other alleged crimes by Joseph, in an article in *The Warsaw Signal*. This paper was edited by Thomas Sharp, a man described by the non-Mormon sheriff of local Hancock County as "an infamous black-hearted murderous scoundrel, guilty of all crimes known to our laws." An agitator, Sharp had been expelled from New York State. Jealous of the growth of rival Nauvoo, he had several times tried to stir up mobs against Mormons through provocative articles and editorials. On June 12 he editorialized: "War is inevitable! Citizens arise! Can you stand by and suffer such infernal devils to rob men of their property and rights, without avenging them? We have no time for comments; every man will make his own. Let it be made with powder and balls!"

Joseph responded by placing Nauvoo under martial law and calling out the Nauvoo Legion. On June 18 he addressed 10,000 townspeople and 1500 legionnaires: "All mobmen, priests, thieves, apostates, and adulterers who combine to destroy this people now raise the hue and cry throughout the state that we resist the law, in order to raise a pretext for calling together thousands more of infuriated mobmen to murder, destroy, plunder, and ravish the innocent. Will you stand by me to the death?" Thousands responded "Aye!"

Joseph continued: "Come, all ye lovers of liberty, loose the iron grasp of mobocracy. This people shall have their legal rights, or my blood shall be spilt upon the ground like water. I am willing to sacrifice my life for your preservation. May the Lord God of Israel bless you forever and ever. I say it in the name of Jesus Christ of Nazareth and in the authority of the Holy Priesthood he has conferred upon me."

Governor Ford later described the hectic activity to stir up the people against the Mormons through public meetings, inflammatory speeches, and wild messenger rides. False rumors described Mormons burning homes, looting, and murdering innocent people. Ford said that people opposed the Mormons because of their violation of freedom of the press, their use of the Nauvoo Legion, and their religious views, particularly their stand on polygamy. Other complaints he listed were the statement that Joseph had been crowned a king, the belief that God had consecrated all property to the Saints, and perhaps worst of all, the practice of bloc voting that kept any state official from being elected without their approval.

Ford himself believed that many actions of the Nauvoo city council, mayor, and municipal court were illegal, and that the Nauvoo charter should be revised or revoked. He asked Joseph and all others involved in destruction of the press to go to Carthage to stand trial "to prove their wish to be governed by law." He told Joseph: "Your conduct in the destruction of the press was a very great outrage upon the laws and liberties of the people. Submit yourselves to be arrested. If no such submission is made, I will be obliged to call out the militia." He promised the Mormon leaders protection against any bodily injury.

Feeling that they were the key targets, Joseph and his brother Hyrum crossed the Mississippi River into Iowa the evening of June 22. Later, Ford admitted that might have been the best resolution of the crisis.

But many Mormons felt deserted by their leaders in a time of urgency, and pleaded for the Smith brothers to return. "Let us go back," suggested Hyrum. "We shall be butchered," Joseph replied. "The Lord is in it," responed Hyrum; "if we live or die, we shall be reconciled to our fate." Reluctantly, they returned to Nauvoo.

On June 24, with a guard escort provided by Ford, Joseph, Hyrum, and five other leaders rode the twelve miles to Carthage. Before leaving Joseph told his mother: "It shall yet be said of me, 'He was murdered in cold blood.' I go as a lamb to the slaughter, but if my death will atone for any faults I have committed during my lifetime I am willing to die." A Mormon messenger, arriving from Carthage, said, "They will kill you if you go to Carthage." But the die was cast.

Ford ordered the Nauvoo Legion to surrender all state-owned firearms. Joseph countersigned the order, but told the Mormons to have a stockpile of secret weapons ready for use on short notice.

When Joseph arrived in Carthage at midnight, the mob wanted to see him. "Tomorrow," said the governor, and the crowd dispersed.

On June 25 the Mormon leaders were charged with riot in destroying the press and released on bonds of $500 apiece. Most of them went back to Nauvoo, but Joseph and Hyrum stayed to talk to the governor. That evening a constable notified them that they were charged with treason, and they were put in the Carthage jail to await trial. The jail was probably the safest place for them at the time.

On June 26 the two brothers were brought before Justice Robert F. Smith, who was also a captain of the Carthage Greys, for a hearing. Trial was set for June 29. Also on June 26 they had a long discussion with Ford concerning the charges against them. The governor was in a dilemma, not knowing whether to fear most the Mormons or their rabid enemies. His first goal was to avoid bloodshed, his second to see justice done to both sides. Despite his obvious neutrality, he clearly erred in providing insufficient protection for the prisoners.

When he left for Nauvoo on June 27 to conduct a personal investigation, his departure was the signal for the murderous crowd to attack the jail. The final speech the governor made at Nauvoo was not conciliatory: "A great crime was been done by destroying the *Expositor* press. Depend upon it, a little more misbehavior from the citizens, and the torch, which is already lighted, will be applied. If anything of a serious nature should befall the lives or property of the persons who are prosecuting your leaders, you will be held responsible."

For all his ineptitude in this crisis, the governor had a high opinion of Joseph. "It must not be supposed," he said, "that the pretended Prophet practiced the tricks of a common impostor." James Gordon Bennett, whose *New York Herald* had often been critical of the Mormon movement, had written on April 3, 1842: "This Joseph Smith is undoubtedly one of the greatest characters of the age. He indicates as much talent, originality, and moral courage as Mohammed, Odin, or any of the great spirits that have hitherto produced the revolutions of past ages." General Moses Wilson, who had seized Joseph for trial in Missouri, testified as to Joseph's charisma: "He was a very remarkable man. I carried him into my house a prisoner in chains, and in less than two hours my wife loved him better than she did me."

After the murder of the Smith brothers, the word spread quickly that "the Mormons are coming" in revenge from Nauvoo to Carthage. With the militia disbanded, people in Warsaw and Carthage were frightened, thinking that the Nauvoo Legion and the Sons of Dan would be riding soon. But it did not happen.

The Mormons in Nauvoo were also scared, feeling that the assassination of their leaders was but the beginning of another wholesale slaughter. Willard Richards, who had survived the jail massacre, recommended caution, leaving vengeance to God. Another jail survivor, John

Taylor, lay gravely wounded in a Carthage tavern — further violence could cost him his life.

In accordance with Joseph's wishes, his body and Hyrum's were secretly buried in the basement of Nauvoo House. The graves were disguised with wood chips and rubbish, so no hostile person might find them.

The official church announcement said of Joseph: "He lived great, and he died great in the eyes of God and his people, and like most of the Lord's anointed in ancient times, has sealed his mission and his works with his own blood."

A movement severely fractured by June 1844 was suddenly given new vitality and new faith. Martyrdom saved a cause that was dying of civil strife, and turned it into one of the most significant religious groups in the modern world.

The murders shocked the nation. No other leaders of the myriad religious groups had ever been so persecuted. The excessive violence used to try to retard this sect suggested that perhaps there was something unique in this religious approach. If it indeed seemed such a portent of evil doctrine, how was one to account for its meteoric rise? Was it possible, perhaps, that here was some type of restoration of New Testament Christianity?

Instead of stamping out the Mormons, the murder of the Smith brothers assured their survival, according to Wallace Stegner: "It tempered their already well-tempered steel in the blood of martyrs, and made zealots out of men and women who might otherwise have been only die-hards; and it assured the carrying out of migration plans that had been fitfully contemplated long before Joseph's death."

Investigation revealed that the murders had been committed by members of the Warsaw militia, instigated by Sharp and the *Warsaw Signal*. Five men, including Sharp, were indicted by the grand jury and tried for murder. Defense attorneys argued that a conviction could lead to civil violence, since the community at large approved of the defendants' acts. The jury verdict was "Not guilty."

Who was to assume leadership in place of Prophet Joseph? Sidney Rigdon said that he had received a divine revelation that he was to be the new church president. When he was turned down he moved to Pittsburgh where he started his own church, attacking the Mormon leaders as apostates and polygamists.

Martin Harris and others said that Joseph had selected David Whitmer as his successor in 1834, and so a new church was started under Whitmer in Kirtland. David's brother John broke off with yet another splinter group. James Strang, a Wisconsin lawyer, took a group of his followers to Beaver Island in Lake Michigan; when Strang was murdered by one of his followers in 1856, the colony died out. Lyman Wright took a small polygamous group to Texas, but the church collapsed at Wright's death in 1859.

In a letter from Liberty jail in 1839 Joseph had said, "Appoint the oldest of those twelve who were first appointed, to be President of your Quorum." Following this advice the Twelve Apostles chose Brigham Young as the new church president.

Joseph's family refused to accept Brigham Young. Joseph's brother William drew a number of followers when he set up a separate church. Joseph's widow Emma insisted that their son, Joseph III, should be the new church leader, even though he was only twelve years old. Unworried by Joseph's revelation that she would be destroyed unless she accepted polygamy, Emma repudiated it after Joseph's death. Both she and Joseph III said that Joseph had never advocated nor practiced plural marriage, but that the practice was Brigham Young's idea. Emma had a happy marriage then with Major Lewis Bidamon, who helped her rear Joseph's children.

In 1852 the followers of Emma and Joseph III established what they felt was the rightful successor to Joseph's church. They called it the Reorganized Church of Jesus Christ of Latter-Day Saints. An Ohio court decision in 1880 substantiated this claim, giving church property to the new group. Thus the reorganized church, with headquarters in Independence, Missouri, now owns the Kirtland Temple and important property in Nauvoo such as Mansion House and the grave sites of Joseph and Hyrum.

Civic unrest continued in Hancock County after Joseph's death. By September 1845 mobs were beginning to trouble the Mormons again. Occasionally there were shootings. A group of 200 Mormons had to be rescued from the village of Lima and brought to Nauvoo for their safety.

Although the Illinois legislature had revoked Nauvoo's charter in January 1845, work continued on building the temple. Outsiders did not realize the importance of the temple to Mormons—it was the center of salvation. Only from the hands of its own ordained priesthood could one get "the rites and endowments that meant salvation," Mormons believed. The only true priesthood, they felt, had been restored through Joseph by the angel of God. Only in the temple could they receive their endowments, and travel westward a saved and covenanted people. Illinoisans feared that a completed temple meant that the Saints would not leave their state.

A commission of four men, including Stephen A. Douglas, was sent by Governor Ford to persuade Brigham Young to move his people out of Illinois. Young promised that the Mormon leaders and 1,000 families would leave in the spring, to be followed by the rest as soon as possible. The commission mentioned the danger of violence again breaking out unless the Saints left.

Young had acted quickly after gaining leadership. Parley Pratt was sent to New York City to be sure that the Eastern press was properly informed concerning church developments. Heber Kimball was assigned the task of getting church members ready for the westward trek.

By December 10, 1845, the upper rooms of the temple were sufficiently finished that the endowments could begin. Night and day church members crowded in to receive baptisms, sealings, washings, and anointings, to see the symbolic Adam and Eve playlet, and to be initiated as full members of the new dispensation. Church rituals, adapted by Joseph from Masonic ones, are kept secret from non-members. Plural marriages were also an important part of the ceremonies performed at that time.

On a cold February day in 1846 Young led his advance party out of Nauvoo, stimulated by threats of arrest on false charges of counterfeiting. The total party had 16,000 persons, with 3,000 wagons, 30,000 cattle, plus many horses, mules, and sheep. Heavy snowfall slowed the march; it took four months to cross Iowa. In June they arrived at Winter Quarters, now a part of Omaha.

Not only the weather hampered progress. Apostates invited church members northward to Wisconsin and southward to Texas. Non-Mormons in Missouri offered former Mormon land free to those who would renounce their faith, but few left the caravan.

What impelled these hardy souls to an unknown destination in the West was deep faith in a new start, free from hecklers—faith in a new dispensation, a move to the literal Kingdom of God on earth. On their way west, they seemed to encounter signs and wonders. Rivers froze to make crossing convenient. Quails fell among them as if manna from heaven. Seemingly their sick quickly recovered when the elders laid their hands upon them.

They proved to be "the most systematic, organized, disciplined, and successful pioneers in our history," Stegner believes. The trail they took was not new. What was new was that a whole people moved, as if a village on the march—grandparents, parents, children, property, customs, and religion. Hardship was interpreted as sent by God to help build strength of character and deepen faith.

Their trek opened a path westward for other pioneers. One-third of all travel to California and Oregon after 1849 followed the Mormon Trail.

A bastion of strength was their leader. Brigham Young endured every hardship and calmed every tempest. "I will do the scolding to this camp, no other man shall," he declared, and he was obeyed. When invited by the U.S. Army to provide a Mormon Battalion as a part of General Kearny's expedition into New Mexico and Arizona, Young overruled his advisers and accepted the offer. The army would provide the 500 soldiers food, shelter, and pay—and furthermore, this would prove the Saints' loyalty to the government.

Even at Winter Quarters the Saints knew not their ultimate destination. Should it be Vancouver, Oregon, California, or where? Since the Mormon Battalion was due to be discharged in California, most people assumed they were headed there. But Young wanted to avoid the large number of emigrants headed for California. He knew that more isolation would produce a better environment for Zion.

While at Winter Quarters Brigham Young announced his only revelation from God, on January 14, 1847. He said God told them to organize into tens, fifties, and hundreds in preparation for the great journey through the Rockies. He assigned caretakers for widows and orphans. He said that they must persevere, that a people must be tried in order to be worthy of the glory of Zion.

The Saints back in Nauvoo still encountered persecution. Homes were burned, and occasionally Mormons were killed. After a three-day battle, the last ones left Nauvoo in September 1846. An arsonist burned the temple in 1848, and in 1850 a tornado further damaged the remains. Faithful believers were grateful that it would thus be spared additional defilement.

In July 1847 the ill Brigham Young was carried into Salt Lake Valley, and announced the site as the city of Zion. But he cautioned that the Kingdom of God would arise there only as the Saints made themselves completely self-sufficient, entirely independent of Gentiles (non-Mormons). The area was still a part of Mexico but was annexed to the United States the following year as a part of the Treaty of Guadalupe Hidalgo, which ended the Mexican War.

There were hardships enough: further emigrating caravans to assist; learning new types of agriculture in a barren land; arranging for converts to get to Deseret (Utah) from Europe; continual problems with Indians and with the federal government. But the Saints felt that God sent miracles to help them in their times of greatest need. When hordes of locusts began to destroy their new crops in 1848, they prayed, and as if in answer to their prayers, thousands of sea gulls from Great Salt Lake flew in and ate the bothersome locusts. The following year gold-rushers came with wagon-trains of provisions, which they sold to the Saints at nominal prices, now that they were getting close to their California goal. "Gold," said Young, "is what streets are paved with," and very few Mormons succumbed to the greedy lure of instant wealth.

Later a good business was made off of the travelers, who needed further provisioning as they traveled west. Profits from this enterprise set up a Perpetual Emigration Fund, used to help European converts come to Utah. In the years 1850–1852 a sum of $750,000 assisted 22,000 new Mormons who arrived from England and Europe. Sometimes shiploads of Mormon emigrants so impressed the crew by their orderliness, cleanliness, and piety that by the end of the voyage the officers and seamen had joined the converts in the new faith.

In 1856 over four hundred emigrants walked 1400 miles from Iowa City to the new Zion, pulling handcarts laden with belongings. Morale was so high that the handcart company sometimes passed up a wagon-train along the way. Later handcart companies, however, experienced too many casualties, and that mode of transport had to be abandoned. When spirits flagged along the way, a few rousing choruses of "Come, Come Ye Saints" (which English convert William Clayton had written at a caravan campfire) seemed to vivify the group into almost superhuman exertion.

By 1855 Salt Lake City had a population of 35,000. That year one-third of all British emigrants to the United States were Mormons; an additional 35,000 lived in England. By 1868 50,000 converts, chiefly British, Scandinavian and German, had arrived in Utah.

In 1857 President Buchanan sent federal troops into Utah to enforce better cooperation with the federal government. There were charges of destruction of federal records and of denial of minority group rights. When the army arrived in Salt Lake City, there were no occupants — Young had moved his people forty miles south to Provo. A truce was arranged, and the Saints moved back into Salt Lake City.

In the period from 1862 to 1870, although outwardly submitting to the territorial governor appointed from Washington, the Saints operated a ghost government under Young. This shadow government met after each session of the state legislature to affirm or deny laws recently enacted. Although this was certainly civil disobedience, it can partly be understood as an effort to place citizenship in God's Kingdom ahead of citizenship in the secular government. It can also be understood as a reaction to misuse of government by anti-Mormon groups in the past.

No doubt the most contentious issue raised by the Saints was the practice of celestial polygamy. In August 1852 Young had formalized the doctrine in an article in *The Deseret News*, for which Orson Pratt had supplied the theological justification. Missionaries prudently soft-pedaled mention of the troublesome concept.

In 1862 the United States Congress passed a law against polygamy, but Mormons and others said that it was an unconstitutional violation of religious freedom. Jerome Clark, no believer in Mormonism, admits that "the spiritual aspect of plural marriage was the one that was emphasized, especially after the move to Salt Lake. The practice was open only to those who were deemed spiritually worthy of such a privilege."

In 1882 the Edmunds Act stated that persons practicing or believing in polygamy or cohabitation as a religious principle could not vote or hold office. Its revision, the Edmunds-Tucker Act of 1887, was much more severe. According to Robert Mullen, "it dissolved the Church as a corporate entity; it seized the property of the Church and ordered it sold for the benefit of public schools in the state; it dissolved the Perpetual Emigration Fund; it disinherited children of plural marriages, abolished the right of women to vote, and placed all the schools under federal officials."

Driven into a corner, church president Wilford Woodruff in 1890 issued a manifesto promising to obey the laws outlawing polygamy, and asking the church to do likewise. The general conference of the church unanimously endorsed Woodruff's position. Fortunately the government was lax in administering the new laws, and existing families were generally not disturbed but new polygamous marriages were forbidden. Finally the church was getting around to the viewpoint on polygamy that Joseph Smith stated shortly before his murder.

Although Salt Lake City continues to be the center of the church, only one million of today's four million Mormons live in Utah. There are church members on every continent, and temples are being built throughout the world to accommodate believers.

What makes Mormonism different from other approaches to Christianity? The prophecies of Joseph Smith, including the *Book of Mormon* and other revelations announced by him, for one thing. Joseph taught that human beings lived with God as children, in the spirit world before coming to earth. In this pre-world, some humans accept life in this world, realizing that the separation from the heavenly parents is only temporary. Although humans will be punished for their sins, "even the meanest sinner will receive a greater gift in heaven than he can imagine," Joseph said. Those whose lives have been more fruitful here will gain greater rewards in heaven.

Countless spirits in the pre-world wait for earthly tabernacles, or bodies, in which to dwell. Woman's highest glory is to bestow such tabernacles, "and her exaltation in eternity would be in proportion to the number she had provided. Hence, the larger her family, the greater her glory." Needless to say, the church opposes birth control.

When Joseph learned that the Hebrew word for God, Elohim, as used in some of the Old Testament books is a plural form, he spoke of the Gods who organized the earth from already existing matter. Adam, the supreme God of this earth, is under Jehovah, who governed many worlds. Jehovah, in turn, is under the Supreme God, Elohim. Sometimes Elohim summons lesser Gods to Him in the Grand Council. Elohim created the other Gods, all of whom have bodies and passions like humans. The Gods' chief function is to create souls to inhabit bodies in this and other worlds.

Human beings, Joseph said, can advance by successive degrees until they too become Gods and receive worlds to govern.

Joseph's teachings were by no means confined to the spiritual realm. Of his 112 announced revelations, 88 deal wholly or in part with economic matters. The L.D.S. Church is listed among the nation's top 50 corporations, with assets well over two billion dollars. Included in its assets are banks, retail stores, ranches, television and radio stations, and an insurance company. Chief internal source of income is tithing, which Mormons practice more faithfully than do most church groups.

Great stress is placed upon family values. Mormon divorces are rare. Sexual activity outside wedlock is discouraged. Mormons are also urged to abstain from the use of alcohol, tobacco, coffee, and tea.

In 1978 church president Spencer W. Kimball announced a revelation removing the restriction of black men entering the priesthood, and there are now a number of black priests. Women, however, are still denied the priesthood, and there is current controversy in the church over this doctrine.

Following I Corinthians 15:29, Joseph recommended baptism for the dead, and hence the great stress in Mormonism on geneology. When one is baptized for the dead, however, the dead person is then offered salvation to accept or reject.

The unusually deep faith of these people, their record for conduct as sober and righteous citizens, the efficient church organization and zealous missionary thrust, and their belief in Christ's return soon, mark these people as unique. Most orthodox Christians do not consider this faith to be an authentic arm of Christianity, largely because of Joseph Smith's additions. But without those additions there would be no Mormon church. "The more the outside world bites its knuckles in existential despair," says Wallace Stegner, "the more the Mormon is convinced of the value of his special sustaining faith as the basis for a healthy society."

# 4
## America's First Feminist

A tall, attractive woman walked into the office of Horace Greeley, editor of the *New York Tribune* in September, 1844. She wore an orange dress, and a white japonica was atilt in her luxurious blond hair.

"Margaret," said Greeley, "I want you to write for the Trib. Your *Summer on the Lakes* is very perceptive, and your *Dial* article — what was it? I think you called it 'The Great Lawsuit' " — Greeley chuckled — "I would like to see you expand it into a book."

Unsurprised, Margaret was nevertheless thrilled. As editor of *The Dial*, America's leading transcendental journal, she had never had more than a few hundred readers. Now she was going to reach many thousands. Nor would she have to pull her punches to do it. She knew that Greeley was rapidly building circulation by confronting civic and national issues in a fearless fashion.

A special attraction was the opportunity to expand her essay into book length. She often had wanted to do this, but an article stating that women were men's equals — and in some respects their superiors — was not likely to be recommended by a male editor to a male publisher in masculine-dominated America. But here is my chance, she thought. Her eyelids fluttered, and she looked at Greeley through half-closed eyes. It was a habit that some of her friends found offensive.

"What do you want me to write?" she asked, leaving her major concern, about her book, to be discussed later.

"Well, I have in mind three articles a week," Greeley responded. "Let's say two on literary topics — Goethe, German literature, American literature, whatever you wish — and one on a current social problem."

"Current social problem?" Margaret's eyelids fluttered. "What, for example?"

"Well, maybe treatment of prisoners, or of inmates at state asylums. Maybe the condition of Irish immigrants. Or maybe the status of women in our society." Greeley knew he had baited his trap properly.

"I'd love the opportunity," Margaret replied quickly. "When should I start? And — what about the book?"

"Are you ready to write it?" he asked. "Do you have enough material? Are you clear on what you want to say?"

Eyelids aquiver, she replied, "Oh, I'm clear enough on what I want to say! And I'm ready to say it, too. Could you give me a couple of month's time to get the book finished, before I start at the Trib?"

"Sure. Sounds great." Greeley chuckled again. "Won't some folks roast over your ideas on women's equality!" He slapped his knee. "I can hardly wait to see them squirm."

Thus did Margaret Fuller, America's first important feminist, get an opportunity to reach a broad audience with her avant-garde ideas. It marked a turning point in her life. So far her audience had been Emerson, Thoreau, Bronson Alcott, and Ellery Channing. Now she was prepared to broaden her interest. She would always love the world of books, but a chance to confront the real world – the world of business and crime, of prostitutes and the poor – made her feel like a female explorer about to sail on a perilous but thrilling voyage.

Margaret, after all, was something more than the leading American woman intellectual of her time. Along with Poe, she was the first important literary critic in her country. Sent by Greeley, she was about to be America's first female foreign correspondent. As her concern for the poor and the oppressed deepened, she was going to become a vigorous opponent of injustice wherever she found it. But perhaps most important of all, she was going to do a great deal toward removing the barriers that had kept American women from being considered free and important individual human beings.

What was Margaret Fuller really like? Was she a cold blue-stocking who never had a close friend? Could she love, and be loved? What role did she play in the Italian revolution? What was the significance of her forty brief years of life? Does she still have a relevance for us as we near the end of the twentieth century?

Margaret's tradition was one of dissent. Her paternal grandfather had been driven out of town for preaching against the Revolution to his congregation of Minutemen. Later, restored, he opposed the federal Constitution because it did not outlaw slavery. His son Timothy, Margaret's father, later opposed the Missouri Compromise for the same reason.

Timothy had been denied valedictorian honors at Harvard in 1801 because of the part he had played in a student rebellion. He always seemed to be swimming against the stream. A New Englander, he supported Jefferson. The Unitarian church gave him the freedom his unshackled spirit demanded. His successful political career was remarkable, considering his independent stance and his rather abrasive personality. In 1817 he was elected as a Representative to Congress. In 1825 he became Speaker of the Massachusetts House of Representatives. But his support of John Quincy Adams in 1828 meant the end of his political career, because of Jacksonian "spoils system" appointments.

Since Margaret was the oldest child, Timothy vowed to make her "heir of all I know." Her start as heiress was untimely early. At 5 she read

Margaret Fuller. (Courtesy Brown Brothers.)

English very well. By the age of 6 she knew Latin grammar, and was memorizing Virgil. He would make her stay up until he returned home late at night, so that he could hear her recite her Latin lessons. Expecting perfection, he corrected her slightest error. Overwrought and under recreated, she began to have nightmares and to walk in her sleep. Her keen intellect was abnormally stimulated, but the price paid was headaches, a nervous stomach, and an underdeveloped emotional life. Sometimes she had convulsions.

Her dreams brought such vivid visions of death that at times they seemed more real than life. She did not get rid of her nightmares and sleepwalking until adulthood. Headaches plagued her throughout her life.

Sabbath was strictly observed by the Fullers. The long morning sermons would be followed by an afternoon devoted to reading religious books. When he caught her reading Shakespeare on the Sabbath, Father reprimanded her, but she continued to smuggle her profane reading. From the Romans she learned the importance of will and resolution. Although she disliked Greek philosophers she loved classical fables and stories of the Greek gods. In later years she often showed admiration of Aspasia, courtesan of Pericles, for her bold wit and intellect. Her favorite writers soon became Shakespeare, Cervantes, and Molière.

"I do wish that I had read no books at all till later," she confessed afterward, "but that I had lived with toys and played in the open air. With me," she continued, "much of life was devoured in the bud."

In 1823, at the age of 13, she attended a girls' school in Groton. Disliking school routine, she attracted her schoolmates' attention by bizarre antics and theatrical manners. Later, as a teacher, she became an early believer in progressive child-centered education, which sought for a unique unified development of the child's emotional and intellectual nature.

At the age of 16 Margaret had decided to be "bright and ugly." True, her tight corsets accentuated her stoutness, and her face was overdone ruddy. But she had dazzling white teeth, and beneath the fluttering eyelids sparkling eyes. She was, however, a perfectionist. If she could not be the most beautiful, she would not deign to enter the lists.

Her daily schedule was rigorous. Up at five o'clock, she helped her mother with household chores, including supervising her brothers and sisters. In the morning she studied Greek at Mr. Perkins' school in Cambridgeport. She impressed fellow students Oliver Wendell Holmes and Richard Henry Dana with her sagacity. In the afternoon she studied two hours of Italian and two hours of French. Before bedtime at eleven o'clock she found time for walks, philosophy lectures, piano playing, entries in her journal, and an hour or two of conversation, at which she excelled. Her favorite confidant was Henry Hedge, newly returned from five years in Germany. Through his influence she developed her lifelong love of German literature. She also became fond of Italian literature, not only Dante but also Petrarch, Tasso, Ariosto, and Manzoni.

Women writers had also attracted her attention. She admired Madame de Staël's brilliant conversation and her stress on spontaneity and imagination. She applauded George Sand as a courageous trailblazer but the Puritanical streak ingrained in her by her father would not let her accept the French novelist's unorthodox love life.

Cambridge in the 1820's was bristling with intellectual activity. The Unitarian belief in human perfectibility led to agitation for many reforms: prison, education, care of mentally ill, temperance, abolition of slavery, and ultimately, women's rights. Besides Hedge, Margaret's friends included Elizabeth Peabody, William Henry Channing, and Lydia Maria Child.

Margaret early flowered as a conversationalist. She was amazingly well informed, and seemed to be interested in everything. She could not only develop an idea logically, adding specific bits of information, but she could also appropriately toss the idea to the proper member of the group who at that point could make the maximum contribution to the idea's maturation. Thus, people always wanted to be in her discussion groups.

She could also be unduly frank. Her ability to destroy an opponent by one incisive thrust got her a reputation for having a sharp tongue. Later, as her friends counseled her to be less rash in her manner, she found that critical comments were more effective when tempered with uncompromising fairness.

She always loved controversy. At her last visit to the Emersons, in 1844, she told Emerson that she could not live in Concord because it lacked "the animating influence of Discord." But she was everywhere a welcome guest, Emerson said.

Margaret helped her mother with the supervision of five younger brothers and a sister. It was said of her that she could "rock a cradle, read a book, eat an apple, and knit a stocking, all at the same time." Her two oldest brothers ran off to New Orleans at an early age. Margaret helped the next two brothers get an education, at considerable financial sacrifice to herself. Her youngest brother, who was mentally incompetent, required special care. She tutored him and kept him company, until finally he was sent to Brook Farm where the Ripleys boarded him at no cost. Sister Ellen married the poet Ellery Channing, who could never keep a job, preferring long solitary walks to everyday routine. Since her mother was sickly, it was up to Margaret to help her father hold the family together.

Despite her frankness, Margaret was a good friend. "What should I have ever been but for you?" queried James Clarke. "You inspired me to distinguish myself above my fellows, and made me see the worth and meaning of life." Clarke confided all his problems, especially those involving love, to Margaret, and she became his confessor, a role she often played for both male and female friends.

In 1831 she had her first love affair. A distant cousin, George Davis, attracted her by his serious outlook on life, but he never seems to have returned the affection. When he announced his engagement to another girl, she suffered a feeling of rejection. Religion pulled her out of her depression.

The crisis came that year on Thanksgiving Day. After church, while walking through a dull grey field, she was flooded by instant sunlight. It seemed to warm her whole being with a newly found faith. She recorded the transformation in her journal: "I saw there was no self; that selfishness was all folly; that it was only because I thought self real that I suffered; that I had only to live in the idea of the All, and all was mine. I was for that hour taken up into God."

It was a familiar New England experience, like Jonathan Edwards discovering the beauty of holiness, or William Ellery Channing experiencing the glory of an impersonal God while living on the very estate that Margaret now called home. Although the ecstasy was short lived, it was sufficient to see her through commonplace experiences of countless mediocre days. She was learning to temper self-love with altruism and was developing a reservoir of inner strength that would help her in later crises.

Her native independence fought against a spirit of submission, even to God. Nevertheless, this mystical transcendental union with God was a state she often tried to capture during these years. For the surrender of one's identity was only that of one's selfish self. One's higher self could only soar upward as it gravitated toward the Source of its being.

She now began a systematic study of the Bible, to see if she could recapture the innocence and the wonder of her childhood faith. She finally grew to accept everything in her life, pain as well as pleasure, as part of a divine plan for her. This religious equilibrium reinforced her natural patience and perseverance. It was in this vein that she announced, "I accept the universe!" Carlyle quipped, "By Gad, she'd better!" perhaps not realizing that she was simply publicizing her intention not to renounce the world through escapism but to squarely face whatever circumstances came her way. In this respect she resembled her friend Emerson, although she lacked his ability to get soul-healing through communion with nature. Also due to her upbringing, she had a lifelong tendency to identify God as the Father.

Andrew Jackson's re-election in 1832 marked the end of Timothy Fuller's political aspirations, so he moved the family to rural Groton. Margaret missed the stimulating conversation of Cambridge. In the daytime household work kept her busy but evenings she read Goethe, Schiller, European history, and the life and letters of Jefferson. Margaret was concerned that Catherine Beecher's axiom would prove to be true for her — that American women were old before their time because of housework. She was also beginning to fear that permanent spinsterhood might be her lot.

Still smarting from the rejection by Davis, she wondered whether she would be better off single. So far she had never met a man who would let her be herself in marriage. In her imagination she became the chaste virgin of Goethe's heroines Iphigenia and Ottilia. Her early writings stress the exalted purity of chastity.

A series of articles on German writers in English periodicals, written by Thomas Carlyle, honed her appetite for German literature. She and James Clarke began an intensive study of the German language, and by the end of the year she had read most of the better known works of Goethe and Schiller in German. The German Romantics gave her an affirmative warmth and a sense of spiritual discovery that she had never felt in Unitarianism. They stressed things that appealed to her: one's responsibility for one's own moral development; a joyful acceptance of a mysterious but orderly universe; and a new way of explaining God's relationship to creation.

She became a disciple of Goethe. His intellectual virtuosity overwhelmed her. She liked his stress on faith in one's ability to surmount obstacles. After reading his "Second Residence in Rome," she said: "I shut the book each time with an earnest desire to live as he did—always to have some engrossing object of pursuit." She decided to emulate his "extraordinary, generous seeking."

As a starter, she translated Goethe's *Tasso*. She was determined to write a comprehensive study of his life. In 1839 she published her translation of *Eckermann's Conversations with Goethe*.

In 1834 she had first appeared in print, in a letter to the *Daily Advertiser* defending Brutus from the attack on him by historian George Bancroft's article in *The North American Review*. Someone from Salem, in response to her letter, which had been signed simply "J.," called her "an elderly gentleman," and she felt, at that time, flattered.

Feeling lonely, she once again turned to the consolation of religion. In her journal she wrote: "Please God to keep my mind composed that I may store it with all that may be hereafter conducive to the best good of others. Thou art my only Friend! Vouchsafe then Thy protection, that I may hold on in courage of soul!"

She studied Christianity seriously, comparing it to Plato's writing on the soul. The deistic overtones of her day, coupled with her native skepticism, led her to raise questions that orthodox religion was not prepared to answer. At this stage she tended to follow William Ellery Channing's version of Unitarianism, which saw Jesus as a perfect ethical model, neither God nor man but someone in between. Her God, however, was a personal one, and she looked forward to meeting Him in the hereafter.

In 1835 she published several articles in a new Unitarian journal, *Western Messenger*, edited by her friend James Clarke. He gave her valuable advice on the necessity of getting rid of loftiness and obscurity in her style.

In June she met Harriet Martineau, the Englishwoman who had written books on social reform. Her rise, overcoming a Calvinistic background, poverty, illness, and lack of acceptance, inspired Margaret. When publishers rejected her book *Illustrations on Political Economy*, Harriet published it herself, and it was a success.

They were a strange pair. Harriet, older, had little interest in literary and esthetic matters; she wanted to reform society. She scoffed at Margaret's recommendation for a gradual phase-out of slavery — she wanted immediate emancipation. Their discussions, however, sharpened Margaret's awareness of social issues, and demonstrated to her that a woman could be in the vanguard of social change. She decided to sail back to England with Harriet.

But the trip never materialized, because Margaret grew gravely ill. Childhood headaches came back to plague her. Part of her problem was a feeling of guilt over having written a thinly disguised love triangle tale, in which three friends — James Clarke, George Davis, and Harriet Russell — had been the principals. When she saw how their feelings had been hurt, she resolved never to write fiction again.

It greatly helped her to hear the words of her father, always a fair even if somewhat severe critic: "My dear, you have no faults. You have defects, of course, as all mortals have, but I do not know that you have a single fault." It was great praise, coming from him, and it acted like healing balm to her troubled conscience.

Recovered from her illness, she once again spoke of traveling to England. But the trip was not to be. On October 1, 1835, after a short illness, her father died of Asian cholera, leaving her to take over management of family matters, since her mother was sickly and retiring in nature. Father left no will and little estate, and Uncle Abraham, the estate trustee, was very stingy. When he decreed no further schooling for Margaret's brothers, she overruled him, stating that she would somehow provide funds for them. But the trip to England was out.

Paradoxically, it had been Goethe who had said, "Enjoy the present and leave the future to God." Although it was bitter medicine, Margaret did what she always did in a crisis — she turned to religion. The night after her father's death she saw that she must synthesize "what is due to others with what is due to myself." She asked God for His help in achieving and retaining this synthesis.

She was beginning to realize how adversity, properly fronted, can lead to ever greater achievement in life. Her constant enemy, the inner prideful desire for intellectual superiority, needed to be toned down by a judicious concern for other people's welfare and other people's rights. Maybe all the problems of the world were not going to be solved solely by intellect. Maybe moral concerns outweighed intellectual ones. "I shall be obliged to give up selfishness in the end," she said. "May God enable me to see the way clear, and not to let down the intellectual, in raising the moral tone of my mind."

Her father gone, Margaret was more than ever determined to meet the sage of Concord, Ralph Waldo Emerson. She persisted until she finally received an invitation to spend three weeks with Emerson and his new wife Lidian at their Concord home in July 1836. Emerson's first wife had died shortly before he left the ministry in 1832.

At first Emerson was repelled by Margaret's nasal voice, and by her fluttering eyelids. Soon, however, both he and Lidian esteemed her highly. He too was seeking a balance, one between society and solitude. He knew he became sterile in his thinking unless he was stimulated by contact with people. Margaret was a good influence on him, for she forced him to remain in society. She also kept him from being too comfortable in his optimism.

He not only deepened her appreciation of nature and of solitude, but he also gave her entry into the masculine-dominated literary world. Their backgrounds complemented each other — Emerson's strength was English and classical literature, whereas Margaret for years had concentrated on German, French, and Italian literature. They exchanged books in their respective fields, and helped complete each other's education.

Realizing that she was not prepared to play the role of her husband's intellectual companion, Lidian accepted Margaret as if she were a family member. Margaret had early learned to sublimate her sexual desires, a factor which intensified her friendship with both sexes. Emerson understood that in Margaret's satire lay little malice. He called it "a superabundance of animal spirits." To his mind it was one facet of a very generous nature underlying the somewhat brusque exterior. How else could one account for the fact that within an hour's acquaintance, total strangers found themselves confessing their life-tragedies to her? No doubt here they found someone who understood, someone who cared.

In time a platonic love developed between these two transcendentalists. One evidence of this was the external bantering between the two, as so often is true in this relationship. Emerson's reserve was almost aloofness — her fervor was too undisciplined for his taste. They had the underlying acceptance that permitted them to be critical of each other. Many friendships would not have been deep enough to stand their frank exchange.

When he first met her, he said he felt her to be a foreigner, perhaps a visitor from another planet. The strangeness about her both attracted and repelled him. She, like Thoreau, admired Emerson so much that she wanted him to be better than he already was. In 1842 she invited herself again to his home. He readily agreed. To her surprise, upon her arrival there she found two other star boarders, Thoreau and Ellery Channing. Despite their proximity, Emerson and Margaret communicated with each other by writing letters, dropping them off at each other's room. Emerson says they would "meet and treat like foreign states, one maritime, one inland, whose trade and laws are essentially unlike."

Once she left this note for him in his library: "I like to be in your library when you are out of it. There is so much soul here that I do not need a book. When I come to yourself, I cannot receive you, and you cannot give yourself; it does not profit. But when I cannot find you the beauty and permanence of your life come to me."

He invited her to move to Concord permanently, but she withdrew from constant close exposure to him. "I get, after a while, even intoxicated with your mind, and do not live enough in myself," she replied. Again like Thoreau, to carry out Emersonianism meant separation from Emerson.

One advantage in knowing Emerson was to be invited to meetings of the Transcendental Club. Here Margaret met men like Alcott, George Ripley, Orestes Brownson, and Theodore Parker, and such women as Elizabeth Hoar, Sarah Ripley, and Elizabeth Peabody. There were few more stimulating contributors to an intellectual discussion than Margaret. She confessed to the group that Emerson had taught her the meaning of an inward life. "The mind is its own place," he had said.

Some members of the Transcendental Club were occultists. This struck a responsive chord in her. She had had a childhood fascination with mythology. She suspected that there was something basically true even in astrology, mesmerism, and extra-sensory perception. She had sympathy for Goethe's belief in demonology, which was itself related to the Greek belief in daemons or indwelling spirits. She often felt possessed by a demonic power, which probably helps account for periods of inactivity and depression she experienced. She certainly had unusual runs of bad luck. Some of these things explain the strangeness that Emerson noted in her.

On the brighter side, she felt that her demon gave her the power to attract people to her and to speak to them in an inspired way. No one ever questioned that her conversation had a power and a charisma not found in her writing.

She was seeking a unique synthesis. She wanted to be a woman, and she wanted to be an intellectual force in a man's world. Other creative women, like the Brontës, Emily Dickinson, and Elizabeth Barrett Browning, either withdrew into seclusion or had protective and supportive husbands. She was determined not to withdraw, and she refused to accept the notion that a creative woman could succeed only when abetted by a devoted man.

Emerson was unable to see that his world had no place for the creative woman. Margaret's classmates, who acknowledged her superiority, went to Harvard and entered professions. Neither goal was open to her. When Oberlin College pioneered by accepting women students in 1833, it drew up a separate simpler curriculum for them, assuming they were unable to meet men's standards.

A man, her father, had decided to give her "a man's" intellect. Her childhood male friends had stimulated her curiosity and encouraged her ambition. Her intellectual endowment could not be fully realized in the kitchen — although she spent plenty of years there as a dutiful family member. Society was designed to deny her natural fulfillment, and then criticize her for not being creative.

It is little wonder that she developed neurotic symptoms. Her strident self-confidence led her to write to Emerson: "I see no divine person. I myself am more divine than any I see." Of course, he would applaud *that*. She had supercharged feelings at times, and moods varying from lassitude to restless high spirits. Her headaches can no doubt be understood as a psychosomatic product. But one wonders whether there was as much illness in the woman as in the society which produced her.

When Elizabeth Peabody left Alcott's Temple School in 1836, Margaret replaced her as teacher of German, French, Italian, and Latin. Evenings she tutored students, and offered a class in German and Italian literature for women students, since Harvard was closed to them. One evening a week she translated from the German with William Ellery Channing.

Angry at Harriet Martineau's attack on Alcott's school in her book *Society in America*, Margaret wrote a stinging letter to Harriet, which marred their friendship for years. Margaret told Harriet that her book lacked order, completeness, and patient investigation. She said that Harriet should have commended Alcott for his high ideals and his deep understanding of children.

Overworked, Margaret nearly had a nervous breakdown. Her headaches intensified, and now seemed to have migrated to her spine. She had curvature of the spine, a malady she felt was cured by mesmerist Theodore Leger in 1845. Feeling depressed over her illness, she developed the theory that illness fostered creativity. But she knew she was rationalizing. "I have as little chance to think," she said, "as a haberdasher's apprentice or the President of Harvard University."

Already suffering criticism, Alcott accepted a mulatto girl into his school in 1839. This proved to be too much for Boston. Parents withdrew their children, and the school closed. Margaret, as chief support of her family, wondered what to do next.

Fortunately she received a teaching assignment at a school in Providence run by Hiram Fuller, no relation to her. The pay was good, but she missed the stimulating conversation of her Cambridge friends. Hiram gave her wide latitude, so she pursued lofty goals for her students: "general activity of mind, accuracy in processes, constant looking for principles, search after the good and the beautiful." Although her pupils seemed to make progress, she herself felt unrealized. "Every year I live," she grumbled, "I dislike routine more and more, though I see that society rests on that, and other falsehoods."

Now she was about to experience another great frustration. Her long friendship with Samuel Ward was blossoming into a romance, she thought. He had paid a lot of attention to her, and she willingly fanned the flames of his ardor. But then he met her beautiful friend Anna Barker. In a short time he and Anna were engaged, and he abandoned his career as a painter to enter his father's bank. Once more Margaret wondered if she would ever be loved.

She took this rebuff with "nun-like renunciation," she said, but the inner pain broke through at times in excessive self-praise. Eventually she found her peace. She told Emerson: "I thank nightly the benignant Spirit, for the unaccustomed serenity in which it enfolds me." But in her journal she confided: "No one loves me. But I love many a great deal. I am myself growing better, and shall by and by be a worthy object of love. I have no child, and the woman in me has so craved this experience that it has seemed the want of it must paralyze me."

In December 1838 Margaret resigned her teaching work in Providence. She missed Emerson and her other friends in the Boston area. She wanted to do more writing, and she realized that teaching and writing did not mix. She moved her family from Groton to Jamaica Plains on Long Island.

By now Margaret was a true transcendentalist. She was too much a romantic idealist to be satisfied with Dr. Channing's logical Unitarianism. She was little worried when Harvard's conservative Andrews Norton attacked transcendentalism as pantheistic and immoral. As Harvard Divinity School grew increasingly scientific, she instead looked inward for intuitive flashes of divinity. Even Emerson's God, the Oversoul, was too impersonal for her. "I would now preach the Holy Ghost as zealously as they have been preaching Man," she opined, "and faith instead of understanding, and mysticism." Mankind, she felt, had a two-fold relationship — to nature beneath and to God above. For man, "the earth is his school, if not his birthplace; God his object; life and thought his means of interpreting nature and aspiring to God." Thus her fundamental quest was religious, although it early took literary and later political form.

Like other transcendentalists, Margaret believed that material prosperity had undermined America's concern for spiritual values. She helped spearhead a revolt against the idols of the marketplace. She knew that once God was displaced as the granter of human dignity, the individual was ultimately doomed. The transcendental hope for man, she said, "is grounded on his destiny as an immortal soul, and not as a mere comfort-loving inhabitant of earth, or as a subscriber to the social contract. Man is not made for society, but society is made for man. No institution can be good which does not tend to improve the individual."

In May 1839 her first book appeared, the translation of *Eckermann's Conversations with Goethe*. Although it brought her no money, it helped consummate her interest in Goethe. Many friends, including Emerson and James Clarke, praised her introduction for throwing new light on Goethe, defending him in his later years when he had been said to be no Christian, no democrat, no idealist, and no Schiller!

In November Margaret began a series of Conversation Classes for women that ran for five winters. A course consisted of 13 two-hour noon meetings. The function of the classes was to report on the changing status of women. Margaret's goal was to get women to alter their image of themselves. Women considered themselves intellectually inferior to men — even she herself had doubts at times. She admitted that "insofar as she was bright she was not quite a whole woman." "If I had been a man," she told William Channing, "then there would have been a man!"

Margaret wanted to give women the opportunity to systematize their thoughts and then to express those thoughts clearly. She wanted women to realize that any deficiencies they might have were not innate but were the result of superficial education and a self-deprecation brought about by social custom and conformity.

Core members of her group were the Peabody sisters, Anna Barker, Sara Clarke, Ellen Hooper, and Sarah Ripley. As the idea took hold, many of the social aristocracy of Boston attended. Names represented included Bancroft, Channing, Higginson, Lee, Parker, Quincy, Russell, and Shaw. Margaret's transcendental seeds were beginning to sprout an unexpected crop.

The first subject for discussion was Greek mythology. Margaret showed how the Greeks used their gods to express certain universal aspects of human nature. In 1840 the topic was fine arts. Many of Boston's young men were studying sculpture and painting in Italy, and the city was in a love-Italy craze.

In 1841 men were invited to attend, and Emerson, Alcott, Ripley, Hedge, and Clarke occasionally attended. But the presence of men stifled spontaneity and frankness among the women, so Margaret went back to the all-female format.

Although discussion was free and sometimes roamed far afield, the unifying factor was always Margaret's stress on human integrity. Her basic position was that all human beings, being God's creation, have a certain fundamental equality. He who is Justice would not be unjust to a part of His creation. Thus, difference of race, sex, or financial status has no bearing on the spiritual freedom that we all carry within ourselves. Art, she said, was valuable mostly as a vehicle for spiritual concepts. Poetry and religion should be one, she thought, although rarely is the unity achieved.

The Conversation Classes had some important consequences. To a surprising extent, they achieved their goal of helping women develop self-respect and self-confidence. They fed the fire of incipient feminism. As Elizabeth Cody Stanton later remarked, "they vindicated woman's right to think."

They also played a part in Margaret's own development. They drew more heavily on her resources than anything she had previously done. They built up her own confidence, and they gave her a reputation as leader in this important field. Perhaps most important of all, they led her to esteem women even more highly than she originally had done, thus preparing her for future more eloquent assertions about woman's capability and role in American life.

The transcendentalists needed an editor for their new journal in 1840, so Margaret became editor of *The Dial*. She was to receive $200 per year after all expenses were paid, but she never received a cent. Since she always had trouble getting material from contributors, she often wrote a good deal of each issue. As editor, she showed good judgment in avoiding the ephemeral crankiness of the 1840's. But she had high standards and strictly observed them. She criticized Emerson for word choice and trite-ness, and she miffed Thoreau by rejecting several pieces of his that she thought were not of high quality. Probably her most reliable contributors were Emerson and Theodore Parker. She also was able to print a number of articles by women.

Her own writing for *The Dial* was of varying quality. Generally her views on literature were sound but when she wrote about music and art, of which she knew little, she was a less trustworthy guide. Nevertheless it gave her valuable experience, preparing her for her later role as a literary critic for Greeley.

After two years she turned the editor's job over to Emerson, who paid for the final issues out of his own pocket. Knowing of the need for material, Margaret continued to write for *The Dial*. No doubt her most important article was in the July 1843 issue called "The Great Lawsuit: Man vs. Men. Woman vs. Women." In the most extensive statement of women's rights yet to appear in America Margaret developed the point that to restrict women's self-development was to restrain the entire human race.

As usual, Margaret's starting place in the article is the equality of God's creation. All souls, she says, including those of Negroes, Indians, and women, are equal in His sight. She points out the inconsistency of Uni-tarians and transcendentalists who exalt mankind to the exclusion of womankind. She asks why women's rights should be man's last concern. She points out the typical male doublethink of the period: Although women helped set up the 1840 World Anti-Slavery Convention, not a woman was invited to attend as a delegate! She asks for equal educational opportunity for women, and then for equal vocational opportunity. These things, she says, lead naturally to equal legal and political opportunity. Sounding very modern she says that "there is no wholly masculine man, no purely feminine woman." A woman who remains single should suffer no social ostracism, she holds. The article not only brought wider notice to Margaret and her work but it reminded the transcendentalists to practice their stated ideals.

Admiring the relationship between German poet Karoline von Günderode and Goethe's young admirer Bettina von Arnim, Margaret pub-lished an anonymous translation of the correspondence between the idealistic Karoline and the earthy Bettina in 1842. She was probably trying to vindicate the friendship role between two women deeply attracted to each other.

Like Emerson and Thoreau, she was too much an individualist to join Ripley's Brook Farm or Alcott's Fruitlands. Questioning her own radi-cality, she found that Utopias were too simplistic, on the one hand, and ex-cluded too much, on the other.

She farmed her cow at Brook Farm, and Hawthorne said it had all the mulishness of a transcendental heifer. Some of her visits to Brook Farm, however, were to see Hawthorne, who had not yet married pretty Sophia Peabody. In August 1844 Margaret and he went for a long moonlit row on

Concord River. They walked together through the woods, and talked far into the night. In her journal she wrote of Hawthorne: "I love him much."
By now her ideal man had Emerson's mind, William Channing's "pure and
passionate beauty," and Hawthorne's mellowness.

Alas for Margaret—little of that mellowness appeared in his portrait
of her as Zenobia in *The Blithedale Romance*. Zenobia, the brilliant conversationalist and champion of women's rights, is prideful, egotistical, and
tactless. History unkindly confuses Margaret with Zenobia, and perpet-
uates an inaccurate and unfair stereotype. Hawthorne denied that Zenobia
represented Margaret, yet even his journals contain a vicious attack on her.
He states that she thought she was her own Creator. But strong as were her
convictions, Margaret always stood in true humility before God.

In the summer of 1843 Margaret joined James and Sarah Clarke on a
tour of the American Northwest, which at that time was the western side of
Lake Michigan. Material gathered on the trip was the basis for the next
book, *Summer on the Lakes*, which was published on her thirty-fourth
birthday, May 23, 1844. To do research for the book she got rare female
permission to use Harvard Library.

Her book describes the multi-cultural setting of the frontier, with
Irish, German, and Scandinavian settlers each forming their own cultural
oases. She was impressed by the contrast between the beauty of God's
nature on one hand and the sordid ugliness of the cities on the other. But
unlike Jefferson she accepted the evils of the city as the price of
progress—hopefully cities would some day be civilized. The forthrightness
of Chicagoans appealed to her. She felt that in the West there was a better
opportunity than in the East for America to develop a truly indigenous
culture.

Not all the comforts of home were found in this sparsely settled
region. One night all rooms were taken at a town's only tavern. So the bar-
tender chivalrously evicted his customers so that Margaret and Sarah could
sleep on the barroom tables.

Women suffered more on the frontier than men, she found, because
they often had to do men's work as well as their own. No household help
was available. To men, hunting and fishing are partly recreational but there
is little glamor in housekeeping. Continental women, accustomed to field
work, endured the rigors of frontier life better than did English women.

Horace Greeley, after offering Margaret a job as a writer for his
*Tribune*, had granted her several months to convert the article into book
form. Thus she and Caroline Sturgis spent seven weeks at Fishkill, above
New York City, in October and November of 1844. Severe migraine headaches were the outward manifestation of Margaret's great inner struggle.
When people told her she had a man's mind she would reply, "I love best to
be a women, but womanhood at present is too straitly bound to give me
scope."

"Shall life never be sweet?" she asked. " 'Tis an evil lot to have a man's ambition and a woman's heart." Her childhood nightmares now returned. One constantly recurring dream was a vision of falling off rocks into the ocean and drowning.

The interior struggle between feminine submissiveness and masculine assertiveness was devastating, but somehow Margaret trusted in the outcome. "The Woman in me kneels and weeps in tender rapture; the Man in me rushes forth, but only to be baffled. Yet the time will come when, from the union of this tragic king and queen, shall be born a radiant sovereign self."

The work involved in writing *Woman in the 19th Century* gave Margaret the opportunity to achieve the long-sought synthesis. The "masculine" creativity and boldness poured itself through her "feminine" tenderness and sensitivity to make her the needed mouthpiece of her sex. Now her pen could repeat what her tongue had long since learned — that no matter how good a better half a woman made, she made a best whole, apart from any need to define herself as man's dependent.

The writing, though intense, seemed never difficult, but poured from her pen as if she were in automatic writing. There were pleasant interruptions by visiting friends. But by mid-November she was finished, and she was satisfied. "I felt a delightful glow," she said, "as if I had put a good deal of my true life in it, and as if, should I go away now, the measure of my foot-print would be left on the earth."

Since Margaret's feminism was built on a religious base, one might ask what were her religious views at this time. Speaking through her main character Miranda, Margaret says: "Religion was early awakened in my soul — a sense that what the soul is capable to ask it must attain." Orthodox Christianity seemed somewhat thin to her, in the light of her early exposure to the rich Greek pantheon. She had written her religious credo in 1842: "I believe in Christ because I can do without him. But I do not wish to do without him. He is constantly aiding and answering me. When he comes to me I will receive him; when I feel inclined to go by myself, I will. Jesus breaks through the soil of the world's life, like some great river through the else inaccessible plains and valleys. I bless its course. I follow it. But it is a part of the All.

All future manifestations will come, like this — not to destroy the law and the prophets but to fulfill. But as an Abraham called for a Moses, a Moses for a David, so does Christ for another ideal. We have had the Messiah to reconcile and to teach; let us have another to live out all the symbolical forms of human life with the calm beauty and physical fulness of a Greek god, with the deep consciousness of a Moses, with the holy love and purity of Jesus."

Before she had started writing her book, Margaret had reviewed the current status of women. Had her zeal ever been tempted to flag, the remembrance of that status could only spur her onward.

Abigail Adams had asked in vain for her husband John to present women's need for equal treatment to the Continental Congress. As if in reply to Thomas Paine's *The Rights of Man*, Mary Wollstonecraft answered with *A Vindication of the Rights of Women*, published in London in 1792. She asked for women to be allowed to be educated, to vote and hold office, and to have access to industry and the professions. The Scottish feminist Frances Wright arrived in the United States in 1819, and immediately pressed for equal educational opportunities for women. Lydia Maria Child in 1832 published *The History of Women*, surveying women's role in society and showing the need for greater gains to be made toward equality.

Some progress was being achieved. Emma Willard opened Troy Seminary for women in 1819, and Mary Lyon founded Mount Holyoke Seminary in 1836. Female academies, giving the equivalent of high-school education, were beginning to appear in many states.

Some of the leading women reformers were Quakers, who gave women equal treatment with men. Acquiescent women considered women's-rights advocates as hussies for concerning themselves with men's affairs. The Grimké sisters, Angelina and Sarah, moved from repudiating their slave-holding family to an attack on slavery itself. When they were told to be quiet, they responded by expanding their definition of slavery to include the status of shackled women. As women were denied their right to speak against slavery, they were reminded of how many other rights were also denied them.

For example, in most states women could not vote or hold public office. In the eyes of the law they were considered minors. Unmarried, they were wards of male relatives; married, they were part of their husband's chattel. When a women with property married, the property automatically became her husband's. All married women's acts were performed under the protection of her husband — her condition was called coverture. A married woman's earnings belonged to her husband; a married man's earnings belonged to himself. If a wife died intestate, the husband received all her property; if a husband died intestate, the wife got one-third of his property. At the husband's death his will could take away all their children from the mother and give them to a guardian selected by the husband. According to Alice Tyler, "wife beating 'with a reasonable instrument' was legal in almost every state as late as 1850." Was there any wonder that Margaret was furious as she surveyed the condition of her sex?

In the preface to her book Margaret explained what she meant by the phrase "the great lawsuit." She says each sex is its own worst enemy. Humans, who by living in accordance with the highest elements of their nature could make earth a part of heaven, continually obstruct themselves by their prejudices and passions. Neither sex can achieve its highest form unaided by the other — they are "two halves of one divine thought."

Margaret felt that she was being used as a part of God's unceasing revelation to humankind. "No doubt a new manifestation is at hand, a new hour in the day of Man. As the principle of liberty is better understood, a broader protest is made on behalf of Woman. As men become aware that few men have had a fair chance, they are inclined to say that no women have had a fair chance. This country is surely destined to elucidate a great moral law, as Europe was to promote the mental culture of Man."

But she felt that her country was going to have to rid itself of sexual stereotyping. Alexis de Tocqueville had said that no country had gone so far as the United States had in creating separate lines of action between the sexes. Harriet Martineau added that this stereotyping was crushing American morals. As men were encouraged to neglect religious and esthetic values in an increasingly competitive industrial order, women were being expected to embody these values for their men, to be their "better half." The cost being paid, as America created "a cult of Pure Womanhood," was that women were excessively cultivating submissiveness, piety, and domesticity as if these were exclusively feminine virtues. The teeter-totter was dangerous at both ends; as men's morals declined, women's went up only at the price of a loss of independent strength and self-reliance. To restore the balance for both sexes, stereotyping had to go.

Emerson's self-reliance was what women now needed. Seeking, like Thoreau, to find a lowest common denominator for living, she says: "What woman needs is not as a woman to act or to rule, but as a nature to grow, as an intellect to discern, as a soul to live freely and unimpeded." She blames women as much as men for the cliché that women's minds are inferior to men's. "Man is not willingly ungenerous," she says. Women's willing subservience is greatly responsible for women's restricted role in human society. She cites examples to show that men are capable of recognizing women's true capacities. Also, she shows examples in history when women have wielded power foolishly, in those rare cases when they had it. But man's need to dominate women had even distorted woman's image of herself. What women want is simply "the birthright of every being capable of receiving it—the freedom, the religious, the intelligent freedom of the universe to use its means, to learn its secret, with God alone for their guide and their judge."

No woman who is properly enlightened concerning her nature and its potential, she says, would want to be a man or to usurp man's role. Each sex should develop its unique potential: "The Power who gave a power signifies that it must be brought out toward perfection."

America's history, founded in religion, meaning equality before God, and political liberty, makes it the country with the proper ideas for the emancipation of women, she felt. Quoting Emerson, she says, "Union is only possible to those who are units."

She shows how women's work in the abolitionist movement reminded them of their similarity to slaves: they cannot own or inherit property, or keep their own earnings, or keep their own children if their husbands are faithless or abusive. So she advocates legal safeguards for women. And she asks for equal opportunity for education and for vocation for women.

Although she celebrates a kind of virginity, she realizes that woman can best achieve her highest nature through an equal union with man. She lists five types of marriages, on an ascending scale of preference: worst of all is the marriage of convenience; not really good is the state of mutual idolatry; a much better arrangement is one of household partnership; an excellent union can be built upon one of intellectual companionship; best of all is the "religious marriage," which combines the household partnership with the intellectual camaraderie.

She asks for complete vocational equality for women. At a time when women were having some difficulty being accepted as nurses and teachers, she says gaily, "Let them be sea-captains, if they are able!" As a matter of fact, when she saw the French frigate Hercules anchored in Narragansett Bay she had remarked to a friend, "I should much like to command such a vessel."

Margaret identifies three prophets of the new age. Emanuel Swedenborg, the Swedish mystic, not only synthesized science and religion, but he also early realized that women must be encouraged to develop their fullest potential. François Fourier, the French socialist, not only stressed the growth of the individual but also stressed equal treatment of the sexes. In Goethe she admired the different types of feminine temperament found in *Wilhelm Meister*, and liked his stress upon self-development for women as well as men.

Realizing now that women have the Minerva or masculine aspect to their nature as well as the muse or feminine aspect, she now forgives her father for his strict tutorage of her. Accepting sexual equality and knowing there was inadequate educational opportunity for women, he had made up for society's lack by his personal concern for her education. This gave her, she now realizes, the ability to take her place easily in the world of the mind, and so she offers him her belated thanks.

One can see in the book Margaret's growth in the direction of social action. She praises abolitionist leaders like Angelina Grimké and Abby Kelley. She calls upon women to rise up against the annexation of Texas, which she saw as a pretext for the expansion of slave territory. In order to make their full moral force felt, she recommends public speaking and petition carrying by women.

To refute the charge of contradiction and betrayal of her sturdy defense of individualism, she says society needs to blend the wisdom of Fourier, who saw the need for social measures, with the wisdom of Goethe, whom she calls the soul's critic.

The women she praises were largely rebels, like Madame de Staël, George Sand, and Mary Wollstonecraft. This had to be so, because a man's world would not accept their advanced views.

She denies that prostitution is a necessary accompaniment of civilization, stating that were wives and husbands true partners, there would be no prostitution. She attacks the double standards of morals, asserting that the sex drive in women is every bit as strong as it is in men. She believes women need better sex education, and that men should learn to practice sexual restraint.

Her summary is eloquent: "I wish Woman to live *first* for God's sake. Then she will not make an imperfect man her god, and thus sink to idolatry. By being more a soul, she will not be less Woman, for nature is perfected through spirit. Now there is no woman, only an overgrown child. That her hand may be given with dignity, she must be able to stand alone."

Published by Greeley at 50¢ a copy, the edition sold out in a week. Poe called the book "nervous, thoughtful, brilliant, and scholarlike," but he felt that Margaret had assumed that all women were like her, whereas in reality there were only a dozen or two women like her in the world. The book was widely read, even in England where it appeared in a pirated edition.

Soon a number of women's rights societies began to appear, many of them named after Margaret. The organizers of the first women's rights convention, held at Seneca Falls in 1848, paid tribute to Margaret. At the 1850 convention in Worcester Paulina Davis lamented Margaret's death at a time when she was looked up to as the national leader in the drive for women's rights. Sarah Grimké in 1852 urged the first women's rights convention in Pennsylvania to adopt as its motto the words of Margaret's: "Give me truth; cheat me by no illusion." Nearly forty years later, Julia Ward Howe said of Margaret's book, "Nothing that has been written or said in later days has made its teaching superfluous." A crusader for women's rights, Ednah Cheyney, said in 1902: "To this day I am astonished to find out how large a part of me I have derived from her."

By 1850 a number of states passed laws granting property rights to married women. In 1853 Antoinette Brown became the first ordained woman minister in the United States. She later married Dr. Samuel Blackwell, brother to two doctors of medicine, Emily and Elizabeth, who set up an infirmary for women and children in 1857 that was staffed entirely with women. Women first got the right to vote in Wyoming in 1859, and then a number of western states pioneered in granting women suffrage.

Although there were many other important influences on the progress of women's rights besides Margaret's book, it was a landmark for its courageous trail-blazing in a much-needed direction. Where Mary Wollstonecraft had tried to reason with men to grant women equality, Margaret had taken the attack directly to women, calling upon them to liberate themselves.

Greeley's wife, Mary, impressed by Margaret's courage, persuaded her husband to let Margaret live with them in their ramshackle mansion on the East River. Greeley himself whimsically remarked, when she waited for him to hold a door open for her, "Sea-captains, indeed! A good husband and two or three bouncing babies would have emancipated her from a good deal of cant and nonsense." Nevertheless, like Emerson, he supported the action programs of the various women's rights groups, and he called her book "the loftiest and most commanding assertion yet made of the right of woman to be regarded as an independent, intelligent rational being."

Margaret decided to begin her newspaper career in New York City with a series of articles on city institutions that needed reform. She found the Bloomingdale Asylum well run but the other public institution for the insane, on Blackwell's Island, was a terror. Its patients crowded in dingy corners, with no hope for rehabilitation. Of its 1200 inmates, 700 were women, but there was not a single woman custodian. She also visited The Tombs, the city jail, and Sing Sing. Most of the women prisoners were prostitutes, for whom she felt a special sympathy. Like Christ, what she saw in them was the good, the redeemable elements. Many society ladies were only high-fashion versions of them, she felt. She praised matron Eliza Farnham for the reforms she had introduced at Sing Sing: suspension of the silence rule, use of flower bouquets, installation of a library and a school teaching writing and crafts. When Eliza was discharged for reading *Oliver Twist* to inmates, the cause of prison reform was set back several decades.

In 1845 she wrote a series of articles opposing slavery. "Clergymen today command slaves to obey a gospel which they will not allow them to read," she said. "The world ought to get on a little faster than this," she felt, if God's kingdom were ever to come to earth.

She welcomed persecuted Germans and Jews who were arriving in New York, and she championed the cause of the poor Irish, "an oppressed race," as she called them. She attacked employment notices stating, "No Irish need apply," and she helped expose the Protestant die-hards who were instigating anti-Irish riots.

As a reporter, for the first time a woman of her class was seeing problem areas that were formerly ignored: immigrants, blacks, the poor, the blind, the insane. The sensitivity that had quickened at the plight of suffering women now expanded to embrace the entire gamut of suffering humanity. Wherever there was injustice, Margaret was its foe. Friends who criticized her for deserting her high muse, literature, got this response: "I never regarded literature merely as a collection of exquisite products, but rather as a means of mutual interpretation." Mutual interpretation to her meant using her writing to help bring about society's improvement.

Emerson said evil was illusory, ephemeral, unreal. Evil was real enough in the world Margaret saw, but there was a God who would help us overcome it if we trusted in Him, used our brains, and got to work to eradicate it.

Margaret had not, after all, abandoned literature. Two of her three weekly articles dealt with literature and the arts. Greeley helped her simplify her heavy Germanic style into clear and interesting sentences. Her objectivity is seen by her review of Emerson's *Essays, Second Series*. Although she found much merit in them she wished he would keep his feet on the ground and face life's real conflicts head on.

She applauded the practice of American novelist Charles Brockden Brown of putting most of his heroism and nobility in his feminine characters. She admired the poetry of Elizabeth Barrett Browning for its freedom, erudition, and vigor. She found much to praise in the work of George Sand: she knows passion, has great descriptive talent, and exquisite poetic feeling. Nor was the Frenchwoman now to be condemned for her unconventional love life. A victim of a marriage of convenience, she could not stand the hypocrisy of her peers and so had struck back boldly at its falsity. For this, Margaret felt, she should be commended rather than condemned.

As a literary critic, Margaret was severe but sound. She was also quick to recognize and reward merit. She extolled Poe, Melville, and Hawthorne before they had received general acclaim. As a critic, she was less an impressionist than Poe or Lowell, and more logically consistent than her two rivals as America's first important literary critic. Certainly no contemporary American critic had the wide reading background of continental literature that she had.

In 1845 Margaret fell in love with James Nathan, a German Jew who was a commission agent in New York City. Longing to be a wife and a mother, she relapsed into a submissive feminine role to try to attract him. She finally wrote to him: "Are you my guardian to domesticate me in the body, and attach it more firmly to the earth?" Mistaking her meaning, he made sexual advances which she promptly squelched. When he abandoned her and married a German girl it hurt Margaret very much. Now 35, it certainly seemed that a consummate love affair was not going to be hers in time.

During the summer of 1846 Margaret persuaded Greeley that he should use her as a foreign correspondent. He agreed, and on August 1 she sailed to Liverpool, accompanied by her wealthy friends, Marcus and Rebecca Spring. Her articles back to the *Tribune* give a good picture of her reaction to Europe.

She praised the practical curriculum of the Mechanics Institute in Liverpool. The public baths of Edinburgh impressed her. One night, descending Ben Lomond in Scotland after a four-mile climb, she got lost and spent the night alone on a narrow ledge.

She was pleased that her book *Papers on Literature and Art* was favorably received. "I find myself in my element in European society," she wrote Emerson.

The public laundries in London impressed her but she could not stomach "the shocking inhumanity of exclusiveness" — royalty parading down streets lined with beggars and orphans. She described favorably the improvements to tenement districts and especially the role being played by British women, who were active in art, publishing, museums, and in conducting schools for the working people.

She was likewise impressed with Emerson's friend, Thomas Carlyle. Although he was very conservative and gave no one else a chance to voice opposite opinions, she rejoiced in his infinite wit and exuberant vocabulary. "Allow for his point of view," she said, "and his survey is admirable."

Carlyle's wife, Jane Welsh, was an admirer of the Italian patriot, Giuseppe Mazzini, who had been exiled from Italy in 1830. A frail, handsome man with a saintly gaze, Mazzini made an immediately favorable impact upon Margaret. "What impelled him," she said, "was no superficial enthusiasm but an understanding of what must be the designs of Heaven with regard to man, since God is Love, is Justice." His position that one cannot transform the inward person of a factory laborer working fourteen hours a day now made more sense to her than Emerson's grandiose doctrine of "the infinitude of the private man." Mazzini not only reinforced her fundamental values but also gave her new visions of how these values might be achieved in a precarious world. Like Emerson, he saw materialism as the biggest evil of the time, but unlike the American, who felt individualism was the only cure, Mazzini put his faith in society's collective action to restrict industrial evils and prevent political exploitation.

In November Margaret and the Springs went to Paris. The highlight of her stay in France was her meeting the Polish poet, Adam Mickiewicz, who, in exile, was professor of Slavic literature at the College de France. Mickiewicz, inspired by Emerson and other American transcendentalists, was working feverishly for the freedom and self-government of all of the oppressed peoples of Europe. Moreover, he strongly believed in equal treatment for women. He immediately became one of Margaret's closest friends. He urged her to act out her philosophy: "You have pleaded the liberty of woman in a masculine and frank style. Live and act, as you write." He learned soon enough that Margaret meant what she wrote.

As if a premonition of worse things to come, the vessel Margaret took to Naples had a collision and had to be towed into port. She was relieved it was not worse, for she had always feared death by drowning.

Margaret fell in love with Italy, as have so many others. Here nature, history, and the people all seemed to merge into a sensible unity. But with all her early interest in esthetics she found herself going to fewer art galleries and more cafes where rebels were secretly discussing the coming overthrow of the government, to be replaced by a people's republic.

The Congress of Vienna in 1814 had divided Italy into eight separate states, most of which were under Austrian control or influence. The new pope, Pius IX, had liberal tendencies and wanted reform, but of course he would do nothing to harm the Church, and the monarchies of Austria, France, and Spain were all Catholic. When Pius IX, as ruler of the Papal States, granted amnesty to many political prisoners and relaxed the press censorship, he was widely hailed as the native Italian leader who would unite Italy and throw off the yoke of the foreign domination.

Though nominally a Protestant, Margaret felt completely at home during the services at St. Peters during Holy Week, 1847. On Easter Day the biggest event in her life occurred.

After vesper services she became separated from the Springs. Lost, she wandered through dark side chapels. A tall handsome man in his late twenties asked if he could help her. He had dark brown eyes and a full soft moustache. He wore a flowing cravat and carried a bamboo cane. Margaret easily understood his clear and rhythmical Italian.

She replied, "Yes, I need help," and explained her predicament. When no carriage was available, he offered to walk her to her hotel. She accepted.

The Marchese Giovanni Angelo Ossoli was the youngest son of a high functionary at the papal court. He was unmarried. His three brothers were colonels in the pope's guard. But Giovanni did not approve of the pope's temporal power. He admired Mazzini and wanted a united Italian republic. He was overjoyed to hear that she knew Mazzini, and that she had smuggled him into Italy, disguised as a member of her party.

At her door he kissed her hand, conventionally, and went away. She wrote in her journal, "No one loves me. But by and by I shall be a worthy object for love." In a few weeks she would be 37.

As she reviewed her previous love affairs, she could well say: "I have wished to be natural and true, but the world was not in harmony with me — nothing came right for me." George Davis, the brilliant student, had suddenly moved away. Sam Ward deserted painting for banking and married the beauty, Anna Barker. Emerson had told her he could love her courage, her enterprise, her thoughts, her prayers, but assuredly not her body. James Nathan, who had mistaken her tender phrase, now wanted a payment in return for the love letters she wanted back from him.

As she reflected, out of her window she recognized *his* graceful form. She snatched shawl, bonnet, and gloves and hurried down to where he was waiting. He smiled, and the melancholy cast in his eyes vanished. It would be a pleasure to show her the sights of Rome.

She was aware that he was eleven years younger than she. He felt there was nothing unusual in a young man courting an older woman, something often done in Italy.

Mickiewicz understood what was happening. He wrote from Paris: "Don't leave lightly those who would remain close to you. In this I refer to that young Italian whom you met in the church. Absorb from Italy all that you are able to take."

What should she call him? She finally settled on "Caro Giovane" (Dear Youth), and he called her "Cara Amica" (Dear Friend) or simply Cara. He had little book education but he knew practical things, such as estate management and care of horses.

The family name, Ossoli della Torre, was recorded in the Golden Book of Italian Nobility. But he did not introduce her to his family. They would not have resented his affair with an American woman — even an older Protestant one — as long as marriage was not mentioned. But a liaison with a republican woman — never! There was always the danger of contamination by close association.

She told him, "You are the only one I have seen here in whose eye I recognize one of my kindred. I want to know you and to love you and to have you love me."

One day they spent together in the country. Not trusting her oral Italian, she wrote out to him: "Soon I must leave here. Do not let me go without giving some of your life in exchange for some of mine. I feel I have something precious to give and that you are not unaware of this." So he proposed marriage; with his father's help he could get papal dispensation to marry a Protestant.

Strangely, she turned him down. He was hurt, but patient. "You will return to me," he said.

The Springs wondered why she was so peevish when they left Rome together in June. She had said previously: "Once I was almost all intellect; now I am almost all feeling. I feel all Italy glowing beneath the Saxon crust. This cannot last long; I shall burn to ashes if all this smoulders here much longer. I must die if I do not burst forth in genius or heroism." Or love, she could now add.

In Bologna, Margaret was pleased to find a high regard for women. Its women painters had been widely known throughout 16th century Italy. At the university there had been female professors of Greek and of anatomy. In Milan she met a group of young republicans who impressed her by their idealism and their bravery. Her knowledge of the language improved, drawing her closer to the people. In Florence Margaret met the Marchesa Costanza Visconti, just returned from 26 years of political exile. The Marchesa introduced her to many Italian writers, political activists, and women intellectuals. Margaret by now was a part of the movement to set up an Italian republic.

There was still high hope that Pius IX would unify Italy. He promised his people a representative council, and he permitted political opponents to return from abroad. But he knew his limitations. He confessed, "They want to make a Napoleon of me, a poor country priest!"

In October she returned to Rome, to her lover. This time she permitted herself to fall deeply in love with Ossoli. The two men who had been most attracted to her as a woman, Nathan and Ossoli, were Europeans who knew nothing of her repute as an intellectual. Thus, she would not have to choose between being a wife and a creative thinker. She wrote to her mother in December that she had never been so happy in all her life.

But they kept their relationship secret. By the end of the year she was quite certain that she was going to bear Ossoli's child.

Pregnancy out of wedlock brought guilt feelings to this former Puritan. Marriage seemed out of the question. But she had written in *Woman in the 19th Century:* "Woman is born for love, and it is impossible to turn her from seeking it."

At times she was greatly depressed, and had intimations of death. She often inserted the phrase "if I live" into her letters. She felt so low as to say, "I think that the spirit that governs the universe must have in reserve for me a sphere where I can develop more freely and be happier."

But the sight of her handsome lover, now clad in the uniform of a sergeant in Rome's civic guard, lifted her out of her depression. She wrote to her mother: "The Italians sympathize with my character and understand my organization as no other people did." To her sister Ellen she later confided: "I acted upon a strong impulse. I could not analyze at all what passed in my mind. For bad or for good, I acted out my character."

She still sent dispatches to Greeley's *Tribune*. A nation absorbed in Mexican conquest and soon to set out on a gold-hunting frenzy might have been startled to read her advice: "Learn to guard the true aristocracy of a nation, the only real nobles—the laboring classes." She spurned Emerson's advice to return to America, where, she said, the spirit of liberty had died out in the race to pile up individual wealth. Italy now harbored the spirit of liberty, while "my country is at present spoiled by prosperity, soiled by crime in perpetuation of slavery, shamed by an unjust war, the aims of politicians selfish or petty, the literature frivolous and venal."

In February 1848 Ossoli's father died, and the estate passed into his older brother's hands, who disliked Ossoli because of his republican sympathies. Since marriage was out of the question, she and Ossoli decided she should have her child somewhere outside Rome. Rebellion had broken out throughout Italy. In Venice and Milan the Austrians had been driven out, and other duchies were also ready to declare their independence. When Margaret heard slurs against the republic, it reminded her of similar attitudes towards blacks and women in America, and she became all the more radical. She began to believe that perhaps some type of Fourier socialism would best safeguard human rights in a democracy.

Living in the mountain village of Aquila, northeast of Rome, she began writing a history of the Italian republic. In July she moved closer to Rome, to Rieti, to be nearer to Ossoli. He was with her when their son, Angelo Eugenio Filippo, was born on September 5, 1848. Margaret was 38; the birth was difficult.

State law required baptism, but there had been no formal marriage. A nephew of Ossoli agreed to serve as a witness, and the baby was baptized. Then a smallpox epidemic broke out, and after great stress, Margaret got the baby inoculated.

She left little Angelo with a nurse and returned to Rome. She wanted to resume her *Tribune* articles, and she wanted to allay her friends' curiosity over her long absence. But she frequently visited her son—in fact, it was torture being separated from him. Motherhood had brought out humility in her. While pregnant she had said, "I am too rough and blurred an image of the Creator to become a bestower of life."

Emelyn Story, wife of the American sculptor William Wetmore Story, now became Margaret's closest friend. "How different you are from what I imagined you to be in America," confessed Emelyn. "My life has new channels now," replied Margaret. The stereotype in America of a haughty intellectual with no sweetness of disposition is not what Emelyn found. Instead, she came to know an affectionate and a sensitive person, "with so broad a charity that she could cover with its mantle the faults of all about her."

Margaret visited Mazzini's mother in Genoa, who suggested to her son that he marry "the tender American." Mazzini, of course, rejected marriage because he did not want to be diverted from his lifelong dedication to Italian freedom. But he fit Margaret's definition of a leader: "Those who would reform the world must be severe lawgivers to themselves. They must be religious students of the divine purpose with regard to man, if they would not confound the fancies of the day with the requisitions of eternal good."

All Europe was in turmoil. Louis Philippe had been dethroned in Paris. Hungary was revolting against the Austrians. In Prussia there was an insurrection against King Fredrick Wilhelm IV.

Italians were choosing sides. Margaret's friend, the Princess Belgioioso, had gone south to spearhead the move to overthrow Ferdinand II of Naples, called "King Bomba" because he had turned his cannons against his people. The Marchesa Visconti supported change but felt that Mazzini's headstrong leadership would ruin Italy. Adam Mickiewicz, on the other hand, felt that only Mazzini had the charisma and strength to unite Italy and drive out the Austrians.

Friend to both the Marchesa and Mickiewicz, Margaret steered a middle political course. She agreed that Mazzini was indispensable at the moment, since he understood how to install the machinery of representative government. What he lacked, she felt, was a realization that simply giving people the ballot would not solve their problems unless it was accompanied by economic steps, such as redistributing the land and giving protection to factory workers.

Coincidentally, Karl Marx and Frederick Engels were giving their solution to "the specter haunting Europe" in the Communist Manifesto they were publishing that year. Margaret seemed to have an intuitive awareness of the thinness of political rights unless they are accompanied by measures to ensure economic and social equality.

When Margaret returned to Rome in November, Pius IX was under attack from both sides. On November 15 his minister, Pellegrino Rossi, was stabbed to death by a mob. The cardinals felt that the pope had given in to the mob too often, and were secretly speaking of electing a new pope. The mob marched on the pope's quarters at the Quirinal Palace, demanding reforms. In an exchange of shots, the pope's confessor was killed. Disguised, Pius IX fled to the fortress of Gaeta in the territory of King Bomba of Naples. Mazzini said that he had abdicated. Margaret felt that he should at least be stripped of his temporal powers.

Back in New York City Bishop John Hughes protested to Greeley about Margaret's attack on the pope, but Greeley continued to print her articles as she wrote them. Margaret asked for an American ambassador to Italy who understood the Italian people and their problems. "Another century," she wrote, "and I might ask to be made ambassador myself. But woman's day has not come yet." A century later, in 1953, Clare Booth Luce became the first woman ambassador to Italy.

Margaret was still separated from her baby, who was at Rieti. She felt she had to confess her condition to someone — but to whom? Finally she told Caroline Sturgis Tappan, but swore her to secrecy.

Emerson, in Europe in 1848, several times volunteered to accompany Margaret back to America, but she refused. "I have much to do and learn in Europe yet," she told him. "I am deeply interested in this public drama. Methinks I have my part therein, either as actor or historian."

She kept her religious faith. She wrote to her mother, "Some higher power leads me through strange, dark, thorny paths, at times opening into prospects of sunny beauty into which I am not permitted to enter. If God disposes for us, it is not for nothing."

In February 1849 a Roman Republic was proclaimed with a constituent assembly elected by all male citizens. Spiritual authority was reserved for the pope, who was still in exile. Pius IX declared that anyone having a hand in setting up the assembly would be excommunicated. Mazzini was called to Rome in glory. There was singing and dancing in the streets.

Giuseppi Garibaldi, who had returned from exile in South America, now led his band of legionnaires around the countryside, taking provisions from the clergy. At Rieti, Margaret feared that some of his band would rape little Angelo's pretty guardian. So when a group of them arrived at her inn, she told the innkeeper to give them food and drink at her expense. Her generosity won them over. They treated her courteously and after eating left, harming no one.

The ephemeral Republic had a Catholic noose around it. King Bomba attacked from the south. In the north the Austrians were regrouping. From the west came Spanish ships with reinforcements for Pius IX. The big question was, what will the new French Republic do? Its president, Louis Napoleon, persuaded the French assembly to send an expeditionary force to Rome. Outwardly, the force was described as a stabilizing factor, to bring peace. But underneath lay Louis Napoleon's desire to re-establish French power and influence in Italy. He also wanted to be emperor rather than president, and for this he needed to have the pope consecrate his rule as divinely ordained.

Therefore the French landed a force of 10,000 troops at Civita Vecchia, the port of Rome. A French emissary met with Mazzini, saying that the French wanted to block Austrian and Bourbon intervention, but that the pope must be restored. The Roman assembly refused, preferring to resist force with force.

On April 30 Garibaldi's troops repulsed the French attack on Rome.

Garibaldi then left Rome, and drove Bomba's troops back into their own territory. During the May lull the French were building up their forces. Their spokesman was Ferdinand de Lesseps, a young consul-general who dreamed of building a Suez canal.

On June 3 the French general, Oudinot, with 35,000 men and superior field pieces, attacked the Roman garrison of 19,000 defenders, armed with outdated weapons. A bitter conflict raged. Margaret chose to remain in Rome. She was appointed manager of the hospital of the Fate Bene Fratelli, located on an island in the Tiber. Her hospital, near the front, handled hundreds of dead and wounded. She became an angel of mercy to the wounded and dying, visiting them around the clock to cheer them and to comfort them. She scanned each new face being brought in — could it be her Cara Giovane?

Fearing that she and Ossoli might be killed during the siege, Margaret confided the news about her baby to Emelyn Story. She told Emelyn that she and Ossoli were married, and she gave Emelyn some papers to give to her family in the event of the death of her husband and herself. She asked Emelyn to see to it that her son got to America.

It was just a matter of time before the French drove a breach in the Roman wall. Garibaldi pointed out that further defense was impossible, so he took what remained of his legion to Venice to help fight the Austrians.

On July 4, Garibaldi's birthday, the French army occupied Rome, and the Republic was dead. At first Mazzini remained in Rome, taunting the French, who dared not imprison the popular hero. Margaret then got an American-protection passport for him, and he returned to live his final twenty years in London.

Garibaldi came to the United States and became a candlemaker on Staten Island. In 1860 he returned to Italy and assisted in the unification of his country under King Victor Emanuel II.

Ossoli's bravery and competence had won him a promotion during the siege of Rome. With the French entry he and Margaret returned to Rieti to be with Angelino. But the baby was ill. He would not take food, and was suffering badly from malnutrition. "If he dies, I want to die too," said his mother. The illness brought the parents even closer together, as worry will.

Finally Angelino grew well. Now Margaret wrote to her mother, saying she had married a marquis and had a child by him. She said that her mother and Ossoli would like each other, both being gentle and sincere people. Mother took the news well, glad to hear they had survived the fighting and the baby was over his sickness. But Margaret's brother Richard, whom she had helped rear and for whose education she had made great sacrifices, refused to send his congratulations to his sister — he found it hard, he said, to forgive her "worldliness"!

There has always been some mystery surrounding Margaret's marriage. Ossoli's sister Angela wrote to Margaret's sister Ellen that the two had been married in Florence shortly after the baby had been born in Rieti.

In the Papal States there was no civil marriage, but it was permitted in Tuscany and the other Italian districts.

On April 12, 1850, Pius IX returned to Rome. Now Ossoli was willing to accompany Margaret back to America. She had lost her position with the *Tribune*, perhaps because of rumors about her love life. She submitted her history of the Italian revolt to an English publisher, who turned it down, probably because of its republican bias.

Her plan was for her to support the family through writing and lecturing on Italian history. They would live near New York City, where Ossoli would find an Italian community. She worried about him. Could he find a job? Would her friends accept him? Would the difference in their ages, plus his living in a strange land, bring separation between them? Thank God there was Angelino as a bond.

In one of her last letters to the Springs she said, "I have become an enthusiastic socialist; elsewhere is no solution for the problems of the times. I am not sure that I can keep my hands free from blood." Thus had the internal struggle between masculine and feminine traits ended in triumph for neither—she had ended the struggle by giving full expression to both aspects of her being.

She never stopped growing. She had been a Goethe advocate, a transcendentalist, a feminist, a crusading journalist, a friend of the poor and oppressed, a fighter for freedom—but withal a lover, wife, and mother. It is unthinkable that she would have ended a normal life span as a Fourier socialist. She would have evolved—mind, body, and soul—into the best that America and the world had to offer in her century. And she would have bravely led the way for more timid souls to follow on the path to a world of justice and equal opportunity.

They borrowed money to pay for their passage to America. Preparing to sail, she had a ten-day headache siege. Her old fear of death by water returned. She saw evil omens everywhere. On May 10 she wrote to Emelyn Story: "Look out for news of shipwreck!"

They planned to sail on the packet ship *Argo* from Le Havre, but it was wrecked crossing from America. She read of other wrecks: the English steamer *Royal Adelaide* and the American packet *John Skiddy*. She said, "My future here on earth now seems to me short. It will not be so very long now. My life proceeds regularly, far more so than the fates of a Greek tragedy."

Their last night in Florence was spent with the Robert Brownings. Elizabeth feared that Margaret's reception in America would be hostile, because of her political opinions and her fearless manner of voicing them. Margaret's own premonitions of tragedy seemed to be unconscious expressions of the fact that the person she had become could not go home to an America of 1850.

The Brownings kidded Ossoli about an old prophecy that he should fear death by water. Margaret laughed, stating that the name of their ship,

*Elizabeth*, would bring them good luck. But after they left, Elizabeth was disturbed by the inscription in the Bible they had given to the Brownings' son. It read: "In memory of Angelo Eugene Ossoli."

In one of her final letters Margaret told Madame Arconati, a friend: "I shall embark praying fervently that it may not be my lot to lose my babe at sea. Or that if I should it may be brief anguish, and Ossoli, he and I go together."

The *Elizabeth* was a nearly new three-masted American merchant-man. It carried but five passengers — the three Ossolis; a nurse girl, Celeste, to help with little Nino; and Margaret's friend Horace Sumner.

On June 3 Captain Seth Hasty died of smallpox, and the ship was quarantined a week off Gibralter. Mr. Bangs, the first mate, who took command, had never guided a vessel at sea.

Nino caught smallpox, and nearly died. Distraught, Margaret nursed him back to life.

On July 18 the *Elizabeth* was off the New Jersey coast, between Cape May and Barnegat. Mr. Bangs promised they would be ashore in the morning. Trunks were brought up from the hold. Margaret selected Nino's frock for landing.

That evening a wind blew up. By midnight it was of gale force. Mr. Bangs, thinking he was still off the Jersey coast, close-reefed the sails. Inexperienced as a navigator, he had underestimated the powerful current along the south shore of Long Island.

At about 3:30 A.M. on July 19 the ship struck a sand bar off Fire Island beach. The pounding waves slammed the vessel hard against the bar, and the stern swung around broadside to the waves. The cargo of marble in the ship's hold broke through the bottom, flooding the hold.

The skylight of the Ossoli cabin was shattered, the door wrenched open. The passengers found a dry spot in a room tilted at a crazy angle. Knowing that the ship would sink, they exchanged messages to families and friends in case anyone should survive.

In a long white nightgown, her wet hair loose around her shoulders, Margaret clutched Nino to her breast and tried to quiet his screams. Ossoli, calm, prayed with Celeste. Separated from the crew, who were forward, the passengers thought the crew had perished, and the crew thought the passengers had drowned.

At dawn, with the gale increasing and the surf relentlessly pounding the vessel, the crew led the passengers one by one into the greater safety of the forecastle. A seaman carried Nino in a bag slung across his back. Margaret left behind in the cabin her treasured manuscript of the history of the Italian freedom fight.

The ship's boats had been swamped. No reserve boats arrived. Beachcombers ashore — less than 100 yards away — gathered salvage into wagons: bolts of silk, flasks of oil, boxes of almonds.

Two sailors rode spars safely ashore. Horace Sumner leaped in with a plank, and drowned. Mrs. Hasty, the captain's widow, rode ashore safely with a sailor, both holding onto a plank. Mr. Bangs urged the Ossolis to do likewise but Margaret refused, fearing for Nino's life. Mr. Bangs safely made shore on a plank, leaving the Ossoli party of four with four seamen.

A lifeboat with mortar gun arrived, but the surf was too heavy to launch the boat. The mortar, fired into the wind, proved useless. For several hours the life-saving crew stared at the wreck and the survivors stared back. Meanwhile the scavengers went about their ghoulish business.

At 3 P.M. the ship began to break up. Margaret, her nightgown clinging to her body and her hair disheveled, sat at the foot of the foremast. The steward pleaded desperately to be allowed to take Nino ashore.

A huge wave swept Ossoli and Celeste into the rigging, where Ossoli clung for a moment, then disappeared. The big wave also washed Margaret overboard. She and Ossoli were never seen again.

On the beach lay the dead bodies of Nino and the steward who had tried to save him.

# 5
## *What Hath God Wrought!*

March 3 was the last day of the Congressional session. The tall, blue-eyed president of the National Academy of the Arts of Design was once again dejected. For five years he had spent much of his time lobbying senators and representatives, assuring them that if they would pass a bill granting him $30,000, he would construct a telegraph line that would prove that his invention really worked.

It had been his idea in the first place. As long ago as 1832, aboard the packet-ship *Sully*, Samuel F. B. Morse had sketched out the plan for an instrument that, impelled by electricity, could send messages that could accurately be recorded at great distances from the sender.

Some people listened, a few helped, but most scoffed. True, Franklin had shown that lightning could transmit signals, but to control the lightning, or electricity, so as to read in Washington what someone was sending in New York — the smiles of incredulity took over. Why doesn't the man go back to painting portraits? You know, he was pretty good at it! He did one of my uncle, you know, the rich banker from Elmira — it was worth every bit of the $100 he asked for it.

And so Finley Morse, as he was called, went home to bed that March night in 1843. Since it was the last session, Congress would not adjourn until midnight. President Tyler had a room in the Capitol, where he would sign bills passed at the last minute.

But there was no hope for Morse's bill, he had been assured by his legislative friends. Another year down the drain. Would it be worth trying any more? Would Fog Smith ever find a capitalist to build the experimental line? Should he give up the whole effort, let the European telegraphs take over, and go back to his work as a painter?

It is so much easier to *say* "Thy will be done, O Lord" than it is to *feel* it, Morse knew. The delays, the discouragements, kept piling up. Would he never be able to provide a decent home for his children? But somehow, beneath it all, lay God's hand. The trials and the frustrations were all for some dimly perceived divine purpose.

Now he finally understood why God was holding back from granting him the opportunity to make the contribution he felt he had been ordained to do. "Not until my impatience has yielded unreservedly to submission has He relieved me by granting light upon my path," Morse said. "Praised be His name, for to Him alone belongs all the glory."

At breakfast next morning a waiter ushered a pretty young lady to Morse's table. He recognized Annie Ellsworth, daughter of his former class-mate at Yale, H. L. Ellsworth, now commissioner of patents. Bubbling with exuberation, Annie told him the good news. The bill had passed the Senate, and was now a law. Morse had the money he needed to prove to the world that his invention was no fluke.

"Annie," he said, "I can't believe it. My friends said it had no chance. That's why I went home before adjournment. But I'll tell you what, Annie – I promise you that the first message to be sent on the telegraph line from Washington to Baltimore will be yours to select."

True to his word, over a year later, on May 24, 1844, Morse invited many Washington dignitaries to the chamber of the U.S. Supreme Court to watch the first message be sent. He kept his promise that Annie would choose the message.

Construction had not been as easy as Morse had supposed. Most of his colleagues had failed him. The underground method of stringing wire did not work at all. Fog Smith, formerly chairman of the Senate Commerce Committee and more recently Morse's business and legal adviser, had turned against him. But as obstacles mounted, Morse fell back on his deep faith in God. He felt the assurance that his Creator had chosen him to be a great benefactor to mankind. And now the great moment to demon-strate his telegraph had come.

Helped by her mother, Annie chose a passage from the prophecy of soothsayer Balaam in Numbers 23:23: "What hath God wrought!" Balaam was carrying God's message that nothing could harm His chosen people, the Israelites. Morse, too, felt chosen.

He fingered the message on his instrument, sending signals to Alfred Vail, his assistant, in Baltimore. Moments later the paper on his receiving apparatus printed the fateful words: "What hath God wrought." Cheers of success surrounded Morse, and his niche in history was secure. He had many battles left to fight, but he was no longer a voice crying in the wilder-ness – crying for America to recognize the value of art or crying for the world to realize what a boon instantaneous long-distance communication would be.

Morse felt that Annie's choice of phrase was most apt. "It is His work," said Morse, "and He alone could have carried me thus far through all my trials and enabled me to triumph over the obstacles which opposed me. To Thy name, O Lord, be all the praise."

What kinds of obstacles had Morse overcome? What sorts of battles still lay ahead? What role did religion play in the life of this many-sided genius – one of America's leading portrait painters who became one of the world's great inventors?

Samuel Finley Breese Morse was born in Charlestown, Massachusetts,

Samuel F.B. Morse. (Courtesy Brown Brothers.)

on April 27, 1791. Samuel Finley, his mother's grandfather, had been president of the College of New Jersey (later Princeton). Breese was her maiden name.

His father, Jedidiah Morse, was called "the father of American geography" because his geographies of the new country were the first and the most widely used in his day. Jedidiah was a Congregational clergyman who stoutly resisted the Unitarian trend of thought in his church. To propagate his views he founded a religious magazine *The Panoplist* and a religious newspaper *The Boston Recorder*. A man with a skill at organization, he helped found Andover Theological Seminary, the American Bible Society, the American Board of Foreign Missions, and the American Tract Society. He and his wife had eleven children of whom only three survived infancy: Samuel and his younger brothers Sidney and Richard.

Samuel grew up in an austere Calvinistic home. Religion was the chief topic at the dinner table. At the age of four Samuel got his first caning for the cause of art—he had scratched a pin portrait of his teacher on a dresser. As his numerous brothers and sisters died, Mother never failed to warn the surviving children—always be ready to meet your Maker, for you never know when your hour will come. Her lessons stuck with the three boys throughout their lives.

When time for college came, Harvard, because of its Unitarian heresies, was out of the question, and so Samuel attended Yale. Nicknamed "Geography" because of his father, Samuel was not a good student, and always suffered scholastically when compared to Sidney and Richard.

He did, however, like Professor Benjamin Silliman's lectures on electricity. And an experiment by Professor Jeremiah Day attracted Samuel's attention: "If a circuit be interrupted by several folds of paper, a perforation will be made through it." Samuel used this principle later in his telegraph.

In his junior year at Yale Samuel began to paint portraits of his classmates. The portraits, for which he charged one dollar for a profile and five dollars for a miniature on ivory, were an instant success. He soon had all the business he could handle.

While at Yale he met America's leading painter, Washington Allston. Allston recognized the talent Morse had, and encouraged him into a career as a painter. Morse asked permission to study under Allston, but Dr. Morse frowned on having an artist in the family and so the frustrated young painter became a clerk in a Boston bookstore.

Young Morse retained his religious outlook, and soon he was superintendent of one of America's first Sunday schools, the one in his father's church. Already as a young man there was growing within him the belief that God was choosing him to be an instrument of His to bestow some great blessing upon mankind.

His heart was set on a painting career—this was the only area in which he had already shown exceptional talent. Finally, under steady barrage from Allston and Gilbert Stuart Dr. Morse relented. Samuel had permission to accompany Allston to Europe as his pupil in 1811.

Samuel was overjoyed. Despite political differences, England was the place for rising American artists to learn their craft. A number of American artists had triumphed there—Allston, Benjamin West, John Singleton Copley, and John Trumbull. Samuel was determined to add his name, showing that the United States was no esthetic desert, but a place of elegance and refinement.

Allston introduced Morse to Benjamin West, who was now president of the Royal Academy of Art, having lived in England since 1763. Morse entered the Academy art school and studied under West and Allston. From them he learned an honesty and integrity of technique that came to characterize all of his paintings.

In 1812 war broke out between England and the United States. Actually, Parliament's council withdrew its war order on June 16, but since it would take several weeks to get the message across the Atlantic, Congress declared war on England on June 18. A patriot, Morse stoutly defended his country's position, but he seems to have avoided public controversy, for there is no evidence that he suffered persecution for his views. Morse differed radically with his Federalist father concerning the war. Dr. Morse strongly supported the views of the Hartford Convention, which went so far as to consider secession and re-merger with England. New England merchants had not thrived under the embargo policies of Jefferson and Madison, and were now bringing home to roost the secessionist views that those two presidents had voiced in the Kentucky and Virginia resolutions when the Federalists had been in power.

The safe distance from home gave Samuel courage to accuse his father of supporting an unpatriotic stance. To buttress his position Samuel quoted a number of Englishmen who admitted that their country was at fault and who hoped for an early peace.

In 1813 Mrs. Morse heard that Samuel was friendly with the American actor and playwright John Howard Payne, whose portrait Samuel had painted. Be careful, she warned, not to keep company with actors like Payne—they will corrupt your morals. Payne, the author of "Home, Sweet Home," would have smiled at the warning, as did Samuel Morse.

That year his first and only sculpture, "The Dying Hercules," won a gold medal award from the Duke of Norfolk. His painting on this subject won a prize from the Royal Academy and the recognition that he was one of the best artists currently exhibiting in England. He was already at 22 being recognized as one of the most promising young artists of the Western world.

Finances, however, were a constant problem. Dr. Morse sent one thousand dollars each year, but Samuel found it to be insufficient. Reluctantly he returned to portrait work to raise funds. But with the war over, he found that the British had little use for an American portrait painter. He spent six months in Bristol, lured by the promise of work, but found none.

He could see that his only hope to support himself by his brush lay in a return to America.

Although the Treaty of Ghent on December 24, 1814, marked the end of the war, communications were so slow that the news did not reach Washington until February 11, 1815. Meantime Andrew Jackson had led American troops to victory at the unnecessary battle of New Orleans on January 8. Morse could see the price being paid for slow communication.

Morse was a friend and admirer of Bishop William Wilberforce, who had played a leading role in getting England to outlaw slave trade in 1807. While visiting Wilberforce in London in 1815, Morse heard a series of cannon blasts, signalling the overthrow of Napoleon and the entry of Allied troops into Paris. Again he reflected upon the primitive, slow system of communication used to transmit important messages.

Reluctantly Morse prepared to return home. He wrote his parents: "Had I no higher thoughts than being a first-rate portrait painter, I would have chosen a far different profession. My ambition is to rival the genius of a Raphael, a Michael Angelo, or a Titian, in all these plans always taking into consideration the will of Providence."

He arrived back home in October 1815. What he had learned about art in England related chiefly to drawing and modeling. He had mastered what even artists like Copley had not achieved — how to render rich tones and avoid harsh ones by blending colors and using gentle, transparent shadows. Perhaps more important, as a person he had learned to take and defend an independent position, even if loved ones like one's parents differed. This inner strength served him well as he later fought many battles over his invention.

In 1816 the young painter opened a studio in Boston but finding no business he took to the road as a portrait painter. Charging fifteen dollars per portrait, he found that he could pay expenses and support himself. Art was not wholly proscribed for puritanical New England. The esthetic creed of the time was that art, and all beauty, were a reflection and projection of God. Art's function, thus, was to evoke a universal sense of beauty, truth, and morality. Morse definitely felt that God moved his brush in every good stroke that he made.

In Concord, New Hampshire, Morse found another beauty, Lucretia Pickering Walker. Though only 16, she was "amiable and handsome," he wrote his parents, and her family checked out on every score except that "they were not professors of religion." Characteristically, he took his problem to God: "I have prayed to the Giver of every good gift that He will direct me in this business; that if it will not be to His glory and the good of His Kingdom, He will frustrate all."

Despite their recent political differences, Dr. Morse had little fear concerning the status of his son's soul. Sidney was editing a religious newspaper and Richard was studying for the ministry but Father felt that Samuel was the most deeply religious of his three sons. He watched admiringly as

Samuel won Lucretia's soul for the Lord. When she had become "a sincere and devout Christian," Samuel married her on October 1, 1818. He must have been pleased that the wedding announcement in the local paper described him as "the celebrated painter."

As a portrait painter he felt that he needed to know the subject's character, in order to paint a faithful representation. Suddenly he felt it more important to be concerned about a person's soul than the person's portrait. He announced to Lucretia that he had decided to enter the ministry. He would be an Episcopalian clergyman, because of his attendance at the Anglican Church in England. He was tired of the controversy his father had to endure as a Congregational minister.

But soon his interest shifted. The new Andover Seminary was looking for a design for its building. Morse decided he would be an architect. He submitted a model for the building, but when it was rejected by the building committee he ended his career as an architect.

Now he felt he would be an inventor. He designed a marble-cutting machine which would make copies of statues, but found that someone already had patented such a device. He and Sidney worked to perfect a water pump to be used on fire engines. He did the drawings and worked on sales, while Sidney did most of the mechanical work. Their only sale was to the Concord fire house. When the pump was tried at a fire, it failed to spout water. Samuel decided that maybe he was not cut out to be an inventor, after all.

In November 1819 Morse and Lucretia moved to Charleston, South Carolina, where he had won a reputation as a portrait painter the previous winter. His mother's uncle, Dr. James Finley, introduced him to Southern society. For the first time his brush brought him considerable financial returns. Within a year he earned $9000 over expenses through his portraits.

When President James Monroe visited Charleston Morse was commissioned to paint his portrait in Washington. Although it bothered him to have the President disturbed from his pose every ten minutes, he was pleased to hear Monroe say that he preferred this portrait of him to the one done by Gilbert Stuart.

In 1821 Morse helped found the South Carolina Academy of Fine Arts. But the Yankee never felt at home in Cavalier culture. The flirting, card playing, and drinking bothered him. He missed the church revivals and the strict Sabbath of the North. Later that year, when business tapered off, he moved back to New Haven.

Dr. Morse succumbed to the Unitarian conflict in 1819, when he was removed from his pulpit by dissatisfied parishioners. The following year he became America's first commissioner of Indian affairs. Son Samuel began his famous painting of the old House of Representatives chamber that year. He often worked fourteen hours a day on it. He had long aspired to leave the field of portrait painting in favor of doing historical paintings. This work, eleven feet by seven-and-a-half feet, had 88 portraits, almost all of whom posed for the occasion. Samuel proudly painted his father, accompanied by a Pawnee chief, in the gallery.

Morse set up exhibitions of the painting in Boston and New York at twenty-five cents apiece, but receipts barely paid for rental space. Everyone agreed that it was well done, but it brought Morse little reward for his years of effort on it. Because of the public apathy, he dropped his plans to paint the Senate chamber and the White House drawing room.

In New Haven Morse, with his wife and two sons, lived with his parents. Sidney and Richard were still at home. Dr. Morse had hit upon a period of financial reverses, with his geographies no longer bringing in much royalty money. Ultimately he was forced to sell his large home to Eli Whitney.

Morse continued to paint portraits. First it was President Jeremiah Day of Yale, then Eli Whitney, then another neighbor, Noah Webster. The portrait of Webster was engraved as a frontispiece of the first Webster dictionary in 1818, a position it occupied for an entire century.

Morse now wanted to go to Mexico, where he felt the reception for painters might be more cordial. In addition, he felt he could display his large painting of the House of Representatives. He was appointed cultural attaché to the first United States minister to Mexico, Congressman Edwards of Illinois. A political squabble canceled the appointment of Edwards, so Morse remained in New Haven.

In the fall of 1824 Morse moved to New York City. When the Marquis de Lafayette visited America in early 1825, Morse was commissioned by the city to paint a full-length portrait of the French general, being selected over such rivals as Rembrandt Peale and Thomas Sully. While working on the portrait in Washington, Morse received word that his beloved Lucretia had died suddenly. News traveled so slowly that she had been buried before the grief-stricken painter arrived home. Two of their five children had died previously, leaving Morse to care for two sons and a daughter. Fortunately his parents provided a home for the children while Morse was away on painting trips.

Morse quickly found himself accepted into James Fenimore Cooper's literary circle in New York. He felt flattered to be among such novelists as Cooper and Richard Henry Dana, such poets as William Cullen Bryant and Fitz-Greene Halleck. His portraits continued: Bryant, General John Stark, De Witt Clinton at the opening of the Erie Canal. He repaid a youthful debt by painting Professor Benjamin Silliman.

Morse now received an opportunity to display his administrative ability. Many art students at the American Academy of Fine Arts, run by Colonel John Trumbull, were dissatisfied. To them it seemed as if the place was run for the patrons and directors, not for the students. Also, topics for paintings continued to be Revolutionary War battles, harking back to Trumbull's youth. There seemed to be a need for a fresh approach for art students.

Accordingly in January 1826 Morse, along with the painter-play-wright William Dunlap and others, organized the National Academy of the Arts of Design (later called the National Academy of Design). Morse was elected first president and was re-elected each year until 1842. Even rival Trumbull grudgingly admitted that Morse was a good organizer.

In 1826 both his parents died. His daughter Susan now lived with her dead mother's sister, and the two boys lived with Richard's family. Restless Morse, who had five different addresses in New York City in five years, paid for the expenses of caring for his children.

A sensation hit New York City in 1827. Madame Hutin from France danced, nearly naked, in the new Bowery Theater. All ladies in the first tier of box seats indignantly left the theater. Morse became the city's chief protester against indecent "French" dancing, using the convenient columns of brother Sidney's weekly religious newspaper, *The Observer*. London itself, said Morse, had only two licensed theaters but New York City, much smaller, already had six. Morse envisioned another Gomorrah, unless Gothamites took care. He enjoyed his crusade against the stage. He told Sidney, "I feel satisfied that whilst engaged for God He will not suffer me to want." In an effort to provide New York readers with a "clean" newspaper, he helped found *The Journal of Commerce* that year.

Likewise in 1827 Morse attended a series of lectures on electricity given by Professor James Freeman Dana of Columbia College. From Dana he learned of some recent discoveries concerning electro-magnetism, such as that bending a wire increases its magnetism, and a spiral wire wrapped around an iron bar also increases the magnetism. Each electrical fact seemed to be stored away for future use.

He now felt compelled to return to Europe for further study of painting. He sold his "House of Representatives" painting for $1100, and paid off his debts. Using $3000 raised by commissions for paintings from friends, he financed a trip to Europe in late 1829. His children remained with his relatives.

In France Morse liked best his visits with Lafayette, now back in the legislature because of the liberal resurgence. At this time only 15,000 Frenchmen out of a total population of 25,000,000 had the right to vote. Lafayette, however, a great popular favorite, had risen in political power to be second only to the king.

Because of the lack of Protestant churches in France, Morse was forced to worship in Roman Catholic churches, an experience that did little for Morse or Catholicism. At Dijon he stopped, refusing to travel on the Sabbath. He disliked the church menials, who seemed to him to wink, leer, and laugh at the crowd during the service. In Avignon he reported a similar experience — the people seemed to him to be in a far from worshipful mood. The great beauty of the church structure led his mind away from God toward a world of sense. Where was the sober, practical religious instruction demanded of a Sabbath, asked the Yankee puritan.

In Rome, Titian and Veronese became his favorite painters because of their use of color. Contemplating Veronese's "Green Picture" done all in green, Morse developed his theory for the distribution of color values in painting: "The highest light should be cold, the middle ground cool, the mass of light warm, the reflection hot, and the shadow negative." Allston later told Morse: "Your theory has saved me many an hour's labor." Praise from the teacher thrilled the former student.

While in Rome Morse painted a portrait of the famous Danish sculptor Bertel Thorwaldsen, which he later personally gave to the king of Denmark. During Holy Week he attended many Catholic services. He noted the colorful robes, the pageantry and ritual, but he missed the spiritual significance of the ceremony. He showed a child-like disrespect for Catholic authority. He spoke of fat friars, gambling priests, and begging monks. Once, when he refused to doff a hat to passing church dignitaries lest it be idolatry, an irate Roman soldier knocked his hat to the ground.

Civil war raged within the breast of the puritan artist. He was fascinated by much of the splendor of the coronation of Pope Gregory XVI. He was grateful for the role of the church as an art patron. The beauty of Milan cathedral led him to express his divided feelings: The Catholic church used a marvelous unity of all sorts of artistic effects in capturing one's imagination — but this is no substitute for the true function of religion: an understanding of the solemn truths of God's Holy Word. Theatrical effects, whether sacred or profane, seemed to him suspect, for they could insidiously undermine one's moral values.

"I am sometimes even constrained to doubt the lawfulness of my own art," he confessed, "when I perceive its prostitution, were I not fully persuaded that the art itself, when used for its legitimate purposes, is one of the greatest correctors of grossness and promoters of refinement." Briefly he pondered whether he could devote himself to adorning church buildings with religious art, but he quickly resisted the temptation, convinced of how readily the imagination seduces the understanding from God's truths.

His sympathies with the rising republican movement in Italy swelled his patriotic heart with pride. At home we hear about despotism, he said, but here we see it all around us. He now defined life's goal in these terms: "The soul of freedom is true religion exerting its moral power on an educated population."

"The patriot of our country," he continued, "to act in character must promote religion and education. These two principles acting together are a salutory check upon each other." Religion apart from education can degenerate into superstition, and education without religion can devolve into a substitution of wild theory for the common sense of Christianity, and thereby undermine the countless secret moral restraints which religion alone can provide.

The beauty of the Swiss Alps moved the puritan painter to religious fervor. Too many viewers accept this beauty, he mused, without a single thought of the Being who created it and what their duty to Him might be.

In Paris in 1830 Morse lived near Lafayette. Together they watched the unhappy news flashed from hilltop to hilltop ("telegraphic dispatch," Morse called it) that the Russians, with Austrian help, had retaken Warsaw, and Polish liberation was again imperiled. James Fenimore Cooper joined in their lamentation.

Lafayette and Cooper were Morse's political mentors. From Lafayette he learned to prize highly democratic practices such as the United States was developing. Cooper, on the other hand, gave him a realistic insight into the dangers of too much political power being placed into the hands of uneducated persons. Like Morse, Cooper sneered at the Roman Church as an unbridled autocracy, and he had little use for titles and nobility. Both artists suffered from the fact that adolescent America preferred the work of European artists over that of native sons.

In the Louvre, Cooper would watch Morse paint and say, "More yellow, Samuel" or "The nose is too short." Morse accepted the amateurish comments graciously, for he liked Cooper. He also liked Cooper's 19-year-old daughter Susan and wanted to marry her. When Cooper issued an adamant "No!" their friendship remained unimpaired.

Discussing what Roger Bacon and Franklin had done with electricity, Morse told Cooper in 1831 that an electric spark could be used for telegraphic purposes. The slowness of the mails irritated Morse. He felt that even the French semaphore system would be an improvement for America, where the skies are generally clearer than in Europe. But even that system needed speeding up. "The lightning would serve us better," he felt. Had he known that the inventor of the French semaphore system, Claude Chappe, had been led into suicide by the controversies engendered by his discovery, his ardor might have been tempered somewhat.

Failure to keep the Sabbath, that "greatest barrier to immorality," had led Europe into moral decline and the resulting political weakness, Morse believed. "Oh, that we appreciated in America the value of our Sabbath!" he pined. As he reflected on July 4, 1831, in Venice about his country — "the one bright spot on earth, truly a terrestrial paradise" — he found a divine mission underlying the United States: "When I think of the innumerable blessings we enjoy over every other country in the world, I am constrained to praise God who hath made us to differ, for 'He hath not dealt so with any nation, and as for His judgments, we have not known them.'"

On October 6, 1832, Morse left Havre aboard the packet-ship *Sully* bound for the United States. On this historic trip he invented the design of a workable telegraph. It is remarkable how few basic changes were made in the instrument through the ensuing years.

A fellow passenger, Dr. Charles Jackson of Boston, remarked that Franklin had demonstrated that electricity passes instantly over long lengths of wire. "If this be so," Morse replied, "I see no reason why intelligence might not be instantaneously transmitted by electricity to any distance."

Although his comment went unnoticed, Morse began to apply the slow sea days to implement his vision. He acted as if he had not known about Franklin's work previously. He called upon what he had learned about voltaic batteries from Professors Day and Silliman. He recalled the information about increasing the intensity of currents, picked up from Professor Dana. Though his own knowledge was relatively meager, he had compensating qualities useful in an inventor: creative insight to see relationships and possibilities, manipulative skill, persistence, and organizational ability.

He began to share his idea with other passengers and respond to their objections. He began to work on a code based on numerical digits, since there are fewer of them than of letters of the alphabet. He used a code based on dots and dashes — short and longer electrical impulses. Adept at drawing, he depicted a strong electro-magnet which moved a lever when driven by a current. At the other end of the circuit, a pencil recorded dots and dashes on a moving paper tape. The marks could be translated by the code into letters, which formed words. A weaker magnet pulled the pencil back into position, ready for the next impulse.

Here was the basic modern telegraph instrument, designed without use of reference books or laboratory equipment. Morse knew instantly that he had stumbled on a great invention. People could see by his dancing eyes that he was in a mood of high excitement.

Later, when it became important to verify the date of the invention, Captain Pell of the *Sully*, along with a number of other passengers, testified that Morse had disclosed all of the basic elements of the telegraph aboard ship.

When he landed and told people about his invention no one seemed impressed. He wondered if indeed the device was so earth shaking. It seemed so simple that surely someone by now had already patented such an invention. If not, certainly someone else would think of this soon.

It is true that as early as 1753 Charles Marshall of Scotland had suggested the use of friction electricity to transmit information. In 1827 Harrison Dyar used friction electricity on a two-mile course to discolor sensitized paper. But friction electricity was too weak to be used at great distances and too unreliable because of its dependence upon weather conditions.

Magnetic needle telegraphs had been developed previously by such persons as Louis Ampère, William Cooke, and Charles Wheatstone. But these instruments were also dependent upon the weather and had the additional inconvenience of showing a needle position for an instant, when it had to be copied down, and then being forever lost. Morse saw the need for a permanent record of the message, which could be consulted for accuracy in decoding the message. One of his early problems was to intensify the electrical impulse so as to have force enough to move the recording lever up and down.

Morse invariably gave credit to God for his invention. Robert Rankin described his frequent conversations with Morse: "He had been long impressed with the belief that God had created the great forces of nature not only as manifestations of His own infinite power but as expressions of good-will to man. Analogically magnetism would do in the advancement of human welfare what the Spirit of God would do in the moral renovation of man's nature. He felt as if he was doing a great work for God's glory. His sensitive and impassioned nature seemed almost to transform him in my eyes into a prophet. There gradually loomed up before my mind a vision of this great globe of ours, prophesying the commingling and unification of nations; of the gospel, on heaven-spread wings, flitting over the earth, and ignorant and uncivilized humanity brought into subjection to our heaven-born Christianity."

When he was appointed professor of the literature of the arts of design at the new University of the City of New York (later New York University) in 1835, Morse became America's first fine arts professor. Since he was not expected to lecture, he received no salary. His remuneration came solely from student fees. His large painting, "Gallery of the Louvre," excited little attention so he sold it for $1200 and went back to portrait painting. Cooper said they both were born thirty years too soon. Morse said it was more like one hundred years, but he planned to cut America's cultural gap from Europe to fifty years, not only by his painting but by his education of the public. The National Academy of Design, as it was now called, gave him a channel for reaching the public.

By now his violent anti-Catholic prejudice had made him a controversial figure. Many fundamentalist Protestants were beginning to express fear and dismay at the large numbers of Catholic immigrants.

In 1800 Roman Catholics numbered tenth among American religious groups, but by 1850 they ranked first. Historically Catholics had been unwelcome in most American settlements. The only New England colony that welcomed Catholics was Rhode Island. Of the half million immigrants to the United States in the 1830's, 44% came from Ireland. The following decade the percentage increased to 49. In 1807 there was only one Roman Catholic see in the United States, with 70 priests and 70,000 church members. By 1835 there were 10 sees, 6 seminaries, 9 colleges, 33 monasteries and houses for religious women, and many Catholic schools and hospitals.

Along with traditional prejudice and ignorance came economic competition. Recent immigrants would undercut the wage markets, since they were accustomed to low wages in Europe. Many signs appeared in city stores: NO IRISH NEED APPLY.

Many immigrants lacked job skills. Germany used the United States as a dumping group for criminals and paupers. In 1831 Jamaica had a law requiring that every ship that docked there had to carry away a number of poor persons. The English poor laws encouraged emigration. The consul at Liverpool estimated that 90% of the poor leaving that port were headed for

America. In 1836 a Congressional committee estimated that over 41,000 paupers were being sent annually from England to the United States. By 1837 over half of all persons receiving welfare payments were foreign-born.

While in Europe Morse had heard of the organization of the Society for the Propagation of the Faith (in Lyons in 1822) and the Leopold Association (in Vienna in 1829) to promote Catholic missionary work in America. During the 1820's the United States experienced a Second Great Awakening, which placed great stress on personal salvation, the Bible, and opposition to Roman Catholicism. Great controversy ensued. The Catholic Tract Society was founded in Philadelphia in 1827 to defend the Catholic position. In 1829 the first Provincial Council of Catholicity in America was held in Baltimore. It issued 38 decrees, warning against unauthorized translations of the Bible and recommending parochial rather than public schools. When a court decided that a bishop, rather than a lay board, had control over church property, nativists (as anti-Catholics were called) used this as an example of how an autocratic church spreads its tyranny.

In 1831 the New York Protestant Association was formed, to give Protestants information about what it called "popery." The leaders asserted that "popery to be hated needs but to be seen in its true character." The first discussion topic was "Is Popery that Babylon which John has described in the Apocalypse?"

In 1834 Morse published two anti-Catholic works. A pamphlet, *Imminent Dangers*, told of problems America had with immigrants. A longer work, *Foreign Conspiracy against the Liberties of the United States*, appeared serially in Sidney's *The Observer* and was reprinted in many Protestant journals. Morse used the pseudonym "Brutus" when the articles appeared in newspapers, but he used his own name when the longer publications were printed.

Morse argued that since religious autocracy threatens political and civil liberties it must be opposed. He saw the Roman Catholic Church as such a threat. In Europe, he said, that church always aligns itself with undemocratic, and frequently tyrannical, regimes. Austria, a Catholic nation, opposed the efforts of Italy and Poland to set up republics. He conveniently ignored the fact that Italy and Poland, Catholic nations, were busily engaged in setting up republics.

He showed what he felt was the mongrelization of American society through lax immigration laws. Catholics, he said, were clannish, often spoke no English, and were not easily assimilated into American society. He deplored the O'Connel Guards, a paramilitary Irish organization in New York City. He accused priests of interfering in elections, thereby violating the American practice of separation of church and state.

His recommendations were to cut down on immigration, require a 21-year apprentice period for citizenship, make public all Catholic records, and organize the Protestants to keep Catholics out of public office.

An impostor, Maria Monk, wrote a supposed exposé of sexual

perversions she had experienced as a member of a Montreal convent. Long after she had been exposed as a fraud Morse continued to support her wild claims. Catholics circulated rumors that he might marry her. Subsequently she was jailed as a pickpocket and died in a home for prostitutes.

Morse's views helped inspire a series of three anti-popery sermons preached by the Congregational minister, Lyman Beecher, in Boston. Aroused mobsters stormed the Ursuline convent in Morse's native Charlestown and burned and looted the building. A committee of 38 Protestant leaders investigated the riot and reported that the Protestant press and pulpit had been responsible for it by promulgating outrageous lies. Nevertheless a Protestant jury acquitted the mob leaders. In 1838 the Mother Superior and her nuns moved to Canada.

Morse quoted Lafayette for support in his opposition to the Catholic church. In supporting republican Italy, Lafayette said that "robbery will always subsist in a country governed by priests and aristocrats, enemies of every liberal sentiment." On the title page of his book Morse gave a statement attributed to Lafayette: "American liberty can only be destroyed by the Popish clergy." Challenged by Catholics to show the source, Morse could find nothing in writing but insisted that Lafayette had often revealed such sentiments to him.

Protestant narrowness was seen further in 1835 when the Presbyterian General Assembly approved a resolution stating that "the Roman Catholic Church has essentially apostasized from the religion of Christ, and therefore cannot be recognized as a Christian church." The Assembly encouraged its ministers to preach against the spread of "Romanism."

To achieve such goals the Native American Association was organized in New York City in 1836. This group opposed the election of any Catholic to public office, on grounds that he had sworn primary allegiance to a foreign power, the pope. The Whigs particularly supported the Association and its goals, largely because most immigrants became Democrats.

Morse was chosen by the Association as their candidate for mayor. In accepting he stated that the Association would not interfere with the rights of naturalized citizens but that it did plan to stress the election of only native citizens to public office. He ran fourth in a field of four, receiving only 9% of the votes cast.

During these years Morse taught painting to support himself, and built his first crude telegraph. His first experiments took place in brother Richard's home. Richard's wife had to chastise Morse for spilling molten lead on her parlor carpet and chair.

To get the up-and-down motion required on the lever which transcribed onto the recording paper, Morse developed a series of cogged or saw-toothed type. Each letter had its own characteristic saw-tooth, which represented a particular dot-dash combination.

At the end of 1835 Morse invented the relay. Since the electrical charge weakened as it traveled the wire, Morse found that he could connect a number of circuits, each with its own battery, so that the magnetism of the current of the first circuit could close and break the second, the second the third, and so on. This, a major discovery in electricity, was independently developed a year or two later by such scientists as Joseph Henry, Charles Wheatstone, and Edward Davy.

Morse's colleague, Leonard Gale, professor of chemistry, now proved to be of great assistance to him. Gale was familiar with the discoveries reported by Joseph Henry in 1831. Henry had shown that greater electrical force was generated by increasing the coils of wire wrapped around an electro-magnet. Gale also got Morse to replace a battery of one cup with a battery of many cups, again making it possible to project the electrical impulse over greater lengths. Soon Morse and Gale were sending telegraphic signals through ten miles of wire strung around Gale's lecture room.

Through these years Morse was nearly destitute. In his campus room he ate, slept, taught, and experimented. He needed to paint, in order to have money for his invention, but if he painted he had no time to devote to improving the telegraph. In addition, there were no electrical appliance stores where he could purchase the needed parts. Everything had to be done laboriously by hand, including wrapping wires around magnets. Had he known how close European inventors were to perfecting a telegraph instrument, his anxiety would have greatly increased.

He decided to work hard at painting so as to have the money needed to perfect the telegraph. Four painters were to be selected to paint historical scenes for the rotunda of the National Capitol. Here, he felt, was his great opportunity to work on a patriotic topic and at the same time earn his needed funds. Building and adorning the Capitol building constituted the largest federal art project of the nineteenth century.

John Quincy Adams, now in the House of Representatives, insisted that the competition for artists be open to foreign painters. Cooper wrote a stinging criticism of Adams' views, but it was falsely attributed to Morse, and he was not chosen. He was stunned and disillusioned. "I have no wish to be remembered as a painter," he said, "for I never was a painter. My ideal of that profession was, perhaps, too exalted."

He was nonetheless forced to continue to paint. A group of friends, to allay his disillusionment, raised a fund of $3,000 to enable him to paint a historic subject. He had long aspired to paint "The Signing of the Mayflower," so he informed them of his intent. Several years later, unable to bring himself to complete the painting, he returned the money to the contributors.

After Morse's brilliant success in 1844, Adams said that men like Morse and Robert Fulton, inventor of the steamboat, had accomplished more than any 200 presidents could ever hope to do. But it was in 1837 that Morse needed help—not in 1844!

In 1837 an important member joined the invention team of Morse and Gale. Alfred Vail was given a contract by Morse to construct instruments and to work on patents. Vail had previously made electrical appliances in his father's iron works. On October 3, 1837, Morse submitted a caveat to the commissioner of patents, signifying his intent to request a patent on a telegraphic device.

Vail added both money and technical expertise to the project. He helped perfect the dot-dash code, he inserted the key into the sending instrument, and he replaced the recording pen or pencil with a blunt stylus. Of all of the colleagues who assisted Morse in his invention, Vail made the greatest contributions.

Vail's father, Judge Stephen Vail, was reluctant to advance further funds until he saw the telegraph demonstrated. When his sample message, "A patient waiter is no loser" was successfully transcribed before his eyes, he became an enthusiastic supporter and his funds were of great assistance to Morse in developing the project.

In January 1838 Morse made a famous demonstration of his machine before Thomas Cummings, who was awaiting promotion to general. Morse chose the significant message, "Attention, the Universe; by kingdoms right wheel!" Cummings and his entourage were duly impressed.

In February came two more successful demonstrations, before a group of scientists at the Franklin Institute in Philadelphia, and before President Van Buren and his cabinet in Washington.

Morse had always hoped that the federal government would buy his rights to the telegraph and develop it as a natural monopoly. Senator F. O. J. ("Fog") Smith of Maine saw a chance to make money, however, so he entered into an agreement with Morse to be his business and legal advisor. As chairman of the Commerce Committee he got the Senate to pass a bill granting Morse $30,000 to build a 50-mile trial telegraphic line.

Morse's partners, Gale and Vail, agreed to revise downward their shares in profits from the telegraph, in order to make use of Smith's position and expertise. Distribution of shares was now Morse 9/16, Smith 1/4, Vail 1/8, and Gale 1/16. Expenses involved in securing American patents were to be borne by Morse and Vail; expenses for foreign patents were to be paid by Smith. Any inventions or mechanical improvements made by one of the partners were to be shared by all partners. This later became a significant burden to Morse.

Smith's Senate bill never passed the House of Representatives. Discouraged, Morse and Smith sailed for Europe in 1838 in an attempt to secure foreign patents.

Morse was gratified to see that his machine was definitely superior to those in use in Europe. Securing patents, however, was another story. In England the Attorney-General, wishing to protect the magnetic-needle telegraphs of Wheatstone and Davy, denied a patent on the grounds that since Morse's invention had been described in British newspapers, it was by now public property.

In September 1838 Morse gave a successful demonstration before the Institute of France, with such celebrities as Joseph Gay-Lussac, Baron von Humboldt, and the astronomer D. F. Arago attending. France granted a patent, but then decided that the telegraph was a governmental monopoly — and the French government would not buy Morse's machine.

Russia gave Morse much encouragement, so that he was prepared to go there in 1839 to install a trial line. But soon came the bad news — the czar had vetoed the proposal, on the grounds that "malevolence can easily interrupt the communication." Russians have always had to be unusually sensitive to malevolence.

In the spring of 1839 Morse met another famous inventor. Louis Daguerre, a French painter, had invented a method of reproducing images by exposing a sensitized plate to mercury vapor. The resulting daguerrotype, as it was called, constituted a primitive photograph. In earlier years Morse had experimented with a similar process but had given it up as impracticable.

Together the two inventors basked in the Parisian limelight. Daguerre taught Morse the art of image-making by his process. When Daguerre's laboratory was destroyed by fire, Morse was gratified to see that the French government liberally assisted him in rebuilding it.

Back in the United States Morse encountered his most depressing years. Europe had given him no more financial encouragement than had his native country. Since his three colleagues seemed to have lost interest in the telegraph while he was overseas, he found no one to assist him.

His imagination piqued by Daguerre's invention, Morse set up a photography studio in his room at the university. He thus became one of America's first photographers. He not only took pictures but also taught photography and wrote articles explaining the process. His picture of the thirtieth reunion of the Yale class of 1810 was the first group photograph of a college class.

In March 1840 Wheatstone and Cooke proposed to Morse that they consolidate their two types of telegraphic instruments. When Morse refused, they secured the first American patent on a telegraph. Morse hurriedly followed suit, later in 1840.

Morse continued to hope that Congress would appropriate funds to enable him to build a trial line. He could not believe that Congress would allow foreign inventors to build a commercial telegraph system before he could do so, considering his earlier precedence in the field.

One might have thought that a portrait painter would view photography as a competitive threat. Not Morse. To him photography was an adjunct to painting. He planned to use photography to store up a lot of model subjects for future painting.

In 1841 he mused dejectedly: I am now 50, my sight is failing, and no one seems interested in my telegraph. I'm separated from my children, and I've lost interest in painting. Will I ever be financially independent?

Despondency was short-lived in Morse, however, because of his deep religious faith. That year he said in a letter to his cousin: "I write not in the spirit of complaint of the dealings of God's Providence, for mysterious as it may seem to me, it has all been ordered in its minutest particulars in infinite wisdom. I rejoice in the midst of all these trials, and in view of my Heavenly Father's hand guiding all, I have a joy of spirit which I can only express by the word 'singing'."

Daguerre had said that portraits could not be taken by his process, since subjects could not sit still long enough. Morse and others disproved this by their success with portraits. Many of Morse's pupils became famous photographers. One of them, Mathew Brady, took portraits of every U.S. president from John Quincy Adams to William McKinley (with the exception of William Henry Harrison). By the first U.S. World's Fair, held in New York in 1853, America led the world in photography. A good deal of the credit belonged to Morse.

Morse's second try to become mayor of New York City, in 1841, was no more successful than his first. As usual, religious consolation carried him through the defeat. Despite many cares, anxieties, and disappointments, he said, "all will work for the best if we only look through the cloud and see a kind Parent directing all. This reflection alone cheers me and gives me renewed strength."

By 1842 England had over two hundred miles of telegraph line in operation. In Bavaria, Professor K. A. Steinheil had been operating a magnetic-needle telegraph since 1838, assisted by generous government grants. Knowing these things kept Morse in a state of constant anxiety.

His remorse was allayed somewhat in 1842 by a visit from Joseph Henry. Henry had kept up with developments abroad; he assured Morse that his instrument was clearly the best, largely because it was unaffected by weather disturbances. Morse was greatly cheered to hear this, for he had a high regard for Professor Henry's scientific knowledge.

In October 1842 Morse laid a cable across New York harbor, from Castle Garden to Governor's Island, but a ship's anchor cut the cable, and the message failed to get through. In December, however, he experienced success with a similar experiment across a canal in Washington.

While preparing for a demonstration before a Congressional committee, Morse entered a basement room of the Capitol building and found there, dusty and cob-webbed, a plaster cast of his statuette, "The Dying Hercules," which had won him the Adelphi Gold Medal in London many years previously. Since it was the last surviving cast, Morse accepted it as an omen that here too he would finally gain recognition, and secure his desired grant from Congress.

During the Congressional session of 1843 Morse received much help from John Pendleton Kennedy, the novelist, who was chairman of the House Commerce Committee. Kennedy got the bill authorizing a grant of $30,000 for a trial line introduced and read the necessary three times, despite much razzing and horseplay. Representative Houston of Alabama added an amendment that mesmerism and Millerism be added to the experiment. The amendment got 22 votes but failed. One of the bill's supporters, General Lew Wallace of Indiana, author of the novel *Ben-Hur*, was later defeated for re-election because of having spent public funds on such an absurdity.

The bill passed the House by a vote of 89 to 83. Commerce-minded states in the North and West supported the bill — all nine Southern states opposed it.

The Senate calendar was hopelessly jammed. On the final day of the session, there were 140 bills ahead of Morse's on the agenda. Little wonder that he went home before adjournment, for it seemed impossible that a vote would even be called for on the bill.

After receiving the great news from Annie Ellsworth, Morse consulted with Secretary of the Treasury J. C. Spencer and decided to use the $30,000 to build a telegraphic line from Washington to Baltimore, where both national presidential conventions were to be held in 1844.

Morse's worries were far from over. Professor J. C. Fisher, in charge of the underground cable, erred by using hot lead tubes which burned the wire's insulation. Trial messages were not getting through, and it was not known where all the breaks had occurred. With $23,000 of the grant already spent, Vail persuaded Morse to follow Wheatstone's technique of stringing wires from poles.

Fisher was fired for his error. Morse's helpers now deserted him. Gale returned to New York to run his father-in-law's factory. Vail demanded and got a salary increase, meanwhile predicting the failure of the project. Smith, left out by the Congressional appropriation, attacked Morse for his treatment of Fisher. Smith wrote newspaper articles against Morse, alleging that Morse had been making money out of sub-contracts, whereas in reality Smith had been the one making a profit from equipment purchases.

But in his hour of trial Morse found a faithful supporter. Ezra Cornell, a plow salesman, took over the cable project. To avoid undue ill publicity, he intentionally broke the main plow against a rock. Using this as a cover-up, he began installing 24-foot chestnut poles, 200 feet apart. The defective pipe was sold, and the wire recovered and strung on poles.

By early March, when the Whig convention was held in Baltimore, the line reached twenty-two miles, to the Annapolis junction, following the right-of-way of the Baltimore and Ohio Railroad. The race was on — would the railroad or the telegraph first bring the news to Washington as to whom the convention had chosen as vice-presidential candidate? Henry Clay was the assured presidential choice of the Whigs.

On May 1 Vail sent the message from Annapolis junction that the Whigs had selected Theodore Frelinghuysen. The telegraph beat the railroad by one hour and four minutes. Morse's stock rose.

What is more, Morse could describe the little-known Frelinghuysen to his Washington listeners. Taking advantage of the religious fervor of the time, the Whigs had selected one of America's leading Protestants. Known as the special champion of religion in politics, Frelinghuysen was chancellor of New York University. He later served as president of Rutgers University from 1850 to 1862. Because of their work together in such common causes as the American Bible Society and the American Sunday School Union, Morse knew Frelinghuysen and could present him favorably to interested Washingtonians.

By May 24 the line to Baltimore was finished and the famous first message was sent. Morse liked Annie Ellsworth's message so much that he announced that it settled for all time the controversy over the telegraph's inventor: "It baptized the American telegraph with the name of its Author," he modestly announced.

Two days later the Democrats met in Baltimore. Again the new discovery played an important role. Martin Van Buren, who opposed annexation of Texas, could not get the nomination but he successfully blocked the choice of ardent expansionist Lewis Cass. The convention chose as a compromise little-known James Polk of Tennessee, who kept the Democratic Party from a North–South split.

Again — who would be the vice-presidential candidate? Vail reported to Morse that the convention had selected Senator Silas Wright of New York. Informed by Morse, Wright declined. Convention leaders told Vail to ask Wright to reconsider. Back and forth went messages of persuasion and rejection. For the first time in history long-range communication was possible while an important political decision was being made. Now everyone in Washington agreed that "Morse's folly" was a great work.

Wright stuck by his decision. G. M. Dallas of Pennsylvania was selected as the vice-presidential candidate and inaugurated along with President Polk the following spring.

Newspapers all over America acclaimed the new inventor and his invention. Little stress was placed on the twelve-year search for support and recognition.

Morse now feared success and its effects. Characteristically he turned to God for strength. "I rejoice with fear," he prayed, "and I desire that a sense of dependence upon and increased obligation to the Giver of every good and perfect gift may keep me humble."

Morse's charity extended even to his chief heckler, Fog Smith. Said Morse, "I pray God for a right spirit in dealing with him." Morse called Smith "the thorn in the flesh permitted by a wise Father to keep me humble."

Fortunately Morse's absorption in the success of his telegraph probably kept him from getting embroiled in the religious turmoil of 1844. Along with the climactic peak of Adventism and the murders of Joseph and Hyrum Smith in Illinois, the country was witnessing a rapid outbreak of partisan religion.

In 1841 Morse had been elected president of the new American

Protestant Union, whose function was to keep public funds from going to sectarian organizations. Under the competition from Catholicism, Protestantism flourished. Whereas only one out of fifteen Americans was a member of a Protestant church in 1800, by 1850 the figure had risen to one out of seven.

In 1844 the American Republican Party, a nativist organization, got its candidate, James Harper, elected mayor of New York City. Nativists were also a force in national politics that year. They helped get Freling-huysen selected by the Whigs. They elected three of Philadelphia's four Congressmen. At huge mass meetings they denounced Catholics and foreigners. Their official song urged "patriots to break the Jesuits' band."

A big controversy broke out over use of the Bible in public schools. Since Puritan times the Bible had had a recognized place in the public school curriculum. Where they were in the majority, Catholics objected to use of the King James version of the Bible, recommending instead the Douay version. When turned down, the Catholics requested the use of state funds to support parochial schools. Governor William Seward of New York, later Lincoln's secretary of state, supported their request, but the legislature rejected the bill. A few rabid Catholics held open "Bible burning" meetings. In 1844 Pope Gregory XVI issued a letter to Catholic officials attacking Bible societies and the indiscriminate use of the Bible by laymen. The American Bible Society, at its annual meeting in 1844, said that "The Bible, from its origin and style is peculiarly appropriate for use in common schools, and cannot be excluded without hazard to our civil and religious liberties."

In 1844 a committee in the Congregational Church in Massachusetts announced that the danger of a Roman Catholic takeover was the greatest since the Reformation. In the Episcopal Church the immediate effect of John Henry Newman's switch to Rome was to strengthen anti-Catholic forces in the United States. The American Protestant Association, no longer headed by Morse in 1844, launched a violently anti-Catholic journal, *The Quarterly Review*, which asked zealous nativists to rally in a new Reformation.

Riots broke out during elections involving German–American Catholics in Louisville, Kentucky. Catholic priests found themselves in a Catch-22 situation: when they called upon Catholics to take no part in the rioting, their church was attacked because it was said that its members had surrendered their liberties to priests.

The religious fervor of the period reached its peak in Philadelphia in 1844. When the public school board permitted Catholic children to use their own Bibles and to be excused from Protestant religious instruction, American Republicans called mass protest meetings. Violence ensued, and a score of people were killed in May. Catholic churches and seminaries were burned. Powerless to keep order, the mayor called for the militia. In July a resurgence of rioting led to thirteen more deaths and many more wounded.

Bishop John Hughes warned New York nativists, "If a single Catholic Church is burned in New York, the city will become a second Moscow."

He stationed between 1,000 and 2,000 armed men around each Catholic church. There were no riots in New York City that year.

The Philadelphia riots hurt the nativist cause. Neutral persons found it difficult to condone violence used in the name of religion. Nativism now went underground until it resurged in the Know-Nothing movement of the 1850's.

It was fortunate for Morse that during this wave of religious antagonism he was almost completely absorbed in demonstrating the effectiveness of the telegraph. So immediate was his recognition after May 1844 that inventors of all sorts of gadgets wrote to him for his advice on their inventions — a flying machine, a caloric engine, a cable-stopper. For the rest of his life he was bothered by such requests.

Characteristically, he gave his first money from the telegraph to God's cause. When he received $45 for use of his patent on a short line in Washington he donated $50 to a Washington church.

He wanted to sell his rights in the telegraph to Congress for $100,000, but there was no deal. Later in his life when Congress contemplated buying all telegraph lines, the cost would have run into tens of millions of dollars. In 1845 Congress appropriated $8,000 to continue the Washington–Baltimore line. Unable to sell his rights to a commercial buyer, Morse went into business with Amos Kendall, postmaster general under Jackson. Together they formed the first successful telegraph company in America, The Magnetic Telegraph Company. Ezra Cornell, superintendent of the new company, made his first investment, $500, in this company. Cornell went on to build a huge empire in the Western Union Telegraph Company, and together with Andrew White, founded Cornell University.

As new telegraph companies were organized, they generally paid Morse's patent fee with stock. In time Morse thus possessed much stock, and was no longer a poor man.

When Congress refused to give him a contract to paint the Capitol rotunda in 1846, Morse left painting forever. He said of his once beloved mistress, painting: "I did not abandon her, she abandoned me."

At the age of 56 Morse had never owned a family home. Finally, in 1847 be bought Locust Grove, a 100-acre estate south of Poughkeepsie. At long last his three children were reunited with him. By the following year the land was free from mortgage.

At the wedding of his son Charles in 1848, Morse was attracted by a pretty bridesmaid, his second cousin Sarah Griswold. He had admired the partially-deaf young lady for years. Within several months the 57-year-old inventor married the 26-year-old Sarah. His first choice, of course, was to intensify her religious faith! At last he was supremely happy. His lifelong quest for recognition and security had been achieved.

Tranquility, however, was never Morse's lot. In 1848 the first of many lawsuits involving the telegraph broke out. Henry O'Rielly, who had a contract with Morse to extend telegraph lines west from Pittsburgh, decided to run a line, competing with Morse's, south to New Orleans. Morse sued O'Rielly and won.

A battle broke out between Professor Henry and Morse. Vail, in his *History of the American Electro-Magnetic Telegraph* published in 1845, had failed to give Henry credit for his scientific foundation of Morse's invention. Henry blamed Morse for the omission. In many lawsuits Henry testified against Morse, at times making it sound as if he himself had invented the telegraph. Angry, Morse responded with a long pamphlet, *A Defense against the Injurious Deductions drawn from the Deposition of Prof. Joseph Henry*, in which Morse questioned Henry's veracity and stated that he owed nothing to Henry. The latter statement was of course an error, and Morse paid dearly for it in later years when the Smithsonian Institution, which Henry then headed, issued a study placing most of the blame for the misunderstanding on Morse.

Newspapers tended to be hostile toward Morse. Some disliked his nativist politics. Many felt that his telegraph was making their news technique too slow and thus obsolete. Most seemed to feel that Morse was reaping a profit out of what should have been a natural governmental monopoly. They neglected to state that Morse had worked in vain for years to convince Congress of just that point.

Largely to coordinate their use of the telegraph, a number of New York City editors formed the New York Associated Press in 1848. Later this organization grew to be national in scope.

When the O'Rielly case was appealed to the U.S. Supreme Court, Chief Justice Roger Taney issued the court's decision in 1854, upholding Morse but granting others the right to use their forms of electromagnetic telegraphs, lest Morse have a monopoly. Also in 1854 Morse received a seven-year extension on his patent, assuring him of considerable royalty income for that period.

A retired paper manufacturer, Cyrus Field, was determined to lay an Atlantic cable. When his company was formed in 1854, Morse was named chief electrician and vice-president. Morse spent several years assisting in this project, but in 1857 he left Field's company when he was not named a director of the company.

The national debate over slavery caused Morse to switch political parties. When he was nominated for Congress by the Democratic Party in 1854, he once again had an opportunity to make public his conservative views. "Slavery is not sin," he said. "It is a social condition ordained from the beginning of the world for the wisest purposes, benevolent and disciplinary, by Divine Wisdom." Morse vigorously opposed immigration and supported the Know-Nothings, whose object, he said, was "to resist the aggression of foreign influence and its insidious and dangerous assaults upon all that Americans hold dear, politically and religiously." Again he was soundly trounced in the election.

Morse, however, was given a regal welcome in Europe in 1856.

The czar feted Morse at a lush banquet, and even the British, who had never been cordial to him, had a public dinner in his honor in London. His former rival, W. F. Cooke, was chairman at the dinner. Cooke publicly acknowledged that Morse was the one who had done most to advance the telegraph, and that his form of the telegraph was superior to all others. Morse modestly gave all credit to God and stressed the simultaneity of inventions: "Man is but an instrument of good if he will fulfill his mission; He that uses the instrument ought to have the chief honor. It is surely sufficient honor for any man that he is a co-laborer in any secondary capacity to which he may be appointed by such a Hand in a great benefaction to the world."

Despite the warm welcome they gave him that year, the British were conspicuously missing from the list of governments that contributed 400,000 francs to Morse in 1858 as a token payment of their use of his telegraph. Among the many other rewards and recognitions Morse received, at least one might have given him pause to reflect — Spain issued him "The cross of Knight Commander de Numero of the order of Isabella the Catholic."

Each time Morse received financial payments, Fog Smith would sue for a share, and win. Morse willingly shared receipts with the heirs of Gale and Vail. His experience in litigation reduced his estimate of lawyers: "I have not lost my respect for the law, but I have for its administrators; not so much for any premeditated dishonesty as for their stupidity and want of just insight into a case."

In 1859 Morse bought a winter home at 5 West 22nd Street in New York City. He became active as a civic leader and philanthropist. His philanthropy focused on three fields: religion, art, and women's education. He gave gifts of $10,000 each to Union Theological Seminary and the Yale Divinity School, $5,000 to his Poughkeepsie Presbyterian church building fund, and many other religious contributions. He purchased Allston's painting of Jeremiah for $7,000 and gave it to Yale. He often contributed to the artists' fund of the National Academy of Design. In 1851 he gave $1,000 to the Cleveland Female Seminary. He assisted Matthew Vassar in the founding of Vassar College at Poughkeepsie in 1861. In 1871 he helped found Rutgers Female College.

During the Civil War Morse became president of the national Society for the Diffusion of Political Knowledge, which opposed Lincoln as having usurped too much authority. It sought to bring about peace through conciliation. Morse once again became an unpopular figure — in the North, for opposing abolitionism, in the South, for opposing secession.

Morse felt that the Bible clearly condoned slavery. "If the Bible be the umpire, as I hold it to be, then it is the abolitionist that is denounced as worthy of excommunication. Not a syllable of reproof do I find in the sacred volume administered to those who maintain, in the spirit of the gospel, the relation of masters and slaves." He felt that "slavery is necessary to the Christianization and civilization of a barbarous race," and that God had ordained slavery as a means of benefiting the enslaved. His son Edward, who wrote a lengthy biography of Morse, said, "For those who believed in a literal interpretation of the Bible there was much excuse."

In 1864 Morse supported General George McClellan for president, since he considered Lincoln to be weak, vacillating, and in error for the Emancipation Proclamation. Abolitionism, said Morse, is the logical progeny of Unitarianism and infidelity. It blinds Christians' eyes from "their sad defection from the truths of the Bible." The following year he avoided the class reunion at Yale because he feared jingoistic trappings: "The loudest boasts of patriotism do not come from the true possessors of the genuine spirit. It is no improvement for Christian America to show less humanity than heathen Rome. The Romans never made demonstrations of triumph over the defeat of their countrymen in a civil war."

Carleton Mabee, author of *The American Leonardo*, says: "Like so many stern Calvinists, he obviously found a moral exhilaration in his incessant battles. In art he fought Trumbull and the American Academy, in religion Channing and all his followers, in public morals the theater and lottery, in politics the Irish. He went through the Civil War assailing the 'usurpations' of the Lincoln administration."

In his final years Morse received many honors and tributes. He must have especially enjoyed the dinner describing him as the Father of Modern Telegraphy in 1868, since it was presided over by Chief Justice Salmon Chase, the very person who had been chief counsel against Morse in the O'Rielly trial.

On June 10, 1871, a statue of Morse by the sculptor Byron Pickett was unveiled in Central Park. The presentation speech was by William Cullen Bryant. That evening Morse sent his name world-wide on the telegraph, and congratulatory messages arrived from New Orleans, Quebec, San Francisco, Halifax, Havana, Hongkong, Bombay, and Singapore.

The recognition took its toll on the aged inventor. "Strange as it may seem," he said, "this universal laudation is rather depressing than exhilarating." Success had been so slow in coming that it seemed a stranger at his door.

But his faith never wavered. "The nearer I approach to the end of my pilgrimage," he told his grandson, "the clearer is the evidence of the divine origin of the Bible, the grandeur and sublimity of God's remedy for fallen man are more appreciated, and the future is illumined with hope and joy."

His last public appearance was at the unveiling of a statue of Benjamin Franklin at Printing House Square in New York on January 17, 1872. It was fitting for Morse to do the honors, since, of all Americans, only Franklin had received more international recognition than had he.

The doctor attending him for pneumonia in his final illness tapped his chest, saying, "This is the way we doctors telegraph." Morse's final words were "Very good," accompanied by a faint smile.

He died April 2, 1872. Pall-bearers included Peter Cooper, Cyrus

Field, Ezra Cornell, and William Orton, the president of the Western Union Telegraph Company. By then 75 million messages were being sent annually over 310,000 miles of telegraph line throughout the world.

Congress held memorial services for Morse on April 16. All telegraph offices in America were draped black in mourning. Condolence messages poured in to his widow from North and South America, Europe, Asia, Africa, and Australia.

Calling him "the most illustrious American of his age," the *New York Herald* said that he was more important to the world than Napoleon, who had brought widespread death and suffering. "We sum up his life," said the editorial. "We see that the world is better, society more generous, and mankind nearer the ultimate fulfillment of its mission because he lived and did his work."

The *Louisville Courier-Journal* said that judged by the magnitude of his achievements, "the greatest man of the nineteenth century is dead. His mission was fully completed. It has been no man's fortune to leave behind him a more magnificent legacy to earth, or a more absolute title to a glorious immortality. His life monument will endure as long as the human race exists upon earth."

# 6
## John Henry Newman's Conversion to Catholicism

The Anglican priest held his head in his hands. He mused silently, "What hope have I but in Him? All is against me — may He not add Himself as an adversary. May He tell me, may I listen to Him, if His will be other than I think it to be."

It was 1844. The previous September John Henry Newman had resigned his position as rector of St. Mary's, the University church at Oxford. His request to retain the suburban parish of Littlemore had been turned down by his superiors. They had doubts about Newman — he seemed to be leading many of his young followers in the direction of the Church of Rome. Was he too contemplating such a move?

The immediate cause of his resignation had been the conversion of one of his admirers into the Roman Catholic Church. Newman had promised his bishop that he would not advise any of his protégés to make the switch. Young Lockhart had said he would remain an Anglican for at least three years, but within a year's time he found he could no longer resist the lure of Rome. To keep his word, Newman left the pulpit where he had become noted as one of England's greatest preachers.

For years he had lived in a state of what he called "moral sickness, neither able to acquiesce in Anglicanism nor able to go to Rome." His divided mind was beginning to lead to physical breakdown.

Since the earliest days of the Oxford Movement, when Newman and his friends John Keble and Richard Hurrell Froude had demanded reform in the Anglican Church, he had been a center of dispute. For over ten years they had insisted that the Church was too worldly, that it had to assume a serious purpose in order that the way of Christ would become a part of the believer's everyday life. Boldly had they challenged church practices and beliefs. Finally church and university united to squash their movement. Their series of tracts ended with controversial Tract 90, in which Newman had tried to show that nothing in the Thirty-Nine Articles of Anglican faith was inconsistent with Roman Catholic doctrine. Newman and his friends were silenced, at least for the time.

For his faith Newman endured much. His sisters prayed for his soul,

John Henry Newman. (Religious News Service Photo.)

his brothers abused him, his friends seemed to desert him, no matter which side of the argument he took. Gossip ran that he had secretly converted to Rome years ago, but had retained the Anglican surplice in order to win more converts away from the Established Church. Forced as he had been to openly declare his loyalty to Her Majesty's Church, he had made statements against Rome that had made most Catholics out of patience with him. Well could he now hold his head and pray for divine guidance out of his dilemma. Worldly resources had certainly failed him. Only God could now direct his troubled spirit.

Although he had resigned his living at St. Mary's, he still attended Anglican services. This year was to be his year of decision. He would have to decide whether to be Anglo-Catholic or Roman Catholic. His chief complaints against Rome lay in the veneration showed Mary and the saints. There was enough protestant in him that he felt nothing could come between the worshipper and his Maker. As closely as he followed the teachings of the Church Fathers of the early Christian centuries, he parted from them in their defense of exalting humans, no matter how virtuous or how closely connected to Christ.

A deep sense of guilt captured Newman. Had he misled others in the past? If so, it was certainly unintentional. But would he lead more astray if he made the big move he was contemplating? And would he be satisfied as a Roman Catholic, or would his restless soul look beyond the fold, never satisfied with its current status?

As he re-examined himself and his motivation he returned to basics. What he truly sought was the position of the early church, the church at the time of Christ. He resented the subsequent accretions, feeling that they interfered with the constant clear vision of the only supreme Good. He decided to make a careful study of the accretions and their causes. But one thing was clear: if deep study revealed justification for them, as he now believed it would, he would ask to join the Church of Rome, at no matter what cost to him. After all, his very soul hung in balance. What cost could compare with the prospect of eternal bliss in heaven with the Holy Trinity?

What specific factors had brought Newman to this crisis in his life? Would Roman Catholicism be the solution to his perennial gnawing search for ultimate certitude? How would the church of St. Augustine and St. Thomas Aquinas accept this enigmatic convert?

The eldest of six children, Newman was born in London on February 21, 1801. His father was a banker, his mother from a Huguenot family. He attended Ealing School from the age of seven until nearly sixteen. He not only loved to read the Bible, but he knew the catechism perfectly. In his childish imagination the Arabian Tales became as real as life. Scott's novels developed in him a lifelong love of medievalism. He was superstitious, often crossing himself before entering a dark place.

By the age of 14 he had read Voltaire, Hume, and Paine, and was growing in skepticism. The growth was arrested when Newman read essays written by Dr. Thomas Scott, rector of Aston Sandford. The essays cured him of "the detestable doctrine of predestination," Newman said. "I almost owe my soul to him," he added. Dr. Scott also implanted in Newman a deep reverence for the Holy Trinity, leading him to probe into the Athanasian Creed and the milieu which produced it.

Another book leading Newman to study the Church Fathers was Joseph Milner's *History of the Church of Christ*. Milner's thesis was that God selects certain periods in history to release "large and temporary Effusions of divine grace." Pentecost was the first such period—others had occurred throughout the life of the church. Newman had a lifelong belief that he lived in such a period, and that he had a somewhat prophetic role to play in helping bring Christians back to a firmer faith in God.

Likewise very influential on him was *Dissertations on the Prophecies* by Thomas Newton. Assigning literal roles to the prophecies of Daniel, John, and Paul, Newton convinced Newman that the Antichrist they spoke of was the pope. This belief "stained his imagination" until 1843, Newman said. In autumn 1816 he experienced a deep conversion experience. God was asking him to remain single throughout life in order to better serve Him, Newman believed. Perhaps he would dedicate his life to missionary work, working to convert the heathen.

To enter Trinity College, Oxford, in December he submitted to the Thirty-Nine Articles of Anglican faith. Unlike some students, Newman felt no difficulty in accepting them. He studied hard at Trinity, often spending twelve hours a day at his books. With a friend, John Bowden, he wrote a poem "St. Bartholomew's Eve." The poem describes an ill-fated marriage between a Protestant man and a Catholic woman—both die tragically because of the efforts of a cruel, fanatic priest. The poem is a satiric attack on the St. Bartholomew's Day massacre of 1572, in which thousands of French Huguenots had been slain by Catholic order.

At Oxford Newman often took his daily walks alone. He was impressed by the views of Edward Hawkins, later provost of Oriel College. Hawkins helped Newman supplant Calvinist ideas concerning predestination with the doctrine of regeneration from sin through baptism. Newman also began to accept Hawkins' stand on the importance of tradition in religion. The Bible does not teach doctrine, said Hawkins, it proves it—it is up to the church to do the teaching. Newman began to feel that a strong, unified, consistent church was needed to keep religious dogma pure and unsullied through the ravages of time.

In 1820 Newman's health broke down as a consequence of heavy study for his exams. He received his B. A. degree but without the honors required for continuation in the law curriculum. In April 1822, however, came what he called the turning-point in his life. He was accepted as a fellow by Oriel College, Oxford. Oriel became his intellectual and spiritual home during his crucial years of development. Many of his lifelong friends he met at Oriel.

Another fellow, William James, in 1823 introduced Newman to the importance of the doctrine of apostolic succession. Newman came to believe that it was very important for the priesthood to have descended in unbroken line from the foundation of the church in Christ's designation of Peter as His vicar.

Newman patiently worked his way through the Anglican hierarchy. He was ordained a deacon in 1824, and the following year he was ordained to the Anglican priesthood. He served briefly as a curate at St. Clement's Church in Oxford.

He was proud to be selected a tutor at Oriel in 1826. At about this time he came under the influence of Dr. Richard Whately, principal of St. Alban's Hall. Whately helped convince Newman of the need to keep secular authority from dominating the church. This became nearly an obsession with Newman although, like Whately, he believed that the church should derive financial support from the government.

Briefly in 1827 Newman drifted toward liberalism, questioning the Church Fathers and doubting the miracles of the saints. He was rudely shocked back into orthodoxy by two personal events. In November he grew gravely ill, a compound of physical and mental malaise. Then in January 1828 his youngest sister, Mary, died at the age of 19. He had always felt family ties strongly. Now his sister's image haunted him. He suddenly perceived what a veil this world of sense is. The reality of the unseen world overpowered him. He never again suffered any religious skepticism.

That same month Hawkins retired as vicar of St. Mary's, the University church, and Newman was appointed his successor. Overjoyed at the pulpit experience, Newman began to pack the church with crowds eager to hear his impassioned poetic delivery. He got much of his sermon inspiration and material from the Church Fathers. He focused especially on the period of the Arian heresy. The fourth-century priest Arius had argued that Christ, though divine, was not made of the same substance as God the Father. Athanasius, Greek bishop of Alexandria, led the church in squashing the Arian movement and having it declared heretical. Newman felt that Athanasius had thereby saved the church from grave internal split. As he looked at the modern church, Newman saw a parallel. A number of heretical Protestant bishops had infiltrated the Anglican Church, and he saw himself as a modern Athanasius, saving the church from schism and impure doctrine.

In 1827 the Tory Prime Minister, Robert Peel, asked for liberals to support the Catholic Emancipation Act, which would make it possible for Roman Catholics to vote, to sit in Parliament, and to hold most public offices. As recently as 1778 Parliament had passed an act permitting Catholics to operate schools and to own property. In 1815 Parliament demanded the right to veto papal appointments in Ireland, in exchange for granting funds to the Irish Catholic churches such as Protestant churches received.

Daniel O'Connell led Irish Catholics in resistance to this measure. Elected to Parliament, O'Connell was able to pressure Peel to support the Emancipation Bill. Although King George IV opposed the measure, he feared the Whigs even more, and so he supported it.

Newman, like many Anglican leaders, opposed the bill. Newman felt that it would weaken his church and that it would set a bad precedent for future political interference into university affairs. Although the bill passed, Newman's side could point to a local victory at the defeat of Peel as a candidate for re-election from the constituency of Oxford.

Newman and several of his friends began to see their tutorships at Oriel as quasi-pastoral in nature. Resenting this, the authorities deprived the ardent young men of their assignments as tutors in 1830.

Richard Hurrell Froude, one of the dismissed tutors, had introduced Newman to John Keble in 1828. Keble, a fellow of Oriel, had written an influential book of daily devotional verse, *A Christian Year*, in 1827. Keble made a deep impression upon Newman. He taught Newman the doctrine of probability—that in the spiritual realm, the convergence of many probabilities gives a kind of certitude to a belief. He also demonstrated how the sacraments worked, that material objects could stand for real but unseen things. Newman learned that the communion of saints meant first of all a spiritual union between Christ and every Christian, and thus by extension among all Christians. Keble said that certain mysteries of the faith, such as the doctrine of the Holy Trinity, could never be known by reason but could be known by revelation.

A romantic at heart, Newman readily accepted the reality of the unseen. Like Emerson, he believed that all of nature was a parable, an outward sign of a deeper reality, God. His study of the Church Fathers convinced him that despite all errors and false starts, there really was one universal, eternal church which was superior to any established church. His job in life was to discern clearly what that church was, and then announce his discovery to a confused and apathetic world.

As his faith deepened, he developed an antipathy towards certain kinds of religious liberalism, which he called "false liberty of thought." "Liberalism," he said, "is the mistake of subjecting to human judgment those revealed doctrines which are in their nature beyond and independent of it." He satirized the liberal position by asking how one could pray effectively the typical liberal prayer: "Oh God (if there be a God), save my soul (if I have a soul)."

Nevertheless there was a kind of liberalism in Newman's outlook. He strongly defended individual freedom of conscience. He advocated separation of church and state, except for financial support. And he increasingly came to feel that laymen should be given a more prominent role in church affairs.

For several years Newman worked on a book dealing with the Church Fathers. The book, *The Arians of the Fourth Century*, was published in

1833. What impressed Newman about the early church leaders was their active humanity. They were not only ascetics but doers — they demonstrated human nature in a purified and exalted state. Leaders like Athanasius realized that it was the church's duty to formulate creeds and settle doctrinal controversy, unpopular and unattractive as the job may be. Newman watched how dogma grew slowly, being accepted only after careful weighing and sifting the contributions from many sources.

Exhausted from working on his book, Newman left on a Mediterranean tour with Froude in December 1832. Froude's health was very bad, and Newman was glad to be in his presence. Although he was fascinated to visit Paul's missionary sites and the places where the Church Fathers had lived, Newman felt that Rome was "a city under a curse." He did not see many Catholics or engage in dialogue with them. In a letter home he wrote, "As to the Roman Catholic system, I have ever detested it so much that I cannot detest it more by seeing it."

In Sicily he became so seriously ill that he thought he would die. He left instructions on what should be done if he died. But saying, "I shall not die; I have work to do in England," he soon recovered.

In June 1833 the orange-boat on which he was sailing from Palermo to Marseilles was becalmed for a week in the Straits of Bonifacio. Though downcast, his heart was lifted to recall how God had led the fleeing Israelites in a pillar of cloud. He felt inspired to write a poem. The poem, called "The Pillar of the Cloud," has buoyed many Christian hearts for decades:

> Lead, Kindly Light, amid the encircling doom
> Lead Thou me on!
> The night is dark, and I am far from home —
> Lead Thou me on!

Upon his return to England Newman found the Anglican Church in bad shape. Thomas Arnold, the headmaster at Rugby said, "The Church, as it now stands, no human power can save." The Whigs, who were now in power, talked of disestablishing the church which meant, among other things, the loss of governmental financial support. The bishops, most of whom were Tory appointees, had been more noted for their political patronage and nepotism than for dedicated Christian administration.

The very spirit of the times ran counter to the church. The American and French revolutions had popularized liberal ideas. Deism was still in the air. The 1830 revolution in France, called by Newman "the triumph of irreligion," once again had people shouting reform slogans involving "reason" and "disestablishment." August Comte won many converts to Positivism, his substitute for religion. The Christian world was being startled by the findings of German theologians who were employing historical methodology to Bible study. Chartists paraded, asking for fair shares of industrial riches. Thomas Carlyle called the era "destitute of faith and terrified at skepticism."

The spark that ignited the religious conflagration that came to be known as the Oxford Movement was the decision by Parliament to eliminate 10 of the 22 Irish bishoprics. Although on a population basis the decision seemed reasonable, Newman and his friends saw the action as another political infringement upon religious prerogative.

On July 14 Keble preached a famous sermon on "National Apostasy." Keble argued that in view of the supernatural origin of the church, going back to Christ, the government had no right to intervene in religious affairs. Keble attacked the secularism that grew out of the so-called Enlightenment of the previous century. Jeremy Bentham, in his Utilitarianism, had postulated only two absolutes, pain and pleasure. The Christian view, that human beings were God's children, Bentham called "nonsense on stilts." Not only the Whigs and other liberals but Anglican leaders as well drew Keble's wrath. They had become complacent, he said, they ignored their responsibilities, and their lives showed a lack of piety and self-renunciation. In their effort to compromise with liberal Christians they had debased church dogma and weakened its authenticity. English political leaders, said Keble, had loosened church ties in a "direct disavowal of the sovereignty of God." If it continued he could describe the action only as "national apostasy."

The common room at Oriel became a meeting place of High Church Anglicans who were looking for a leader to point the way back to the practice of the primitive church of the first Christian centuries. Newman became that leader. Since he did not wish to form an official faction, Newman recommended individual action through preaching, writing, and discussion. The goal was a "Second Reformation" of the Anglican Church, carrying it back to the glory days of Lancelot Andrewes, William Laud, and other 17th century leaders, who had successfully charted a course between doctrinaire Roman Catholicism and anarchic liberal Protestantism. It was believed that those great Anglicans had best carried out the church practices that had developed in the early church.

In September Newman began the issuance of pamphlets on the doctrine, history, and practices of the early church. These tracts, distributed free, led to the group's being called the Tractarians. They were also called the Newmanites, or after Edward Pusey joined them in 1835, the Puseyites. Of the 90 tracts that appeared from 1833 to 1841, Newman wrote 29. Their purpose, he said, was to "rouse members of our Church to comprehend her alarming positions, as a man might give notice of a fire or inundation."

Newman stated that there were three beliefs behind the tracts. First, a belief in Christian dogma, and an attack on liberals for opposing it. Next, a belief in the visible church, with its rites and sacraments, as a channel of the invisible grace of God. Finally, a belief that the Roman Catholic Church, largely because of its Mariolatry and veneration of the saints, represented the Antichrist of biblical prophecy.

When efforts were made to remove religious requirements at Oxford and Cambridge in 1834, Newman vigorously protested. To remove these tests, especially subscription to the Thirty-Nine Articles at entry, would "make shipwreck of the Christian faith," he said.

The following year Pusey joined the movement. As professor and canon of Christ Church, he gave the group increased prestige. His influence upon the tract writers was to move them toward deeper scholarship and heightened responsibility.

As time went by, the tracts became increasingly Catholic in tone, making Anglican bishops desirous to silence these young "Romanizers." Some tracts even recommended now that the Anglican Church be disestablished, something the comfortable bishops dared not contemplate. Although Protestants like T. B. Macaulay and Thomas Carlyle had portrayed the Church Fathers as ignorant and self-seeking, Newman was educating his readers to believe that their lives and works were models of Christian virtue.

Opponents lampooned the tract writers. Thomas Arnold called them "The Oxford Malignants." Whately designated them "Children of the Mist." Low Church Anglicans circulated rumors that they had close ties with Jesuits. On the other hand militant Tractarians, like William George Ward, criticized Newman for his opposition to the Roman Church. When Ward said that it was the Anglican Church, not the Roman Catholic Church, that was on trial, Newman was forced to reluctantly agree.

The death of Richard Hurrell Froude in 1836 came as a great blow to Newman. Froude had been more influential than anyone else in moving Newman toward Rome. Among Froude's beliefs that Newman was increasingly adopting were a preference for church tradition over the Bible as an ultimate authority and a belief in the need for an authoritative hierarchy to prevent relativism and anarchy. Newman was also moving toward a belief in the Real Presence of Christ in the communion sacrament, a veneration of the Virgin Mary, and a belief that it would have been better had there never been a Reformation, since it had done more harm than good.

In 1836 Newman began editing *Library of the Fathers*, an English translation of writings by early church leaders. He also started writing for *The British Critic*, a journal which became the movement's official organ. And he continued his very popular sermons. At four o'clock each Sunday St. Mary's would be packed with eager listeners. As a rule, his sermon topics avoided dealing with subjects covered by the tracts.

For several years he had been working on defining Anglicanism as a proper middle way between the superstitious practices of Rome and the chaotic relativism of the Protestants. In 1837 he described what he called this "Via Media" in a book called *The Prophetical Office of the Church viewed relatively to Romanism and Popular Protestantism*.

In this work Newman said that the authentic original Roman church had been diverted by historical accretions of a non-religious nature.

Protestants, on the other hand, had whimsically subtracted important truths from essential church doctrine. Only the Anglicans had maintained a safe middle ground between these extremes.

After pointing up the need for authority in religion, Newman said that the Roman church had ignored postulating the consent of the Church Fathers as necessary historical evidence for belief, as it endeavored to state its infallibility. Protestants, on the other hand, went to the absurd extreme of trusting individual judgment to determine doctrine, something not done in any other field of human activity. Once again the Anglicans had sought and found middle ground on the question of authority, "thereby conforming to the early church, which claimed authority but not infallibility."

Newman never liked the term "Protestant" because he said it was purely negative, not indicating any specific profession of religion, and in opposition to the Roman church could equally be applied to an infidel. He felt that all three branches of the original church—Greek, Roman, and Anglican—were equally authentic, since each rested its ultimate claim to authority upon the apostolic succession. Their points of disagreement, he now said, were on non-essentials. He said Romans and Anglicans agreed on the important Christian doctrines: the Holy Trinity; the Incarnation of Christ; Christ's Atonement for man's original sin; man's need for spiritual rebirth; the supernatural grace of sacraments; the Apostolic succession; and the eternity of future punishment.

In 1838 Newman began editing *The British Critic*, and continued until 1841. Of the many articles he wrote for the journal none ever recommended to readers that they join the Roman Catholic Church. As an Anglican clergyman, he felt he could be loyal to only one church. His honest mind probed ever deeper, always coming nearer Rome. But for the time the Via Media seemed to him to be God's intention. His publication of *Letters of Justification* in 1838 showed how Anglicans also achieved the golden mean on the question of whether faith or works brought salvation. The Roman church stressed works too much, whereas the Lutherans stressed faith to the exclusion of works. The Anglicans properly stressed faith plus works. Newman believed in verification of salvation through baptism, which elevates man from a state of nature to a state of grace, thereby opening to him a supernatural faith and the power to act virtuously.

By the spring of 1839 Newman was at the height of his influence in the Anglican Church. Many Anglicans adopted his Via Media as the rationale for their church preference. Newman feared radical Protestantism more than liberalism, which he said was "too cold to prevail with the multitude." Again the Via concept applied. The evangelicals were very emotional and since their positions suffered from lack of internal consistency and intellectual depth, they would spend most of their time fighting among themselves. Newman's prediction of the fragmentation of Protestantism has proved to be accurate.

A chance discovery in 1839 of a fifth-century sect called the

Monophysites started Newman on his road to Rome. The reasoning used by this group, who asserted that Jesus had a divine but not a human nature, was based upon the authority of the Church Fathers and the support of the civil government. Ultimately, however, the church found them to be in heresy. If a fifth-century Via Media had not been successful, maybe the modern Anglican one would similarly fail, he began to fear.

A second blow followed immediately. Catholic Bishop Nicholas Wiseman, in an article in *The Dublin Review*, recounted how St. Augustine had dealt with the Donatists, a fourth-century group who taught that sacraments performed by unworthy priests were ineffectual. No, said Augustine, since sacraments are instituted not of man but of God, they communicate grace no matter who performs them.

In putting down this schism, Augustine used a phrase that greatly impressed Newman: "The whole world judges correctly that they are not good who separate themselves from the rest of the world." Wiseman held that the Anglican Church, like the Donatists, was in schism by refusing to submit to papal authority. Newman was shocked to realize that the Church Fathers, on whose authority his Via Media had been erected, had repeatedly used as the ultimate test of Catholicity recognition of the See of Peter as the final world-wide authority. "By those great words of the ancient father," Newman said, "the theory of the Via Media was absolutely pulverized."

He acknowledged to a friend, "I have had the first real hit from Romanism. It has given me a stomach ache. We have sprung a leak. There is an uncomfortable vista which was closed before."

But he was not yet ready to switch churches. In 1840 he still felt that the edge belonged to the "primitive" Anglican church, because it had avoided the improper accretions that made Roman worship a type of idolatry. He told a friend that "in the end he might find it his duty to join the Roman Catholic Church," but his long-held prejudice caused him to add that if ever such a time should come, he hoped that God would mercifully carry him away before the event!

From this time on the chief goal of the Oxford Movement shifted. Where it had previously sought for reform of the Anglican Church from within, it now devoted its efforts to keeping its followers from flocking to the Roman church.

Newman was thrown back upon the three fundamental bases of the Movement, but examining them he found that the Roman claim was sounder than the Anglican concerning the first two, dogma and sacraments. So he took a look at the third principle, which was anti-Romanism. True, pagan Rome had entered and corrupted the early church, but is the pope really Antichrist: "The true Vicar of Christ must ever to the world seem like Antichrist and be stigmatized as such, because a resemblance must ever exist between an original and a forgery."

Still led by his heart to love his ancestral church, but increasingly being thrust by his intellect toward Rome, Newman prayed fervently for a merger of the two churches as the best means of bridging the ever-widening chasm between his thoughts and his affections.

True to his Anglican vows, Newman tried to stem the tide toward Rome. It now seemed crucial to him that if the Anglican Church were to be saved it would be necessary to show how its Thirty-Nine Articles of faith, adopted at the time of the split from Rome under Henry VIII, were really Catholic in intent and content. He and other leaders realized that unless they could satisfy some of the radical pro-Romanists in their group, people like Ward, there would be a wholesale defection from their ranks to Rome.

Out of this background Newman wrote the famous Tract 90, "Remarks on Certain Passages in the 39 Articles." It caused such a sensation that it proved to be the last tract written in the Movement.

Newman knew that most Anglicans had relied upon the 39 Articles to give their quasi-Catholic church a peculiarly Protestant bent. Newman stated that the articles were not directed against the early church teachings but rather against accretions, which he called "dominant errors." These were popular beliefs and usages which had steadily infiltrated into Roman Catholic dogma. The articles, said Newman, were directed against the pope but not against the Church of Rome. Newman said there was nothing in apostolic teaching granting the pope authority over the whole church. The pope's supremacy was thus not a matter of faith, but rather a long-standing custom and an expedient ecclesiastical arrangement. Anglicans, who were subject to Henry VIII's Oath of Supremacy, which forbade a foreign prelate from having jurisdiction over Englishmen, were free from the pope's authority but not from that of the Roman Church.

Newman felt relieved, since he felt he had freed the Anglican Church from charges of schism. He felt he had demonstrated that the essence of the primitive church was contained in the 39 Articles. "It was a matter of life or death to us to show it," he believed.

Reaction to Tract 90 was immediate and largely hostile. Newman was branded a traitor to his church, an advocate of popery and Romanism. He was accused of betraying the 39 Articles, which he had sworn to uphold. One prominent clergyman said, "I should be sorry to trust the author of that Tract with my purse." Newman was labeled "a subtle-minded ecclesiastical hairsplitter and special pleader." Even some modern Anglicans have felt that Newman's position in the tract shows signs of "double dealing."

Newman took the criticism calmly. "I have asserted a great principle," he said, "and I ought to suffer for it. I am now in my right place," he added, "which I have long wished to be in."

He may have underestimated the storm of reaction that was brewing. His superior, Bishop Bagot, who had always treated him kindly, asked him not only to discontinue the tracts but also to withdraw Tract 90. When Newman refused, Bagot offered a compromise: Discontinue the tracts, and write a letter to him repudiating the Roman Church.

Newman's response was to end the tract series and to write Bagot a letter which stated, "I think that to belong to the Catholic Church is the first of all privileges, and I consider the Church over which you preside the Catholic Church in this country."

Newman's fond hope was still a reconciliation between the two churches. As he later reflected on the tract he said, "No. 90 then was not a resolution of the 39 Articles into the Council of Trent, but an experimental inquiry how far they would approximate to it, under the notion that the Church of Rome would have in her turn to approximate to Protestants." The Council of Trent had been the Roman Catholic response to the attacks made by Luther and other Reformation leaders.

Under pressure to recant, Newman stood adamant. "I have no intention whatever of yielding any one point which I hold on conviction," he stated, "and that the authorities of the Church know full well." Admirable as his stand for personal integrity must have been, one might have asked him how, in principle, it differed from stands taken by liberals or evangelicals like the Methodists, whom Newman opposed because of their reluctance to abide by decisions of the church's hierarchy.

"Rationalism," said Newman, "is the great evil of the day. I am more certain that the Protestant spirit, which I oppose, leads to infidelity than that which I recommend leads to Rome."

His view of society was of a Christian community in which the highest value was individual faith in God, bound up in a collective fabric called the church. Normally the church hierarchy must be obeyed, lest the fabric collapse, but when the hierarchy takes steps which will lead ultimately to the loss of the individual's faith in God, someone must correct the suicidal step taken in error by church leaders. Newman felt God's hand on his shoulder as the one to prevent this grave error. If the cost was loss of family, friends, living, and church – so be it. The goal was worth the risk.

The Heads of Houses at Oxford, those who initiated all university legislation, censured Tract 90 as injurious to the Anglican Church. To Newman, the truth as he saw it was more important than approval from university officials.

He now wondered whether the Anglican theory, which he felt had never been given a fair chance, would forever remain untried. The whole point of the Oxford Movement had been to remind Anglicans that although their church was corrupt, it had great potential to be Christ's vicar on earth. When the Anglican Church showed its opposition to the path to which Newman and his friends had pointed, he felt that the same path was equally open to the church of Rome.

"Whatever be the influence of the Tracts, great or small," he warned, "they may become just as powerful for Rome if our Church refuses them as they would be for our Church if she accepted them."

But he was still of a divided mind. What forces had caused the Protestant movement in the first place, he asked himself. Surely so large a part of Christendom could not have split from Rome, remained so for over 300 years, and continued to grow unless there had been some very grave errors on Rome's part. "Protestantism must have in it a great truth," he confessed somewhat reluctantly. As one who prized tradition very highly, he was never able to perceive what that truth might be.

In the latter half of 1841, said Newman, "three blows broke me." As he looked anew at the Arian heresy, he now saw Protestants as Arians, Anglicans as semi-Arians, and the Roman Catholic Church the same as it had always been. Secondly, the Anglican bishops kept Newman under steady attack because of the views he had expressed in Tract 90. Thirdly, the government spoke of setting up a joint bishopric in Jerusalem, to be shared with the Prussian Lutherans. Newman and his dwindling party would have no such cooperation with Protestants, lest Anglican doctrine be further watered down in a vacuous compromise. Newman began to feel as if the very forces of nature were driving him to Rome.

In this state of mind he was visited by Dr. Charles William Russell, professor (and later president) of Maynooth College, a Roman Catholic seminary in Ireland. Russell, said Newman, "had more to do with my conversion than anyone else."

Newman showed Russell through Oxford's buildings. They did not discuss religion. Newman admired the way Russell permitted him to make his own soul decisions. Russell gave him several books and wrote him a few letters. The only part of the book material Newman disliked was the devotion paid to saints. It took him until 1844 to get over this objection.

Since 1839 Newman had wanted to move to Littlemore, a suburb of Oxford, where he had built a church. Realizing that his views were controversial, he felt uncomfortable at St. Mary's, where his sermons often brought out points that were distasteful to university and church leaders. So in early 1842 he moved to Littlemore, permitting his curate to serve St. Mary's parish.

He now felt he was an Anglican only because it was a part of the church universal. But he now considered his church to be in schism. Perhaps like those other great schismatics, the Jews, they were still somehow God's chosen people. Despite all the pain it had caused him, he did not regret the Oxford Movement. One real outcome was that it was forcing the Anglican Church to take a good look at itself, the first step in any improvement process.

He looked trouble in the eye. "Our Church has through centuries," he said, "ever been sinking lower and lower, till good part of its professions and pretensions is a mere sham. The truest friends of our Church are they who say boldly when her rulers are going wrong, and the consequences."

"This age is moving towards something," he felt, and only the Roman church, despite the errors of its system, "has given free scope to the feelings of awe, mystery, tenderness, reverence, devotedness and other feelings which may be especially called Catholic."

He felt no let-up in the attack upon him. He felt badgered and harried by the bishops' continual pronouncements against him. The press gave him no privacy. In April his bishop asked if the newspaper report was correct which stated that he was setting up Roman Catholic monastic cells in the tenements he owned in Littlemore. Denying the charge, Newman added, "I feel it very cruel that very sacred matters between me and my conscience are made a matter of public talk." He pointed out that the Littlemore parish had twice as many members as St. Mary's, and that he thought it best for all concerned to permit the excitement at Oxford to subside.

He had in fact, he told his bishop, talked some of his young followers out of entering the Roman church. He resented being called a bad Anglican. "If all the world agree in telling a man he has no business in our Church," he said, "he will at length begin to think he has none."

At a time when he needed solitude, time for study, prayer, and contemplation, all eyes were upon him. His Anglican friends criticized him for drifting, while his Catholic friends were impatient with his inaction. Good old Keble and Pusey — they understood his dilemma and sympathized with him. "I had to make up my mind for myself," he said, "and others could not help me. I determined to be guided not by my imagination but by my reason. Had it not been for this severe resolve, I should have been a Catholic sooner than I was."

In February 1843 he published an official retraction of all statements he had previously made against the Roman Catholic Church. He said he had been led into error by his readings of the works of early Anglican leaders. His public statement no doubt eased some of the pressure on his conscience but once again many people attacked him for what they called duplicity.

In September 1843 he resigned his position as vicar of St. Mary's. He asked to keep the Littlemore parish but was refused. On September 25 he delivered his last sermon as an Anglican, called "The Parting of Friends." In a touching farewell he showed regret at leaving the church of his birth but felt it lacked adherence to divine truth. He asked all present to pray for this troubled soul, "that in all things he may know God's will, and at all times he may be ready to fulfill it." He continued to attend Anglican services as a layman for the next two years.

He now embarked upon a period of intense study and prayer. Most of his friends expected him to enter the Roman church. When his followers asked for advice he replied, "How could I in any sense direct others, who had to be guided in so momentous a matter myself?"

He described his dilemma. "I had been deceived once; how could I be sure that I was not deceived a second time? How could I ever again have confidence in myself? As in 1840 I listened to the rising doubt in favor of Rome, now I listened to the waning doubt in favor of the Anglican Church. What inward test had I that I should not change again after I had become a Catholic?"

An idea implanted in one of his final sermons haunted him. The sermon, called "The Theory of Development in Religious Doctrine," examined how doctrine grew. "Growth is the sole evidence of life," Thomas Scott had taught him. He had refrained from charting the growth of Christian doctrine, perhaps because of an unconscious fear that what he found would eliminate his objections to Rome. But the time had now come for an exploration of the hitherto forbidden topic.

His sermon had attacked liberals for their relativism, saying it ends in expressing purely human values. Theology based upon dogma, on the other hand, deals with unchanging truth. The dogma needs to be examined to make sure it derives from God, is internally consistent, and has not become perverted or diluted as it is handed down through the centuries. Theology exists not only to expose heresy but to minister to the universal "devout curiosity, an impulse inherent in the life of faith in the human mind."

Newman constructed his argument upon a psychology of knowledge—what is first intuition grows by reflection into reason. He offered the Virgin Mary as "the perfect model of the theologian: first believing without reasoning, next from love and reverence reasoning after believing." Later Newman made his most important contribution to theology by expanding this sermon into a book.

Realizing that religion can never be verified on a material basis, Newman employed the doctrine of cumulative probability to arrive at the highest achievable certitude for a belief. He said, "I believed in a God on a ground of probability, I believed in Christianity on a probability, and I believed in Catholicism on a probability and these three grounds of probability were a cumulative, a transcendent probability."

He was increasingly led to believe that the two logical alternatives were Rome or atheism: "Anglicanism is the halfway house on the one side, and Liberalism is the halfway house on the other."

By 1844 Newman felt that he never again wanted to influence others by his acts or his beliefs. He feared that his own tortuous spiritual evolution had perhaps misled others. "I shall die alone," he said, quoting Pascal, the French philosopher. He added: "They that are whole can heal others; but in my case it was 'Physician, heal thyself'." He had now entered the dark night of the soul, known to mystics and deep religious seekers.

A number of other former Tractarians preceded Newman into the Roman church. Probably the most illustrious of these was Ward, who published a polemical book in 1844 called *Ideal of a Christian Church*. Ward shocked Anglican readers by maintaining his right to continue as an Anglican clergyman "while holding the whole cycle of Roman doctrine." Oxford University responded by dismissing Ward from his professorship and stripping him of his university degrees. Ward chided Newman for his diffidence in taking the decisive but costly step to which his reasoning had led him.

In September Newman sobbed at the coffin of his friend, John

William Bowden: "He left me still dark as to what the way of truth was, and what I ought to do to please God and fulfill His will." The genuine comfort that the Anglican faith provided the Bowden family led him to once again ask himself if he fully appreciated what he seemed about to surrender.

In November he still could say, "I am not moving. Every one is prepared for such an event, next every one expects it of me. I have very little reason to doubt about the issue of things, but the when and the how are known to Him from whom both the course of things and the issue come. I have a great dread of going by my own feelings, lest they should mislead me."

Later that month he was in mental anguish over the perplexity he was causing to so many people. "My one paramount reason for contemplating a change," he wrote in a letter, "is my deep, unvarying conviction that our Church is in schism, and that my salvation depends on my joining the Church of Rome. I have no existing sympathies with Roman Catholics. I know none of them; I do not like what I hear of them.

And then, how much I am giving up in so many ways! My especial love of old associations and the pleasures of memory. Nor am I conscious of any feeling of pleasure in the sacrifice."

When Stanley Faber accused Newman of having been "a concealed Romanist during the last ten years," Newman charted the course of his religious development: During the first four years, he said, "I honestly wished to benefit the Church of England at the expense of the Church of Rome"; during the second four years, "I wished to benefit the Church of England without prejudice to the Church of Rome; in the ninth year, "I began to despair of the Church of England, and gave up all clerical duty; what I wrote and did was influenced by a mere wish not to injure it, and not by the wish to benefit it."

During the tenth year, beginning in September, 1844, "I distinctly contemplated leaving it. During the last half of that tenth year I was engaged in writing a book (*Essay on Development*) in favor of the Roman Church and indirectly against the English; but even then, till it was finished, I had not absolutely intended to publish it, wishing to reserve to myself the chance of changing my mind when the argumentative views which were actuating me had been distinctly brought out before me in writing."

His plan, then, was to expand the 1843 sermon on development of doctrine into a full-length study, "and then, if at the end of it my convictions in favor of the Roman Church were not weaker, of taking the necessary steps for admission into her fold."

As he started his great work, Newman re-asserted his determination to approximate the condition of doctrine in the primitive church. He now believed that although all truth had been given the church at its establishment, subsequent reflection and thought had produced clarification and a better understanding of Christ's teachings. Heresies kept the church on its toes, forcing it to be certain of its verities. Church Fathers such as Origen,

Basil, and Jerome had subscribed to the idea that Christian doctrine was undergoing progressive growth and development.

Finally the puzzle of the accretions was solved to his satisfaction. The expansion of creed and ritual was a normal evolution from the original seed of faith. "Time is necessary for the full comprehension and perfection of great ideas," he now believed. "The highest and most wonderful truths, though communicated once for all by inspired teachers, could not be comprehended all at once by the recipients, but have required only the longer time and deeper thought for their full elucidation. This may be called *The Theory of Development of Doctrine.*"

The background of ideas in which Newman flourished made his contribution simply a religious application of a commonly recognized principle. Immanuel Kant, the Marquis de Condorcet, and August Comte all viewed humanity as a developing organism. Newman's contemporaries, Charles Darwin, Georg Hegel, and Herbert Spencer, were at work on theories of evolution in their respective fields. If biological and social systems evolved, why could there not be a kindred process at work in the area of religious doctrine?

Having discarded secular authority as the basis for affirming church doctrine, Newman sought for a new anchor. Without a firm foundation, the ship of faith would founder in the chaotic tides of individual preference. The opposite of Protestant anarchy was the firm chain of apostolic succession.

He now felt that were his heroes, Athanasius and Ambrose, to return to the modern world, the only church that they would recognize as theirs would be the Roman Catholic Church. Choosing a number of doctrines, such as original sin, infant baptism, communion, the Incarnation, and papal supremacy, Newman showed that the nearest approximation to the church of the Fathers was the Roman church. "Modern Catholicism," he said, "is simply the legitimate growth and complement of the doctrine of the early Church, and its divine authority is included in the divinity of Christianity."

No longer was he troubled by Mariolatry or veneration of the saints. He described the reason for his altered views: "This I know full well now, and did not know then, that the Catholic Church allows no image of any sort, material or immaterial, no dogmatic symbol, no rite, no sacrament, no saint, not even the Blessed Virgin herself, to come between the soul and its Creator. It is face to face, in all matters between man and his God."

The core of his book is a series of tests to determine a faith which, being vibrant and healthy, deserves to be followed. Reasoning by analogy, he draws his criteria from natural organisms. He poses signs of healthy growth as opposed to signs of change that leads to decay and death.

His first test is preservation of type. A faith needs to preserve its essential idea so that despite apparent external change, "the impression the object actually makes on the mind remains essentially the same." Just as it had on the pagan world, he says, the Catholic church "gives to the world around it the impression of a hidden superstition, magical and fanatical." It appears, as it did in the fourth century, as a well organized, compact, and intolerant hierarchy, "among a coalition of heresies which ceaselessly change and disintegrate. It always excites the same sympathies and hatreds, gives rise to the same problems and takes up the same attitude to them. This is possible only if the one animating idea persists under all these phenomena, unweakened and incorrupt." Whoever quarrels with the Church today would have quarreled similarly with the Apostles and Evangelists of the first century, he felt.

His second test is continuity of principles. "The principles and proceedings of the Church now were those of the Church then; the principles and proceedings of the heretics then were those of Protestants now."

The third test of a living organism is power of assimilation. "To assimilate is to incorporate a foreign substance and to transform it organically into one's own." Finding in the world all sorts of opinions, customs, and rites, the Church adopts certain ones, altering them in accordance with its own essential idea.

The fourth test is logical sequence. Since growth involves ingesting outside elements into itself for the benefit of the organism, "the final term is nothing but the natural and logical outcome of the first." Although the growth is spontaneous and natural, upon reflection it is also seen to be a logical sequence.

Fifth comes the test of early anticipation. Doctrines on which the Church formulated clear knowledge only recently are foreshadowed, in dim form, from the very beginning.

The sixth test involves preservative additions. Although growth involves change, the change must strengthen the organism. "The state finally reached is of richer content than the original, though only its fulfillment." Newman gives as an example the high place given the Virgin Mary, which "in no wise lessens the honor given to her Son, but rather confirms it and sets it in a stronger light."

The final test is that of chronic continuance. Its very existence through a long period of time demonstrates that the Church has not suffered deadly corruption and decay.

Having subjected the Roman church to this series of tests, Newman found that it alone preserved the central core of Christian doctrine. Now he understood its accretions: "The differences and additions in doctrinal teaching observable in the history of the Church are only apparent, being necessary for the development of her ideas."

His quest for certainty had finally ended. He could now see that his conversion to the Roman church implied "no substantial change of conviction, but was its logical consequence." By October 1, 1845, he had progressed far enough to know he would join the Roman Catholic Church. So he set down his pen, and the book was published in the incomplete form.

Not all Roman Catholics accepted Newman's theory of development. Many American Catholics particularly objected to it. One American bishop called it "half Catholicism, half infidelity." The recent convert Orestes Brownson said that Newman still reasoned like a Protestant.

Now that his mind was finally made up, Newman moved fast. He resigned his Oriel fellowship, and told two recent converts, Ambrose St. John and John Dalgairns, of his decision. Dalgairns mentioned that Father Dominic Barberi, an Italian Passionist priest who headed a monastic center at Aston in Staffordshire, was going to stop off at Littlemore on his way to Belgium. Newman said, "He does not know of my intention, but I shall ask of him admission into the One true Fold of the Redeemer."

Father Dominic arrived at Littlemore in a downpour shortly before midnight on October 8. He stood with his back to the fire drying himself. He said, "The door opened — and what a spectacle it was for me to see at my feet John Henry Newman, begging me to hear his confession and admit him into the bosom of the Catholic Church!"

The next morning Father Dominic heard the remainder of Newman's confession and admitted him, together with two other Anglican clergymen, Frederick Bowles and Richard Stanton, into the Roman Catholic Church. Newman wrote thirty letters to his family and friends, informing them of his action.

After receiving his First Communion in his new church on October 10, Newman wrote an epilogue to his recent book: "Such were the thoughts concerning the 'Blessed Vision of Peace' of one whose long continued petition had been that the Most Merciful would not despise the work of His own hands, nor leave him to himself. Seduce not yourself with the imagination that it comes of disappointment or disgust, or restlessness, or wounded feeling, or undue sensibility, or other weakness."

Leaving his beloved Littlemore, Newman moved to Old Oscott in Warwickshire. When he was confirmed as a Roman Catholic on November 1, he took the name of Mary. The house that he and seven other recent converts lived in was called Maryvale. Bishop Wiseman rather proudly stated, "I assure you the Church has not received, at any time, a convert who has joined her in more docility and simplicity of faith than Newman."

Newman's family resented his conversion very much. Likewise most of society's elite — lords, ladies, bishops, university leaders — henceforth avoided him. Mark Pattison, a former Tractarian, said, "It is impossible to describe the enormous effect, I may say throughout all England, of one man's changing his religion." The rising statesman William Gladstone wrote to Archbishop Manning, "I stagger to and fro like a drunken man, and am at my wits' end." The popular press attacked Newman, calling him a secret Jesuit and a coward who had surrendered to the pope because he lacked the courage to think for himself.

Newman contemplated entering a lay vocation. But his total being had been immersed in the church so long that he felt alien to the outside world. He went to Rome and talked to many people, including Pope Pius IX. With three other converts he entered the College of Propaganda, preparing for ordination as priests.

Newman was enamored with Philip Neri, the 16th century saint who had founded the Congregation of the Oratorians, so he entered that order. What particularly impressed him about Philip was his openness to all — young and old, clergy and lay, rich and poor, learned and unlearned.

After being ordained a Roman Catholic priest on May 30, 1847, he received permission from the pope to set up an Oratory at Birmingham in 1848. The following year he also established an Oratory at London.

In response to an anonymous novel called *From Oxford to Rome*, which purported to give the inside story of the Oxford defection, Newman wrote a novel called *Loss and Gain*. Published in 1848, it tells of the religious conversion of a man called Charles Reding, who has many of the traits and beliefs of his author. Reding's change of churches is described as sincere, logical, and in many places expected.

In 1850 Pope Pius IX, newly returned to Rome after a year's exile in Gaeta during the Italian republican revolt, called Bishop Wiseman to Rome, elevated him to cardinal, and put him over the entire Roman Catholic hierarchy in England as Archbishop of Westminster. A letter by Cardinal Wiseman acknowledging the restoration of the Roman Catholic hierarchy in England was interpreted as a wholesale attack upon the Anglican supremacy, and much hard feeling between Anglicans and Catholics developed.

Attempting to bring peace between the warring factions, Newman delivered a series of lectures in Birmingham in the summer of 1851. The lecture series, called *The Present Position of Catholics in England*, was published in book form later that year. In this work, Newman showed how rumor, lie, and prejudice often caused misunderstanding of Roman Catholic doctrine and practice.

One of his lectures, however, got Newman into trouble. An ex-priest, Dr. Giacinto Achilli, had been waging verbal war against the Roman church. Cardinal Wiseman persuaded Newman to charge Achilli with gross sexual misconduct, for which there were abundant witnesses. The angry Achilli sued Newman for libel and won. Newman was fined $500, but had to pay $60,000 in court costs. Newman's friends raised the money to pay the bills. Achilli left England, disgraced.

Public opinion sided with Newman. He said, "Sympathy is doing for me here what success would not have done." The *London Times* said of the verdict: "We consider that a great blow has been given the administration of justice in this country, and the Roman Catholics will henceforth have only too good reason for asserting that there is no justice for them in cases tending to arouse Protestant feelings of judges and juries."

In July 1851 Archbishop Cullen of Ireland asked Newman to become the founding rector of the Catholic University of Dublin. Higher education had had a rough time in Ireland. Americo Lapati says that "from 1600 to 1793, the period of penal laws against Catholics, no Catholic could attend a university or go to the Continent to do so." In 1845 Parliament passed a law setting up three state colleges, but the Irish bishops opposed them on the grounds that they were godless. Anglicans found their needs satisfied by attending their own institution, Trinity College in Dublin. Many of the Irish poor had no use for higher education.

In this difficult situation Newman delivered his series of lectures in 1852 that brought him fame when published as *The Idea of a University*. Newman's two goals were to show the need for theology in an educational system and to demonstrate the value of a liberal education in developing one's mind. Calling theology a science, he said it was a hand-maid to other disciplines. Following Aristotle, Newman defines liberal education as that which is worthwhile in itself. The goal of a university, he says, is to enable its students to develop the philosophical habit of mind, showing freedom, calmness, moderation, and wisdom. Education for a profession is acceptable, but it should be built upon a liberal base.

Newman was better as a theorist than as a practical university administrator. When he tried to import English professors, the Irish rebelled. The Irish professors Newman selected were radicals who wanted separation from England. Cullen, tired of putting out fires caused by Newman, started bypassing him in making appointments. Newman spent much time in England, and university affairs languished.

The proposed university was never chartered. Newman resigned as rector in 1857. One tangible thing he had accomplished: money left over from world-wide contributions to the Achilli trial fund was used to build a handsome chapel.

Newman's persistent belief in an enhanced role for the laity kept getting him in trouble with his superiors. In 1859 he wrote an essay, "On Consulting the Faithful in Matters of Doctrine," in which he said that on such matters as educational policy, laymen should be consulted before a doctrine is announced. Although the church now accepts this "theology of the laity," in Newman's day it was premature. The Bishop of Newport accused him of heresy, the pope looked with disfavor upon him, and Monsignor Talbot, private secretary to the pope, began to feel that Newman was probably the "most dangerous man in England."

Rumors spread that Newman was unhappy in his new church, and would soon return to the Anglican fold. To squelch such a newspaper rumor in 1861 Newman replied angrily: "I have not had one moment's wavering of trust in the Catholic Church ever since I was received into her fold. I do hereby profess that Protestantism is the dreariest of possible religions, that the thought of the Anglican service makes me shiver. I should be a consummate fool (to use a mild term) if in my old age I left 'the land flowing with milk and honey' for the city of confusion and the house of bondage."

After nearly two decades as a Roman Catholic, Newman, now in his early sixties, had lived a life of comparative neglect. Henry Manning, converted after he had been, was already a bishop and seemed the likely successor to Cardinal Wiseman. Newman's Oratory near Birmingham never had a large enrollment. When he made statements on doctrine, generally to help his church, he found either isolation or negative comments from church authorities. He seemed destined to be an early bright star that proved to be an ephemeral meteorite.

At this point Charles Kingsley came into Newman's life. Kingsley, Anglican clergyman and professor of modern history at Cambridge, had a vast following because of his novels, poetry, and strong position on social reform. In a review that appeared in *Macmillan's Magazine* in 1863 Kingsley started a storm with an anti-Catholic statement: "Truth for its own sake had never been a virtue with the Roman clergy. Father Newman informs us that it need not be, and on the whole ought not to be — that cunning is the weapon which Heaven has given to the Saints wherewith to withstand the brute male force of the wicked world."

When a friend showed Newman the review, he angrily demanded an apology. Dissatisfied with a semi-retraction from Kingsley, Newman published a pamphlet of self-vindication in February 1864. His appetite whetted, Kingsley responded with a pamphlet called *What, Then, Does Dr. Newman Mean?* Kingsley assumed that Newman was a master with words, but felt that he had nonetheless equivocated and proved Kingsley's point. Worse still, said Kingsley, was Newman's influence on the young men who admired him. He had "injured their straightforwardness and truthfulness," and had spread "misery and shame into many an English home." "The world is not so blind," said Kingsley, "but that it will soon find out an honest man if he will take the trouble of talking and acting like one." Kingsley said that Newman's work in helping write and edit *Lives of the English Saints* had dealt with preposterous alleged miracles by saints — "no such public outrage on historic truth has been perpetrated in this generation." Kingsley also attacked Newman for stating that faith, unaided by works, was sufficient to achieve salvation through Christ.

A bomb of controversy had exploded. People quickly took sides. Alexander Macmillan, the publisher, defended the magazine's position, stating that he felt the review was inoffensive, since everyone knew that Roman Catholics believed truth to be merely "a matter of enactment." On the other hand, R. H. Hutton, a friend of Kingsley and literary editor of *The Spectator*, came out strongly in Newman's defense. He helped sway neutral minds toward Newman's defense.

Newman saw the opportunity for which he had waited for years. Persons of varying religious color had criticized him for not knowing his own mind, or for subtly leading immature minds astray. The time had come for him to clearly and sincerely chart the labyrinthine course his spirit had journeyed in search of religious certitude. So he wrote what has been accepted as one of the world's great spiritual autobiographies, *Apologia Pro Vita Sua*.

This defense of his life was written as weekly pamphlets. For ten weeks Newman worked fervently, often sixteen hours a day, to recall the highlights of his soul's pilgrimage. He checked his facts carefully, having kept copies of letters to and from him. He learned to know his own mind better as he clarified the reason for changes in his position on key issues. As in the book on development of doctrine, the writing confirmed his conviction that his progress had been inevitable, logical, and correct.

"I must now give the true key to my whole life," said Newman. "I must show what I am, that it may be seen what I am not. For twenty years and more I have borne an imputation. I have not set myself to remove it, first, because I never had an opening to speak, and next, because I never saw in them [his critics] a disposition to hear. I am bound now as a duty to myself, to the Catholic priesthood, to give account of myself without any delay, when I am so rudely charged with untruthfulness."

Like a gifted rhetorician, Newman defined his audience. It was not Kingsley, who had simply given him an opening. His real challenge was "the bias of the court," the anti-Catholic atmosphere that prevailed in England. He felt he had to overturn "the plausible but cruel conclusion that it is more likely that one should be to blame than that many should be mistaken in blaming him."

To vindicate his own name, Newman gives a very detailed account of how he acquired each of his major religious beliefs. Since in his early period he had been strongly opposed to the Roman church, he openly confesses the reasons for his opposition. He shows an early sympathy for many Catholic concepts, and a hope that Anglicans will see these concepts as worthy of not only preservation but augmentation.

As his reading, preaching, and writing present him with unsolved theological problems, he searches for solutions and increasingly finds the best ones in the Roman church. Finally, in the 1844–1845 period, he satisfies himself that only that church can feed his spiritual hunger. Without rancor he explains how what some people interpreted as evasion or duplicity was simply the process of keeping options open, of weighing alternate explanations to see which seemed to be more convincing. An utterly honest mind is revealed as it sincerely seeks to find God's light in a darkening world. To allay rumors of his discontent, Newman says that since turning Catholic he had lived in perfect peace and contentment, "like coming into port after a rough sea."

After having defended himself, Newman turns his attention to demonstrating that the whole Roman Catholic system was "in no sense dishonest," as Kingsley had alleged it to be. His defense of the church grows out of his analysis of the condition of modern human society, and of how God's will can help save mankind from the perilous direction in which it is headed.

Man's sinfulness makes the world ever worse, he says, and thus it takes a powerful agency of God to fight the Satan who seems to be winning converts every hour. The church, as God's instrument, needs great power in order to confront the powerful enemy. "She has it in charge to rescue human nature from its misery, not simply by restoring it on its own level, but by lifting it up to a higher level than its own. For this end a renovating grace was put into her hands. She goes on to insist that all true conversion must begin with the first springs of thought, and to teach that each individual must be in his own person one whole and perfect temple of God, while he is also one of the living stones which build up a visible religious community."

When Christ tells you to be born again, Newman says, "your whole nature must be re-born; your passions, affections, aims, conscience, and will must all be bathed in a new element, and reconsecrated to your Maker—and last, not the least, your intellect."

Newman answers charges against the Roman church. Lest its infallibility be considered whimsical, Newman shows how each tentative new doctrine is carefully weighed at countless lower levels so that by the time it reaches the top, for a decision, reason and faith have intermingled in its formulation many times. When it censures books, silences authors, or forbids discussion, although it must be obeyed, "perhaps in process of time it will tacitly recede from its own injunctions."

Of course history shows that it has misused its power—the divine treasure is in earthen vessels. But what authority has not been misused at some time? "We live in a wonderful age," proclaims Newman. The growth of secular knowledge is so rapid as to bewilder us, and what is more, it will continue to grow at a faster rate. New discoveries upset and impinge upon religious truths, but the Roman Catholic Church will carefully work out anew positions of faith for believers to follow.

Newman's position regarding liberals had changed. Although some are atheistic or anti-religious, some are sincere and humane but confused, and the church should continue to appeal to them for conversion.

Newman shows that charges of deceitfulness levied against the church grow out of ignorance, malice, or human frailty. Sometimes the church is criticized when it uses economy—a short form of teaching for initial simplicity. Seekers should probe deeper to learn the fuller version of doctrines which may seem on the surface to be simplistic.

Newman affixed several appendices to his book, one of which contained letters of support on behalf of 558 Roman Catholic clergy in England, about one-half of the total. He wished to demonstrate that although several prominent Catholics had attacked him, the majority believed that he was not only a genuine Catholic but one whose views the Church should listen to.

Although not all reviewers applauded the book, most did, including many non-Catholics. The generally hostile *Saturday Review* said: "An unjustifiable imputation cast on Dr. Newman by a popular writer has produced one of the most interesting works of the age. Dr. Newman is one of the finest masters of language, his logical powers are almost unequalled, and he has influenced the course of English thought more perhaps than any of his contemporaries."

Kingsley was never heard from again on this issue. When he died, Newman said a mass for his soul, remarking, "Much less could I feel any resentment against him, when he was accidentally the instrument, in the good Providence of God, of vindicating my character and conduct."

For years Newman had wanted to install an Oratory at Oxford, particularly now that religious tests were no longer required for admission. But Manning, now the church authority as Archbishop of Westminster, felt it risky to encourage young Catholics to attend a "free-thinking" university, so with Monsignor Talbot's help, Newman was blocked. Said Talbot, "Every Englishman is naturally anti-Roman. Dr. Newman is more English than the English. His spirit must be crushed." When aroused laity protested, Talbot responded, "What is the province of the laity? To hunt, to shoot, to entertain. Keep the laity in order," he warned Manning. Ironically, hundreds of colleges all over the world now have Newman centers as havens for devout Catholic students!

As the pope was losing his temporal power to the Italian government in 1870, the doctrine of papal infallibility on spiritual matters was approved by the church. Although Newman disliked the doctrine, he defended it against an attack by Gladstone, the former and future prime minister. Newman assured Gladstone and other Protestants that Catholics would be loyal citizens to their countries, since the pope's infallibility dealt only with matters of faith and morals.

In 1879 Newman from his sickbed heard that the new pope, Leo XIII, wished to make him a cardinal. It stirred him to read of the support given him by the Duke of Norfolk, a leading Catholic layman. "I do not think that any Catholic," said the Duke, "has been listened to by those who are not Catholics with so much attention, respect, and to a great extent sympathy as Newman." Despite the many converts he had been responsible for, the Duke continued, his reputation had been damaged by some apparently well-intentioned people who said that Newman's views were not those of the church. "It appeared to me therefore," he said, "that in the cause both of justice and of truth it was of the utmost importance that the church should put her seal on Newman's work."

Much as he desired the elevation, Newman could not leave his Oratory at Birmingham to live in Rome, a requirement for all cardinals who do not preside over a diocese. But Leo XIII granted an exception, and jubilant Newman finally got his red hat, with all the acceptance it signified.

Cardinal Newman lived on for more than a decade. Nearly 90, he heard that some Protestant employers required their Catholic employees to attend daily Protestant instruction. When the parish priest's protests were ignored, Newman visited the owners and succeeded in getting them to set up separate Catholic instruction groups. "If I can but do work such as that," he said proudly, "I am happy and content to live on."

He died of lung congestion on August 11, 1890. At a solemn requiem for him in London Cardinal Manning, forgetting past differences, spoke for many when he said: "We have lost our greatest witness to the Faith. No living man has so changed the religious thought of England. No one who does not intend to be laughed at will henceforward say that the Catholic religion is fit only for weak intellects and unmanly brains. Whether Rome canonizes him or not, he will be canonized in the thoughts of pious people of many creeds in England. The history of our land will hereafter record the name of John Henry Newman among the greatest of her people, as a confessor for the Faith, a great teacher of men, a preacher of justice, of piety and of compassion. May we all follow him in his life, and may our end be painless and peaceful like his."

# 7

## *The Tormented Soul of Nikolai Gogol*

People envied him. With the great Russian poets Pushkin and Lermontov dead as a result of duels, Nokolai Gogol had assumed the role as Russia's leading writer. His play *The Inspector General*, performed before the czar, was acclaimed Russia's greatest comedy. His novel *Dead Souls* was called Russia's best fictional work by the impressive critic Vissarion Belinsky. Russian readers eagerly awaited the sequel to *Dead Souls*, which would show the positive aspects of Russian life. By the age of 35 Gogol had a most promising future facing him.

It had not been an easy climb to fame. The dwarfish, long-nosed Ukrainian boy had been mocked by his schoolmates and ignored by girls. Editors regularly returned his early writings, sometimes with caustic comments. His father's death cut away his financial base, and as the only boy, Nikolai was expected to help support the family. Writing seemed an unlikely economic asset, at first.

But Gogol had a shrewdly observing eye, and had a way of phrasing that at once brought out life's ridiculousness and contradictions. His portraits were funny, unless you thought about them, in which case their implications bothered you. So there was, after all, a market for this odd writer: the general public would laugh at the grotesque caricatures, and the intelligentsia would hail the penetrating satire implicit in the gallery of exaggerated personages. By 1844 Gogol was recognized as an outstanding writer of realism, humor, and eccentricity.

Within himself, however, Gogol was undergoing a tumultuous upheaval. His early goal of literary fame was being replaced by a searing religious search which threatened to destroy his great creativity. "The soul is now my only concern," he wrote to his friend, Mrs. Alexandra Smirnov. "If my soul does not strive to attain absolute perfection, all my abilities will become paralyzed. Without this spiritual education every work of mine, though perhaps significant for a time, will be essentially meaningless."

To be a great writer, he now felt, one must first be a great person. And how does one achieve moral perfection? Knowing that we are blind to our own imperfections, he asked his friends to show him his weaknesses.

166

To his mother he wrote: "Rebukes are good for the soul. I'd give a lot to hear people abusing me."

He asked friends to keep a diary of his faults, listing dates and circumstances, and then report their findings to him, so that he could mend his behavior. "Help me now," he told his friend Stepan Shevyrev, "and when I have grown stronger and more intelligent, it will be my turn to help you."

He said to another friend, the poet-translator Vasily Zhukovsky, that his spiritual education consisted in conscious withdrawal from the world, hour by hour. "I have become a better man than the one imprinted on the memory of my friends," he stated. "The heavenly powers will help me to mount the ladder which has been set aside for me. Only then will I have the strength to begin my real work; only then will the riddle of my existence be solved."

As the pieces of the puzzle fell into place, Gogol began to feel that his real calling was not so much as a writer but as a spiritual guide. God had selected him to understand and solve other people's problems, he felt. To fail to follow his advice would be to disobey God.

He now saw life's meaning for him: he was God's messenger, appointed to lead individuals into spiritual reform, and as a summation of individual reform, Russia would again be God's country and its myriad problems would be solved. Friends complained that he quoted the Bible as a cookbook, with a recipe for every malady he identified in them.

The discovery in early 1844 of *The Imitation of Christ* by Thomas à Kempis so excited Gogol that he sent copies of it to his friends. He told them it would alleviate the torment of their souls, as it had done for him. The book would help them achieve an inner peace, a retreat from the din and confusion of life. One of his friends, Sergey Aksakov, responded angrily: "I read Thomas à Kempis before you were born. I fear mysticism like the plague, and it is rearing its head in you. I loathe moral recipes. You are walking on a razor's edge. I fear the artist will suffer."

Gogol felt that Aksakov's lack of Christian humility was the devil's work, so he gave Aksakov advice on how to handle the evil one: "Slap him across the muzzle, the nasty animal. From the age of twelve I have never swerved from my main principles. I call the devil devil; I do not clothe him in some splended Byronic garb."

The death of his oldest sister Marya in June 1844 called forth a sermon from Gogol to his mother and three remaining sisters: "My sister has paid for her earthly errors with suffering. God sent suffering into her life in order to lighten her burden in the next world. Misfortune is sent to us in order that we shall look into ourselves. Be therefore more vigilant toward yourselves. Our enemy, our tempter, never sleeps. He will open up a path to your heart by appealing to your little weaknesses—sloth, idleness."

When the family resented his preachment, Gogol agreed to remain silent on one condition—that they retain his letter and read it as a breviary each day during the first week in Lent. "Whoever loves me must perform

Nikolai Gogol. (Courtesy Brown Brothers.)

what I demand," he told them. After all, he explained, the letter was so pregnant with meaning that it would take repeated exposures to it to get its full force.

Having discovered his role as divinely-appointed adviser, Gogol undertook as his chief project the spiritual education of Alexandra Smirnov. He had her memorize many psalms, for they are "nothing else but the outpourings of a tender and deeply suffering soul, unable to find peace or refuge among men." He would correct her slightest mistake in reciting the psalms.

She was the beautiful and vivacious wife of a high Russian official, who seemed to neglect her. Gogol liked being near her. Able to resist her charm, he tried to teach her to stop flirting and to be unaware of her beauty. In April 1844 he told her, "You are still too ready to let yourself to be drawn by passion. God demands total impassiveness of us and will reveal Himself only in serenity."

He admonished her that she seemed too eager to engage in carnal conversation. "Have you not even incited others to engage in this type of conversation?" he asked. He assured her, however, that she was making some progress. "Remember that we have only recently discovered the language that enables us to understand each other," he told her. "A time will come when your soul will thirst for reproach as for fresh water."

She thanked him for his criticism. "It is not very likely that another Nikolai can be found in this life," she told him. "My soul is open to no one as to you. You have seen it in all its black nakedness. May God preserve me from showing it to anyone else."

In November 1844 she wrote to him: "Pray for me, a sinner, who loves you so much, so much. You know the human heart. Look at the bottom of mine and tell me if you do not see some baseness there. You will not be able to abandon me so soon; you are more necessary than ever to me."

But a great change was occurring in Gogol's life. He was seeking God, he was revising his scale of values, and he was turning his back on worldly acclaim. In June 1844 he chided his friend Alexander Danilevsky: "You have not yet begun to live an inner life. No, you have not yet felt the mysterious and terrifying significance of the word 'Christ'."

Was Gogol about to plunge into a spiritual abyss, alienating friends while seeking God? Would his religious search vitiate his literary creativity? Would he soon lose his reason and then his life as a price of his search for God? Was he indeed living on the razor's edge? What sort of background had produced this bizarre humorist and soul-searcher?

Gogol's father, Vassily, had a vision of the Virgin Mary when he was thirteen years old. The Virgin pointed to a baby, saying, "This is to be thy wife." When Vassily saw his neighbor's seven-month old girl he knew she was to be his betrothed. Throughout her childhood he gave Maria presents and married her when she was fourteen.

Their first two children were stillborn. Maria, deeply religious, offered special prayers before the icon of St. Nicholas, asking for a son. Nikolai was born on March 19, 1809, at Sorochintsy in the Ukrainian province of Poltava.

Vassily Gogol owned 3,000 acres of land and 384 serfs. His father had succeeded in getting the family entered into the nobility register. A successful farmer, Vassily sponsored the village fair and acted in amateur theatricals. He also wrote some verses and several comedies. A sociable person, he seems to have had relatively little influence upon Nikolai.

Worried about Nikolai's health, Maria pampered him from the start. To insure his health, she built a chapel, paying for it by selling the family silver. But Nikolai continued to be sickly. He had asthma, fainting spells, and tantrums caused by scrofula, which left him slightly deaf. Maria petted him, worried about him, and made the sign of the cross over his head.

Maria believed in premonition, and sometimes her dreams forebode disaster to her. She did her best to transfer her intense religious convictions to Nikolai. Of her twelve children, five survived childhood, but he remained her favorite. She described the Last Judgment to him so vividly that he anxiously coveted the bliss awaiting the virtuous, and feared the eternal suffering of the unrighteous. She made Hell look so dreadful to him that he would awake from a dream howling in terror.

Nikolai later described her to a friend: "She does things she never intended doing and, thinking of her children's happiness, makes them unhappy and then puts the whole blame on God, saying that it was God's will that this should happen." Nikolai's own theology bore close resemblance to his mother's.

In his early years Nikolai was tutored by a divinity student. At the age of ten he attended school in Poltava. A year later he was sent to a public school at Nyezhin, about 200 miles from his home, where he attended from 1821 to 1828. His Latin teacher described him as a silent, lazy fair-haired boy, secretive, "as though hiding something in his soul."

Nikolai was overly sensitive about his physical appearance. Classmates called him the "Mysterious Dwarf." When razzed about his long slanty nose, he would defend himself by caustic epithets and epigrams. Resenting the pedantic atmosphere of the classroom, he became insolent toward teachers. He liked to play pranks, such as stuffing a cone of snuff into a sleeping boy's nose, and howling with glee when the boy awoke, frightened and confused.

Once, to escape punishment at school, Nikolai feigned madness. He tossed furniture around, rolled on the floor, and attacked the headmaster. He was placed in a sanitorium for two months. Every time the school doctor checked upon his condition, Nikolai would throw a tantrum. He later admitted it was all a bluff.

As he looked back on his childhood, Gogol admitted that he outwardly paraded vanity as a cloak for a deep inferiority feeling. Like all teenagers, he badly needed peer acceptance. Feeling his classmates despised him, he would intentionally pick a quarrel and be told off — then he seemed relieved to know that his fears had been justified, because they really did dislike him.

Although he learned rapidly, schoolwork bored him. The only part of the curriculum that appealed to him was dramatics. He loved to act, especially in women's parts. The role disguise of the theater gave him a chance to lose that personality that was always being ridiculed. If people laughed at the character he portrayed, they were not really laughing at him. When they applauded, however, he felt that they were applauding him.

His favorite teacher, Nikolai Belousov, taught a course dealing with human rights, during the time that the Decembrists were pressing for constitutional government as Russia was trying to decide who would succeed Czar Alexander I. Belousov was popular with Gogol and his classmates for preaching the revolutionary doctrine that the freedom of human personality was inviolable, even by the government. When the government exiled Belousov, the students protested. Even here, however, Gogol's protest was based more on moral than on political grounds.

Throughout his lonely life, Gogol's one unswerving source of comfort was God. A teacher's scolding, a personal rebuff, even a head cold — all were part of God's divine plan. By ostracizing him his classmates were unwittingly obeying God's will, he felt.

A severe test of faith came at the age of sixteen when his father died. His one brother also had died. Gogol asked himself why God was giving him such trials. At first he contemplated suicide, but he feared the cold black hole of death. As his faith returned he realized he would now have to play the role of masculine leader of the family. So he wrote his mother a letter of Christian consolation, pointing out that even when we cannot understand God's ways we know they are best for us.

Determined to make a name for himself as a writer, Gogol moved to the capital, St. Petersburg, in December 1828. He auditioned as an actor at the Bolshoi Theater, but was turned down. Failing to find a publisher for his long poem, "Hans Kuechelgarten," which described a young German's lament at the recent Turkish desecration of the Acropolis in Athens, Gogol published it, under a pseudonym, at his own expense. When critics properly called it sentimental and puerile, he made the rounds of book stores, collected all unsold copies, and burned them. He had a mania for burning bothersome manuscripts, as if he could expunge them from his memory through fire.

In despair, he fled abroad. He used the money his mother had sent for mortgage payments to pay travel costs. He told her that he needed to visit health spas, and that he was fleeing from an affair with a prostitute. These were lies, of course. He spent six weeks in Germany, Denmark, and Sweden, but realized he would have to go back to Russia and get a job.

He could not understand his own motivation. "Why has God," he asked, "having created an honest soul which is burning with ardent love for everything that is exalted and beautiful, why has He given him such a crude exterior? Why had He clothed it all in such a terrible mixture of contradictions, stubbornness, arrogant self-confidence and the most abject humility? But my mortal reason is powerless to grasp the great designs of Providence."

Humbled, he confessed to his mother, "I have a bad character and have been spoiled. I must transform myself." Despite having several influential friends, he could not get a government job. "Utterly incapable people," he said, "who have no one to put in a good word for them, easily obtain what I could not obtain with the aid of my patrons. Is not that a clear indication of God's will? Are not all my failures meant as a punishment to lead me on to the right path?"

Finally Gogol landed a minor job at the imperial chancery. He also made a few rubles writing stories and doing translations. He became a friend of the poet and translator, Vasily Zhukovsky, who introduced him to Peter Pletnyev, supervisor of the Patriotic Institute for Young Ladies, a boarding school for wealthy girls. Pletnyev gave Gogol a job as history teacher at the institute. Not only did the position pay 400 rubles a year, but it raised Gogol's civil-service rank from grade 14 to grade 9. Gogol was elated. "How grateful I am to the divine Right Hand for the failures and troubles I have endured," he said. "What peace there is now in my heart."

Pletnyev also secured private pupils for Gogol to tutor, and more important, introduced him to the great poet Pushkin. Inflamed by his nearness to Pushkin, Gogol told his mother to address letters to him at Tsarskoye Selo as follows: "To His High Nobility Alexander Sergeyevich Pushkin, for N. V. Gogol."

Pushkin invited Gogol to write stories for *The Contemporary Review*, which he edited. Gogol was pleased, but he resented Pushkin's editorial revisions. In the summer of 1831 the two writers met almost daily. In September Gogol published a collection of short stores called *Evenings on a Farm near Dikanka*.

Pushkin praised the stories, saying that even the type-setters had laughed at Gogol's humor. "I find them entrancing," he said. "There is real gaiety, sincere and spontaneous, without affectation or gimmickry! And what poetry — what sensitivity! It is all so new in our literature that I cannot believe my eyes."

Gogol was perverse concerning criticism of his work. When critics panned him, he resented it, but perhaps not so much as when he was praised. He had high standards for himself. He knew his work was imperfect — to please God he would have to try harder. His dissatisfaction with these stories that mingled pictures of real life with fantasy and rich folklore was that they lacked an important social or moral message.

Most critics liked the odd assortment of Ukrainian goblin stories. At the early age of 23, Gogol had found literary fame. He quickly followed with a second volume of tales in May 1832. These too sold well and were received well by the critics.

To please Pushkin, Gogol re-read Molière, and found great significance in the French satirist. He was coming increasingly to trust Pushkin's judgment. The two were a strange pair: Pushkin, a lover of women and gambling, lived at a whirlwind pace, abandoning himself to his natural impulses — Gogol, who never loved a woman, had a morbid conscience concerning what God would permit one to do. But Pushkin served as a creative catalyst to Gogol, and as a result the development of Russian fiction moved from Pushkin's *Tales of Belkin* through Gogol's works to the masterpieces of Dostoevsky, Tolstoy, and Turgenev.

For all his religiosity, he rarely attended church in Russia. When his mother criticized him for this, his response was that God was everywhere, not just in churches, and that he communicated with God all day long.

For a time Gogol aspired to be a historian. He planned to build a course of lectures around a series of synchronistic tables he had compiled. He was aware of geography's influence on history, and he believed that folk literature revealed more about people than did their official chronicles. He was amused that "trivial causes sometimes lead to great events" and that "great undertakings sometimes lead to trivial conclusions." Life seemed indeed paradoxical.

On the strength of his plan to write a nine-volume history of the Ukraine, relating it to outside world history, he was offered a lectureship in medieval history at the university in St. Petersburg. His university teaching career was a disaster. After a brilliant opening lecture, he had nothing else to offer. He knew little about the subject. He missed two out of three lectures, giving students reading assignments instead of class. When he came to class he often wore a black handkerchief around his cheek, as if having a toothache. He let colleagues conduct oral examinations, lest his ignorance of the field be confirmed. Turgenev, a student of his, said that Gogol was original but ill-informed.

In July 1835 he lost his job at the Patriotic Institute for Young Ladies, because of excessive absences. By the end of the year he was also forced to resign his university post.

Laziness, however, had not been the deterrent from his teaching — he had been writing constantly for several years. In 1835 he published two volumes of miscellaneous prose called *Arabesques* and two volumes of stories called *Mirgorod*. He had also written a play, *Marriage*, and had begun to work on his two greatest works, *The Inspector General* and *Dead Souls*. He had also begun a play about King Alfred, showing how a wise and virtuous Christian monarch should govern. This play was never completed.

The novelette *Taras Bulba*, published in *Mirgorod*, is a swashbuckling tale of adventure as Orthodox Cossacks fight Roman Catholic

Poles in a quasi-historical account. It took Gogol six years to finish *Taras Bulba*, for he believed in constantly altering his text. The progressive revisions show that he grew increasingly intolerant of any religious position but that of the Russian Orthodox Church. Taras admonishes his comrades, "Let us drink first of all to the holy orthodox faith, to the time when it will at last spread all over the world and everywhere there will be only one holy faith." In October 1835 Gogol asked Pushkin for a plot for a comedy. Pushkin told him of an editor in Bessarabia who had been mistaken for a government inspector and had been treated royally in a corrupt town. Pushkin said a similar thing had happened to him recently in Nizhny Novgorod. Pushkin was perhaps somewhat reluctant to surrender the plot, telling a friend, "You must be on your guard with that Little Russian; he skins me so adroitly that I never even have time to call for help."

The plot had been used before. The German dramatist August Kotzebue, the Ukrainian novelist Gregory Kvitka-Osnovyanenko, and the Moscow journalist Nicholas Polevoy had all used it, Polevoy even calling his play, written in 1832, *The Inspector General*. But Gogol seems not to have drawn upon them much for his details.

Gogol's play, *The Inspector General*, appeared in 1836. In it the oafish rascal Khlestakov is thought to be an awaited inspector, in disguise, and is appropriately wined and dined. Each division head of the city government admits his corruption but points an accusing finger at seemingly worse corruption in other divisions. The delightful exposé of universal civic corruption, played marvelously by Danny Kaye in the movie version, also has romance as the Mayor's wife and daughter vie for the affections of Khlestakov. In the final tableau the real inspector arrives, and the crooked officials stand hapless, awaiting their judgment.

The big question was, how could a satire on governmental corruption get past the censors? Pushkin and Zhukovsky got pretty Alexandra Smirnov to intervene personally with Czar Nicholas I. She had similarly appealed on Pushkin's behalf to get his *Boris Godunov* approved. Once again it worked, and the czar even attended the first performance. At first he laughed at the slapstick, but by the end of the play he grew restive over the satire on provincial government. "Everyone has caught it," he said, "but I have caught it more than anyone." Nevertheless he ordered many of his top ministers to see the play and he sent Gogol 800 rubles three days later; he frequently approved other monetary grants to Gogol in later years.

Reaction, pro and con, was vehement. Gogol, who believed in loyalty to the czar, said he was not trying to alter society's institutions but simply shame corrupt officials out of their dishonest behavior. He insisted that his goal was not political but moral reform.

Conservatives attacked the play, saying that provincial Russia was not that corrupt, or if so, Russia was no worse than other countries. Anyhow this was nothing to laugh about—if Gogol had a serious purpose in mind, he should not have written comedy.

Young Vissarion Belinsky, seeing Gogol as "a great comic painter of real life," applauded the play, noting that beneath the comic surface lay a scathing indictment of universal governmental corruption.

"Now I realize," Gogol continued, "what it means to be a comic writer. The least sign of truth and not one man but all classes of the population rise up against you. It is grievous to see people whom you love with a brotherly love attacking you." He shook his head sadly. "To say of a rogue that he is a rogue is considered to be undermining the foundations of the state." As with many great comic writers, Gogol saw comedy as a moral force. Seeing images on stage, he felt, people will avoid ludicrous behavior lest they be ridiculed. Laughter not merely produces pleasure, but it also serves as a lid against excessive and anti-social behavior.

There was a kind of naive honesty in Gogol's approach. Since he had seen stupidity in high places, he thought it was fair game for his pen. He almost adopted the perverse view that there was a direct relationship between stupidity and governmental promotion. "Only when one is angry does one tell the truth," he now believed.

As he had done previously, Gogol fled abroad. From Germany he wrote to Zhukovsky: "My present removal from my homeland has been imposed upon me from above, by that same Providence which has sent every other obstacle in my path for my edification." But he now felt confident of his literary ability. He told Zhukovsky: "I swear I shall do something that no ordinary man could do. I feel a lion's strength in my soul and I can almost hear the transition from childhood to manhood."

In 1837 in Paris Gogol heard of Pushkin's death. Love rivalry had led Pushkin into a fatal duel. Gogol was deeply grieved. "All the joy of my life has disappeared," he said. "I never undertook anything without his advice. I never wrote a single line without imagining him before me. I am broken-hearted." Now, more than ever, he did not want to return to Russia, the country which had treated Pushkin so badly, he believed.

In Paris he met the Polish poet Adam Mickiewicz, and struck up a warm friendship with him. Gogol's favorite spot in Paris was the home of Alexandra Smirnov, who found it refreshing to be with a man who did not fawn at her beauty. His exaggerations she accepted as the price of a creative imagination. She found herself increasingly confiding in him and seeking his advice.

In March 1837 Gogol went to Italy. The country instantly appealed to him. "Everywhere else I have seen things changing," he said. "Here everything has stopped dead." To him, the city was an apt blend of classical and Christian cultures. Also, art and faith were the highest priorities rather than the trivialities of politics. The religious art and architecture were a constant feast. Like Russia, he felt a dominating aura of salvation. A convert to Roman Catholicism, Princess Zinaida Volkonsky, tried to persuade Gogol to take on the church of Rome but he demurred, stating that the two forms of Catholicism were really one, beneath the surface.

In Rome his friend Alexander Ivanov spent years working on a single painting. This Gogol understood, saying, "An artist whose work has been transformed by the will of God into a truly spiritual effort is incapable of any other task." He posed for a figure in Ivanov's painting and was given the privileged position closest to Christ. Ivanov also made other drawings and paintings of Gogol.

Ivanov's masterpiece reminded Gogol of what he himself was now at work on—a novel involving the purchase of the title to dead serfs. Once again the plot had come from Pushkin. Near Pushkin's estate a clever swindler had bought the title to dead serfs whose names would not be removed from official records until the next census. Armed with his purchase deeds, he would mortgage the dead serfs at the state bank at the rate for live serfs, reaping a good profit thereby. Gogol had been overjoyed when Pushkin abandoned the idea of writing a verse comedy on the subject and gave the plot to him. Even the title pleased Gogol: *Dead Souls*.

Gogol had written four chapters before leaving Russia. Now he was busily engaged in working on what he called his epic. The project consumed all of his time; he was happy. He felt as if he was responding to a high call. He said, "Everything I see is Russian: landowners, civil sevants, officers, muzhiks, izbas—in a word, the whole of Orthodox Russia. The novel is huge, and will not be finished for a long time. It will create a host of new enemies for me. But an invisible hand etches the words before my eyes with the tip of its omnipotent scepter. I know my name will fare better in posterity than in my lifetime."

To live, Gogol counted on help from friends. He asked Zhukovsky, who tutored the czarevich, to request a government pension from the czar. Zhukovsky made the appeal, and got the czar to send Gogol 5,000 rubles. Gogol sang fulsome praise of Alexander I, and was roundly criticized by liberals for being a boot-licker.

Feeling the need of a first-hand experience with Russia again, Gogol returned home. But in Russia his muse vanished—he now knew that the proper place to write his masterpiece would be in Rome. Needing travel money, he once again appealed to Zhukovsky. This time the czarevich provided a grant of 4,000 rubles.

Spring of 1838 found Gogol back in Rome, exuberant with the balmy weather and the progress he was making on *Dead Souls*. But as the hot summer came on the inspiration for writing vanished. Fortunately his lifelong friend, Alexander Danilevsky, was with him, and Danilevsky's presence cheered him immensely. When Danilevsky's money was stolen in Paris, Gogol got friends to send him a replacement of 2,000 rubles. Perhaps feeling their relationship was getting too close, Danilevsky left Gogol, and Gogol was heartsick. He immediately transferred his affection to a new friend, the 23-year-old Count Joseph Vyelgorsky, who was dying of tuberculosis. Admiring Joseph's calm acceptance of his fate, Gogol was his constant bedside companion until Joseph's death in May 1839.

Gogol now began working on his famous story, "The Overcoat," which grew out of a true story he had heard in 1832: a poor clerk, after many sacrifices, finally buys a hunting rifle, loses it on his first hunt, and is sorely distressed—but fortunately his friends buy him a new rifle. Gogol made a number of changes. In the first place, the desired object is not a luxury but a necessity, a coat; the object is stolen, not lost; there are no compassionate friends to help him; he does not recover, but dies; and finally, the actual account is prolonged by a supernatural addition.

The hero of Gogol's tale, Bashmachkin, is absurdly pathetic. In Russian, a bashmach is a carpet slipper; everyone walks on him. But the pathos is genuine. Dostoevsky said, "We all came out of Gogol's 'Overcoat'!"

Again he visited Russia, and again he felt estranged. In October 1839 he attended a performance of *The Inspector General* in Moscow. At the end of the play when the audience called the customary "Author!" he ran off, frightened. The audience felt snubbed. The next day Gogol invented the improbable explanation that he had just received bad news from home and had to leave in haste.

Gogol had long been working on a historical play dealing with the Ukraine, but he could not finish it. This bothered him, his health worsened, and he started concocting weird notions about his body. He told one friend that a doctor in Paris had told him his stomach was upside down, and that the irregular shape of his head brought on illness.

Needing money, he got a loan of 4,000 rubles from the writer-editor Mikhail Pogodin. Another friend, Pavel Annenkov, visited him in Rome, and Gogol dictated to him several chapters of *Dead Souls*. Finishing the account of the moldy miser Plyushkin, Gogol felt so light-headed that he began doing a Ukrainian folk-dance with an umbrella. When he twirled the umbrella so violently that it broke in two, he finished the dance with the umbrella handle as his partner.

As Chichikov travels the countryside buying the title to dead serfs in this picaresque novel, he finds it hard to make economical purchases. Each landowner, representing a universal trait in human nature, is clever enough to bargain upward on the purchase price of the serfs. So the reversal occurs, the confidence man is conned.

Gogol explained that the writing of *Dead Souls* was a type of cathartic for him. "None of my readers ever suspected that when they laughed at my heroes they were laughing at me," he said. "In me, there was no outstanding vice that overshadowed all the rest, just as I had no shining virtues. I did, however, possess a complete collection of every possible nastiness, but all in small doses. God gave me a personality in which there was a little of everything."

He then explained how he built his characters. "This is how it worked: I would take one of my failings and pursue it by placing it in a different station in life. I sought to picture it in the features of some mortal enemy who had cruelly offended me; I struck at him with everything I could lay hold of. Already I have divested myself of many of my faults by passing them on to my heroes, have ridiculed the faults in them, and forced other to laugh at them."

In August 1841 Gogol left Rome for Russia, hoping to get his novel through the censors. But the Moscow censors turned down the book. "How can there be dead souls?" raged the committee chairman. "Everyone knows that the soul is immortal!" When it was explained to him that the term applied to serfs, he insisted there could be no criticism of the institution of serfdom. When corrected again he replied that to portray a swindler would encourage crime. Another censor objected that a price of 2½ rubles for a serf was an insult to human dignity — the price should be higher. Gogol could see little hope for his book to be published.

In desperation, Gogol turned for help to the critic Belinsky. Belinsky had early championed Gogol as a critic of the existing regime, but he was angry at Gogol for consorting with such Slavophiles as Mikhail Pogodin and Sergey Aksakov, whom Belinsky considered to be weak-kneed stooges for the czar.

With a friend's help, Belinsky got the book passed by the St. Petersburg censorship. Gogol had to make a few changes, and the title was changed to *The Adventures of Chickikov*. The novel was published on May 21, 1842.

Once again critical reaction was extravagant in both directions. The exiled Alexander Herzen said, "His portraits are amazingly successful; life is shown in all its fulness." Belinsky called it "an immortal masterpiece," profound at every level of thought. Aksakov raved over it, and his son Konstantin said it deserved comparison with Homer and Shakespeare.

Most conservatives, however, resented the book as a gross distortion. One called it "a caricature of Russian reality," and another tore it apart on grammatical grounds. All agreed that its presentation was one-sided, ignoring the positive facets of Russian life.

Reflecting upon the criticism, Gogol reluctantly agreed that his picture of Russian life had been largely negative, showing swindlers and undesirable characters. So he promised to write a sequel to the novel, in which he would focus on the optimistic aspects of Russia. He would show good people working hard to create a better world. He felt confident that since God was so close to him, He would show him how to portray the wondrous beauty of a Russian woman's sacrificial spirit, Russian men endowed with superhuman valor, and the untold riches of the Russian soul. Scoffed Belinsky: "You promise too much. Your patriotism has captured your reason."

His two plays, *Marriage* and *The Gamblers*, were performed in Moscow in 1843, but drew small crowds and thus produced little revenue for Gogol. Also that year a four-volume collected edition of his works was published, but since sales lagged so did income to the author. When royalties did arrive, instead of paying his debts to friends, he set up funds for needy students. Angry, Pogodin got revenge by publishing some of Gogol's works in the journal he edited.

Now it was Gogol's turn to be irate. He complained not only about his works being used without his permission but also of Pogodin's use of a portrait showing Gogol in a dressing gown, with uncombed hair and a moustache. "What will young people do but imitate my worst traits, that I gave up years ago?" screamed Gogol.

Pogodin now accused Gogol of hypocrisy, coldness, and lying. Aksakov agreed, saying that "even with his friends Gogol was never entirely honest."

Gogol was growing apart from his friends but he felt closer to God. He prized the icon which Archbishop Innocent had given him, considering it to be a sign that God had chosen him to do some great work. "Now I must go to visit the tomb of Our Lord," he said. He realized that his friends now accused him of ingratitude and coldness. But he told Alexandra Smirnov: "Since I have left Russia, a major change has taken place within me. The soul has become my only concern."

In 1843 he wrote to Danilevsky that in maturity one no longer lives by impressions but realizes that the soul has only one true harbor, God. Because his earlier writings had been done before he received this awareness, he now repudiated them as sinful.

He believed that the violent political poems written by his friend Nikolai Yazykov came straight from God. The poems attacked Westernizers like Belinsky. Later Gogol pleaded with Yazykov to try to find some middle ground in the warfare between Slavophiles and Westernizers.

The closer Gogol felt to a person, the more obliged he felt to give the person spiritual advice. He lectured Yazykov, who was dying of tuberculosis, on the subject of prayer. Prayer, said Gogol, is ecstasy for God. We give ourselves to His service by first discovering our God-given talents, and then asking His help on how to use them. As God provides the way, we get filled with enthusiasm. Suddenly everything becomes clear to a writer: one's subject, its deep inner meaning, how to develop it. Now all one has to do is pick up a pen and the hand writes the story.

The believer, said Gogol, realizes that even his misfortunes are God-sent. "The cry coming from your heart is destined to be the crucible of your poetry," he told Yazykov.

But this theory was not working in the production of the sequel to *Dead Souls*. Gogol had prayed to God, and had read three works as a part of his spiritual preparation: The Bible, *The Imitation of Christ* by Thomas à Kempis, and *The Meditations of Marcus Aurelius*. Writing was progressing slowly, despite his careful preparation. He was finding that it was much easier to describe man's ludicrous failings than to depict human character in a virtuous and believable state.

By 1844 his conscience was dividing internally, and punishing him from both sides. His writing, being insincere emperor praise, violated his artistic conscience. But his religious conscience told him that one should accept the czar and the czar's God. Seeing the growing radicalism in Frankfurt that year he pronounced that "people were forgetting that the social order was the will of God."

Occasionally he would burn the manuscript of what he had written as a continuation of *Dead Souls*. This oblation seemed to serve as a burnt offering, penance for past sins, for almost immediately his health would improve considerably.

In one sense, God had answered his prayers—He had sent Alexandra Smirnov back to him. Gogol served as her guide to Rome's art treasures, each day's journey significantly ending at St. Peters. By Easter time, however, he had switched back to the small Orthodox church in the Russian Embassy. If one is to write the great religious work about Russia, one must remain true to her church.

Gogol constantly mentioned his coming pilgrimage to Jerusalem, but habitually postponed it, as if fearful of a disappointing outcome.

He saw Alexandra daily. After a meal together, he would read to her from *The Imitation of Christ*, or an extract from the Church Fathers. He copied psalms for her to memorize. Sometimes he would read from his current work on Part Two of *Dead Souls*. Once, while he was reading, a loud clap of thunder broke out. He stopped. "You see," he said, "God has threatened me. God Himself did not want me to read something unfinished which has not been given my inner approval."

At 32 Alexandra was still a woman of beauty, but she too was in deep inner turmoil. Perhaps her search was for a spiritual beauty to match her physical attractiveness, realizing that the latter was destined to vanish. Her mood quickly changed from clever wit to deep melancholy.

Gogol was disturbed over the pleasure she brought him. He vowed never to touch her, but vows are never easy to keep. He told her how beautiful her soul was, but then condemned himself for seeing more than her soul. Never before had he felt this way in a woman's presence.

As a protection, he berated her for her venal thoughts. He admonished her to live more for God and less for herself. It must have given him bizarre sexual gratification to undress her morally while not laying a hand on her. She could not understand his actions, nor could she understand why she suddenly enjoyed her sublimation of erotic love into divine love. One thing she knew and confessed—he was a good influence upon her, and she was experiencing spiritual growth under his guidance.

One day, in half jest, she told him, "Listen, you are in love with me!" He fled in panic, and stayed away three days. When he returned, he could not drive her phrase out of his mind. It bothered him. Pretty women attracted him, but he felt they were Satan's puppets, and had to be fought off.

Alexandra, however, was no devil. The better he knew her, the more he cared for her—not merely the physical presence, although that could never be wholly ignored, but more the intensity of a soul's search for union with God. If he could succeed in this difficult case of conversion, he felt that his whole changed life would be vindicated.

"She is a pearl among Russian women," he said. "I wonder if anyone possesses sufficient moral strength to esteem her at her true worth. She became my consolation at a time when no one else could have comforted me with words. Our two souls were as close as twin brothers."

So the brink had been reached, and the relationship remained platonic. Yazykov had warned Gogol: "She is nothing but a siren swimming in the transparent waters of seduction." Aksakov thought Gogol loved her passionately, "perhaps because he saw her as a repentant Magdalen and himself as the savior of her soul. Despite his highmindedness and purity, he was not insensitive to the still attractive brilliance and vivacity of the lady."

Gogol's spiritual counseling succeeded on no one else. When he tried it on his family and friends, it backfired, producing estrangement and broken friendships. By October 1844 Gogol was receiving such scathing letters from erstwhile friends as this one from Peter Pletnyev: "You are a devious, selfish, arrogant and suspicious creature who will do anything for fame. You have two kinds of friends: some love you truly, for your talent, and have not grasped anything of your inner self. Such are Zhukovsky, Mrs. Smirnov, Pushkin. The others are the Moscow fraternity: schismatics, pleased to have enlisted a man of genius at their side. They hate truth and enlightenment. Now let us see what you are as a man of letters. An individual endowed with a brilliant creative faculty, the foremost comic author of our time by virtue of your way of looking at man and nature and your ability to extract their most comical aspects; but a monotonous writer, unwilling to take trouble to acquire a conscious mastery of your art, and when your fancy turns from the comic to the serious, improper to the point of bad taste, and pompous to the point of absurdity. You are nothing but a self-taught genius, whose creative faculty dazzles but whose artistic illiteracy and ignorance inspire only pity."

Gogol's reaction to this tongue-lashing was relatively mild. "Why," he asked Pletnyev, "after agreeing that I was an odd, peculiar man, do people demand that I behave like everybody else?" Gogol then said that since he had been wrong to live off friends' gratuities, he would do penance by turning over all of the money from the sale of his works to a fund for deserving university students.

Shevyrev refused to set up the fund, saying that Gogol should first pay off his many debts to friends. Alexandra agreed with Shevyrev, adding that Gogol should also consider making some payments to his mother and sisters. Gogol replied that what he did with his money was none of her business. His money, he said, was a sacred trust, and it would be sinful to use it in any way other than to help students. In fact, he added, if his mother knew how he felt, she would not only return any money sent to her but add some of her own in order to further assist students.

To recover from a severe attack of nerves, Gogol spent six weeks at Ostend in 1844. Here he met Count Alexander Tolstoy who had previously been governor of a Russian province. Tolstoy was a religious bigot who deepened Gogol's lifelong tendency towards religious fanaticism. From this time onward Gogol's sense of humor, which had been the balance wheel keeping him from growing lopsided, vanished, and Gogol began the long journey through the deep narrow religious chasm that had no satisfactory outlet in this world.

As he changed, Gogol reinterpreted his previous works. Part One of *Dead Souls*, he now insisted, had nothing to do with Russian provincial life or serfdom. He said he would reveal its secret meaning in the second part of the novel. Inability to keep this secret helped drive him again to the brink of a nervous breakdown. In January 1845 his doctor sent him to Frankfurt for a thorough rest.

In February he went to Paris, where he read the Church Fathers, studied liturgy, and attended services daily at the Russian church. He began to plan a book called *Meditations on the Divine Liturgy*. He wanted to go to Jerusalem, but felt he would die before he could make the trip. He seemed disinterested to hear that he had been elected to honorary membership of the University of Moscow. He did not know that nearby in Paris Louis Viardot, director of the Italian Theater of Paris, was translating a collection of his stories into French.

In March he received a grant of 3,000 rubles from Czar Nicholas I, "in view of his ailing conditions." Expressing his gratitude to Count Uvarov, Gogol said that all of his writings to date were immature and contemptible. "No wonder the majority of people attach a bad meaning to my works," he confessed.

He wrote to Alexandra in April: "When life becomes too bitter for you, I shall fly through space and appear before you and you will be comforted, for there will be a third person beside us: Christ." He then explained his condition to her: "God has long deprived me of the creative faculty. Until I have been to Jerusalem I shall be incapable of saying anything comforting to anyone in Russia."

By May his health had completely broken down. Doctors differed in their diagnoses: one called it enlarged liver, another called it nervous derangement. On June 4 he wrote to Alexandra: "Every work I do increases my hypochondria. I am in a state of complete physical prostration." By the end of the month he again burned his manuscript for Part Two of *Dead Souls*, and again his health temporarily returned.

As the year ended he drew up his usual balance sheet of accomplishments and was shocked to see how little he had done. In his notebook he wrote: "Lord, bless me at the dawn of this new year. May the Holy Spirit descend upon me, may it sanctify my being by destroying my impurities, my vices, my baseness, and transform me into a temple worthy of Your presence, Lord. My God, my God, do not forsake me!"

In 1846 *The Inspector General* was being revived in Moscow and St. Petersburg. Gogol seized the opportunity to write a new ending to the play, in which the inspector is our conscience, calling us to account in the Last Judgment. Will we be ready, he asked, when God knocks on our door? Aksakov pleaded with him not to publish the new version. "It is from beginning to end a lie and an utter absurdity," he said. "If it is published it will make you the laughing stock of the whole of Russia."

In his new role as spiritual counselor Gogol could not see how obnoxious it was for his family and friends to receive unsought-for advice on how to live near to God. His mind became one-track, obsessed with the idea that these people badly needed his religious tutoring. His many letters to his friends constituted four times as much writing as he had put into the continuation of *Dead Souls*.

He suddenly felt that by selecting certain highlights from the letters he could help show Russia its way to salvation. "What comes out of the soul cannot but be of benefit to the soul," he said. He finally felt he was writing a "sensible and useful" book, since it would show readers how to face adversity, how to put God first in their lives, and other beneficial advice. He told Alexandra that "my book was undertaken for the sole purpose of arousing reverence for everything our Church and our Government have decreed for us by law."

Ironically the censors refused to approve three articles that Gogol thought were crucial to the book's success. Gogol wanted the czar to see the articles, for he felt sure that the czar would approve of them.

Even after excisions Gogol thought his book, called *Selected Passages from My Correspondence with My Friends*, would help his countrymen be better Christians and better patriots. He now believed that progress in society depended upon individual reform. "If each individual would consent to serve Christ in his assigned place, society would progress," he said. Years later Leo Tolstoy came to a similar conclusion.

Gogol's acquiescence to absolute rule was astounding. He now believed that "a state without an absolute monarch is an orchestra without its conductor." Could he really believe that "the more deeply one looks into the workings of the administration, the more one admires the wisdom of its founders"? "God Himself," Gogol continued, "built it through the hands of the sovereigns. Everything is perfect. I cannot conceive what use could be found for even one more official." The final statement unconsciously betrayed Gogol back into truth.

Despite all his anguish from the censor's scissors, Gogol praised censorship. Quoting the great writer and historian Nikolai Karamzin, Gogol said that if a writer's motives are pure, no censor seems harsh. "See how ridiculous are those who claim it is impossible to speak the full and complete truth in Russia," he exclaimed, "and say it can only cause trouble!"

When his book was published with the censor's deletions, Gogol speculated that some evil demons must have been responsible. "Certain mysterious parties of Europeans and Asiatics have united to perplex the censor," he told Count Alexander Tolstoy.

Gogol's illness returned, now accompanied by a partial paralysis. His malaise was magnified enormously at the unfavorable reception accorded his book. The public seemed disgusted at his attacks on even such close friends as Pogodin and Count Alexander Tolstoy. Readers were bored at his banal advice, shocked at his assumption that the Church and Government were infallible, and stupefied at his repudiation and misinterpretation of his own previous works, some of which they knew were masterpieces on grounds completely dissimilar from Gogol's claims for them.

Gogol's friends attacked the book. Aksakov accused him of muddled thinking and contradictory statements: "While thinking of serving God and humanity, you only insult God and humanity." Pogodin was enraged. "How can you call yourself Christian?" he demanded. Christ, he said, told us to judge not, to condemn not, but you do nothing but judge and condemn. You never turn the other cheek — the only person not attacked in the book is yourself! You are insincere, only trying to curry favor from the ruling classes. Pogodin even got Bishop Innocent to admonish Gogol: "Do not parade your piety — it loves the inner room."

Belinsky now said that Gogol was either a Talleyrand or a madman. Aksakov agreed that perhaps it would be most charitable to consider Gogol insane. He told Gogol: If your aim was to cause a scandal, you have succeeded. You have been corrupted by Rome. Your attacks are preposterous, particularly those upon Pogodin.

There were, however, enough lucid passages in the book to indicate that Gogol had not yet lost his reason. There are perceptive analyses of works by such writers as Pushkin, Lermontov, Zhukovsky, Griboedov, and others. Perhaps for this reason Pletnyev went so far as to call the book "the true beginning of Russian literature." Other sensible material in the book included a defense of the stage, a request for common ground between Slavophiles and Westernizers, and a warning against traditional Russian chauvinism: "In Russia we boast before we ever accomplish anything."

Gogol resented being called a Roman Catholic for his views. "I have come to Christ in a protestant rather than in a Catholic way," he asserted. "My analysis of man's soul was the reason for my coming to Christ, for I was first of all amazed at His human wisdom and His hitherto unheard-of knowledge of the soul. It was only afterwards that I worshipped Him."

In one chapter Gogol had given advice to a governor's wife. Alexandra Smirnov's husband had been made governor of the province of Kaluga. Dress simply, Gogol advised her, avoid gossip and unnecessary social calls, set an example for all other women, consult the priest frequently, and "look upon the whole town as a doctor looks upon a hospital." Obedient Alexandra tried following Gogol's advice and was soon the center of malicious intrigues. Ultimately she had a nervous breakdown and had to abandon Gogol's political counsel.

In the pages of *The Contemporary* Belinsky, mortally ill of tuberculosis, raged against Gogol, saying he considered himself "the pope of his little Catholic world." Hurt by Belinsky's review, Gogol objected: "I cannot help being distressed when even a spiteful man — and I considered you a kindly man — nurses a personal resentment against me."

It took the dying Belinsky three days to write his final defense of his ideals from the sanitorium bed in Salzbrunn. The reply has become noted as one of the world's greatest letters. On July 15, 1847 he wrote to Gogol:

"I cannot give you any idea at all of the anger your book aroused in every noble heart. Russia does not need sermons (it has heard quite enough of them) or prayers (it has uttered quite enough of them too); it needs the people to become aware of human dignity, a sense that has been lost for so many centuries. The most acute, the most pressing national problems for Russia are the abolition of serfdom and corporal punishment, and the strict observance of at least those laws we have. And this is the moment chosen by a great writer to bring out a book in which he instructs a barbarian landowner, in the name of Christ and the Church, how to make money out of his peasants and humiliate them more adroitly. If you had made an attempt upon my life, I should not have loathed you more than I do for the ignoble lines you have written there! And to say a book like that is the result of arduous inner struggles and divine illumination of the soul? It's impossible! You are standing at the edge of an abyss. How could you, the author of *The Inspector General* and *Dead Souls*, begin singing hymns to the glory of the disgusting Russian clergy? You present the idea that education is not necessary for the people, is actually harmful to it. May your Byzantine God forgive you that Byzantine thought! It was said all over St. Petersburg that you wrote the book because you hope to be appointed tutor to the heir apparent. The public looks to Russian authors as its sole guides, defenders, saviors from Russian autocracy and orthodoxy. That is why it is always ready to forgive an author for writing a bad book, but it will never forgive him for writing a pernicious one. If you love Russia, you ought to join me in rejoicing at the failure of your book. The only people who seek Christ in Jerusalem are those who have never found him in their hearts or have lost him. It is not the truth of Christian doctrine that can be found in your book, but rather a morbid fear of death, the devil, and hell."

Gogol was dazed and infuriated by the letter. He wrote a response to Belinsky. He said Belinsky was unaware of great literature, having been expelled from Moscow University (Belinsky's sin had been to write a play exposing the evils of serfdom). Gogol said that if Czar Nicholas I would read Gogol's censored articles and carry out the reforms recommended there, Russia could still be saved. My works, said Gogol, show that I understand the Russian people, as your own reviews so eloquently stated. But you don't really understand the Russian people. True, our government is a nest of thieves, but is the solution to be found in turning things over to socialist thieves, those who take other people's property? The only hope for social reform lies in individual reform — external controls cannot remake the inner man. Man is really the citizen of a superior heavenly state. "So long as he does not lead, in however small a way, the life of a heavenly citizen, his earthly citizenship will remain in a disordered state." Leave politics, which is ephemeral, in order to serve art, which is eternal, Gogol advised Belinsky.

Having stated what he felt, Gogol tore the letter into pieces. Gogol's first biographer, P. A. Kulish, found the torn pieces and reconstructed the letter.

The official letter Gogol sent to Belinsky on August 10, 1847, was much more conciliatory. "Perhaps there is some truth in what you say," he admitted. He said no two people agreed in their reaction to his book, but "what does seem to be beyond question is that I know nothing of Russia, that many things have changed since I have been living abroad, and that I must learn, starting almost from scratch, what is there now. The coming century is a century of rational awakening. Just as I need to learn many things that you know and I do not, so you ought to learn at least a fraction of what I know and you mistakenly scorn."

But it was Belinsky's letter which became underground inspiration for Russian reformers for decades. The government forbade having even a handwritten copy of it, fearing Belinsky's ideas. A quarter of a century later a periodical was allowed to print parts of it. Finally in 1905, with a new revolt brewing, the entire letter was made public.

Despite all the adverse criticism the book had received, Gogol felt it had been worth writing. Though imperfect, it was serving a useful purpose to himself and others, he believed. Then too, it had been God's will that he should write it. He still felt qualified to instruct people on how to live: "Every one of us, even the lowliest, must teach his fellow by showing him the way, in accordance with the will of Christ and the Apostles."

Russia needed to have this book, Gogol said, because of "the lack of character and the absolute anarchy of our literature." He felt he had been quite objective — "there is neither irritation nor fanaticism in me," he insisted.

He tried to explain to Aksakov how the book had served his personal needs. "My book is in the straight and steady line of my inner formation. If anyone can truly advance me, and if through him my mind is enriched, then I like that person. What a strange creature is man: what counts most with him is his personal interest."

The big influence upon Gogol now became Father Matvey Konstantinovsky, an Orthodox priest from Rzhev whom Count Alexander Tolstoy regarded as the ultimate religious authority. Short, with long fair hair and grey expressionless eyes, he had a coarse mind. His domineering personality quickly made a slave of Gogol's intent but unbalanced search for God.

Father Matvey considered all art to be a sin against the Holy Ghost. He told Gogol to renounce literature, Satan's tool, and enter a monastery in penance. He scolded Gogol for having defended the theater. Apologetic, Gogol said that perhaps he had not made his position clear; he had recommended classical plays in order to keep people away from such worldly pastime as the ballet and French drama. When Father Matvey upbraided Gogol for his arrogant spirit, Gogol asked him to pray for him. Gogol now felt fulfilled. He had finally met "the seer of his soul."

In the fall of 1847 Gogol made his long-postponed pilgrimage to Jerusalem. The sign from God had arrived. Italian rebels were challenging the pope, demanding a constitution. He must now leave Rome. At Malta he was in a state of near collapse, and asked his friends to pray for him.

He was thoroughly confused. He wrote to Father Matvey: "Christ's law can also be obeyed by an author. Could not an author show, in a compelling novel, living examples of better men than those portrayed by other authors?"

The trip to the Holy Land disillusioned Gogol. How could Our Lord's homeland be controlled by Moslems? He visited the usual Christian shrines, but felt that the Presence lived on in His influence, not in stone steps, desert places, and sepulchres. Leaving for home Gogol felt that possibly the true Holy Land was Russia.

He finished writing *Meditations upon Divine Liturgy* but would not give it to a publisher. He now knew that the public did not want to hear of its vices and how to get rid of them.

He began to feel remorse over his attack upon friends in *Selected Passages.* He wrote a small book, not published until after his death, called *An Author's Confession,* in which he apologized to Pogodin for his harsh statements about him. He defended his friends among the aristocracy, saying that they were the only ones who showed sympathy for him and his views.

He must have publicly apologized to Pogodin, for Pogodin took him into his home as a guest. Always ill at ease in society, Gogol seemed pretentious, as though he deserved regal treatment. Ultimately they quarreled over Father Matvey's influence upon him, so he went to live with Count Alexander Tolstoy. Aksakov described the atmosphere of Tolstoy's home as one of "popes, monks, bigotry, superstition, and mysticism."

Gogol continued to work on the continuation of *Dead Souls.* He now felt that Part Two would be his Purgatory and Part Three would be the Paradise. He was finding it hard to create positive characters. To placate Father Matvey, he promised him that at the end of Part Two, Chichikov would be converted to Christianity by the czar himself. Work on the novel went slowly. "I must drag each word out as if by pincers," Gogol said. His divine inspiration seemed lacking. He told Father Matvey: "Never before have I felt my helplessness so much. I am waiting for inspiration from above. God knows, I should not like to say anything that did not serve for the glorification of His holy name. Everything has been thought out but my pen does not obey me. This is the cause of my secret suffering."

He of course disliked the radical movements of 1848. The Petrashev-sky circle deserved imprisonment, he agreed, although he felt sorry for misled young people like Dostoevsky. He grew angry at Herzen for ac-cusing him of deserting the cause of liberalism in Russia. In his defense he showed Turgenev examples of his own early writings in which he had recommended obedience to authorities. Unimpressed, Turgenev argued with Gogol over his defense of censorship. But Turgenev saw no evidence of insanity in Gogol, despite rumors which were beginning to spread about it.

His family noted the change in him. He now never seemed to be cheerful. His sisters collected Ukrainian songs at his request, and sang them to him. But he complained about modern improvements to his family. Did the oil lamp, highways, the daguerreotype, make people any better? No — probably worse! His sister Elizabeth, getting married, asked him to buy her a carriage as a present. He had no money for such things, he replied. Why be wasteful? Instead, he donated 25 silver rubles to the monastery at Optina, imploring the monks: "Earnestly I beg you to pray for this sinner."

At a previous visit to the monastery he had found peace for his troubled soul. The flowers, the buildings, the quiet disturbed only by tink-ling bells, all brought him a surcease from conflict. Here he felt midway between earth and heaven. Looking back over his life he felt he had had only three genuine friends: Pushkin, the painter Ivanov, and young Joseph Vyelgorsky.

It was Joseph's sister Anna who now attracted him. He became her spiritual advisor. He told her to forego dancing, since she was too stout. She was not pretty, he said, but could acquire beauty through noble thoughts. The essential quality of a true Russian, he informed her, was that he under-stood better than anyone else the sublime words of the Gospel. "The seeds of Christ," he said, "well sheltered in our hearts, gave all the best features of the Russian character."

Though he was 41 and in poor health, and she only 27 and the daughter of nobility, he proposed marriage to her. He cautioned her that after marriage they should never submit to the evils of sexual intercourse. Count and Countess Vyelgorsky were shocked to think that a man of such humble origin should think of marrying into the nobility, and promptly quashed the marriage plans.

Gogol tried to complete Part Two of *Dead Souls*, but it was of no use. He told Alexandra Smirnov that when he finished it he would die. "And if I give the world an immature or imperfect work I shall die sooner," he said, "because I will not have performed the task for which I was put on earth."

When Turgenev visited him in October 1851 he was alarmed at the man he found. "Some secret sorrow, preoccupation or morbid anxiety mingled with his ever-alert expression. What an intelligent, strange, and unhealthy person!" reported Turgenev.

In January 1852 he was saddened by the death of the poet Yazykov's sister Katherine. Looking at her coffin he said, "Nothing could be more solemn than death. Life would lose all its beauty if there were no death."

In February Father Matvey visited Gogol in Moscow. His advice was severe: Confess the sin of being friend to the pagan Pushkin. Take no wine, no meat. Abhor pleasure — no laughter, no song.

It was the beginning of Lent. What better way to show one's loyalty to God than to fast. So Gogol started a long fast.

Demonstrate your religious faith, advised Father Matvey, by burning your manuscript of *Dead Souls*. Gogol refused, knowing that without literature he could not live.

But after the priest left, Gogol's conscience seared his soul. The old dread of eternal hellfire returned. He thought he heard voices from the grave. So during the night of February 11 he burned, for the third time, his work on Part Two of *Dead Souls*. Ten years of work and worry vanished in the fireplace flames.

Count Alexander Tolstoy visited him. "Look what I've done!" he told Tolstoy. "How powerful is the Evil One! See what he's driven me to do! When I recover from my illness, I'll put it right again."

"That's a good sign," replied the Count. "You used to burn everything and afterwards you did it much better. You can remember it all, can't you?"

"Yes," Gogol replied. "It's all in my head."

His health grew constantly worse. "A man has to die and I'm going to die," he said. "I'm ready." He made out his will, bequeathing everything to his mother and sisters. He left no estate other than royalty income from his works. He asked that two serfs, his servants, be freed. He hoped that in time his village would become a haven for unmarried girls and orphans, or better yet a convent.

He now refused to eat. Six doctors worked in vain on him. One tried to hypnotize him but failed. His stomach became so soft and hollow that one could easily feel his vertebrae through it. The doctors finally agreed that he was no longer wholly sane. They placed him in a tub of hot water and poured ice water on his head (as Gogol himself had described in his brilliant tale, "Diary of a Madman"). They inserted leeches in his nose to suck blood. Probably the opposite treatment would have been better — forced feeding, with hypodermic injections of saline solutions.

Although he had a lifelong terror of hell, his tortured soul seemed to finally have found its goal. "My soul senses the beatitude to come and knows that we need only to reach out to that beatitude and Divine Grace will let it descend upon our souls," he had written. In *Selected Passages* he had said that God, in love, stands ready to put down a ladder to earth to take us to heaven. Through the night of February 20, 1852, he asked for the ladder. He died the next morning, and was buried in the cemetery of the Monastery of St. Daniel.

There was not enough time before burial to permit his mother and sisters to attend the ceremony. The government outlawed any newspaper obituary. Nevertheless Turgenev purchased space for a brief newspaper tribute in which he wrote: "Our loss is so cruel and so sudden that we cannot yet accept it. He is dead, the man of whom we are as proud as of a national hero." For defying the ban Turgenev was arrested and exiled to his estate.

As if to get perverse retribution for some unknown crime, censors refused to permit publication of his collected works. Finally, nearly four years later, friends of Gogol got the works published.

From his country's standpoint and the world's, Gogol's tragedy was to be so obsessed by belief in a divine purpose in his writing that it divorced him from reality and utterly consumed him. There was exquisite irony in that despite his obsequiousness to authority his very style of writing was so democratic, both in language and in getting to the heart of human foibles and hypocrises, that he was perhaps unknowingly undermining the autocratic government which never understood him.

He had set into motion a rich vein of literary realism that all of Russia's censors could not stop. Each great writer after him—Dostoevsky, Leo Tolstoy, Turgenev, Chekhov—acknowledged how much he owed to the untutored Ukrainian comic writer. He who had complained of being ill-loved in his lifetime came to be doubly treasured after his death—respected not only for his own great works but for what he had inspired others to write.

# 8
## The Taiping Rebellion

The village of Kuan-lu-pu was in an uproar. A meeting of town elders and clan heads was called to deal with the crisis.

"We cannot permit Hung to do these things!" shouted a bearded elder. "Now he has his cousin Li convinced he's right. Where will it all stop?"

"He can accept this pagan faith, this Christianity, if he wishes," replied the mayor. "But we cannot permit him to attack our ancient beliefs and traditions. Even Confucius has been desecrated by this upstart."

"Smashing idols, that's what they've been doing," responded the bearded man. "Soon all of our morals will be destroyed unless we take action right now."

"I think I have just the plan to handle this problem," said the mayor, his eyes sparkling. "Listen to this."

And so the mayor of Kuan-lu-pu, a village 30 miles north of Canton, China, detailed his plan. The troublesome teacher, Hung Hsiu-ch'üan, would be asked to compose the usual poems in favor of the local gods. He would probably refuse, and then he could be fired. With no job, he would no doubt leave town and the problem would be settled.

The solution worked, at least temporarily. Hung and his cousin, Hung Jen-kan, also a teacher, were told to compose the traditional poems. They refused. Immediately harsh poems on both sides of the controversy appeared on the village walls. Hung and his cousin removed the time-honored idols from their classrooms. Several town bullies threatened to beat them. Enraged, Hung destroyed the altar holding the table of Confucius in his school.

The mayor's plan had worked. Hung and his cousin were dismissed as teachers. The faith of the forefathers had been preserved.

Out of this simple beginning in 1844 came the Taiping rebellion, one of the greatest revolutionary movements in recorded history. Before it was over more than 20,000,000 Chinese would be dead—twenty times as many people as in all American wars combined.

Hung left the village, as predicted. He took with him another teacher, Feng Yün-shan, who had also been converted to Hung's version of Christianity. Hung and Feng began a missionary journey westward to Kwangsi province. As they traveled they preached. While making converts

德天

Hung Hsiu-ch'üan, the "Heavenly King," in a contemporary drawing (from life) at the height of his power. From Callery and Yvan's "History of the Insurrection in China," 2d ed., translated from the French by John Oxenford (London: Smith Elder & Co., 1853).

they continued smashing idols. By the end of the year two goals had crystallized in their minds: conversion of China to Christianity, and overthrow of the ruling Manchu dynasty. As is so often true, religious ideals of peace and love led to untold carnage, bloodshed, and destruction.

How did this all come about? What motivated Hung so deeply in his new religion? How did politics merge with religion as Taiping goals? Had he succeeded, as he nearly did, in seizing control of the government, would modern China be Christian instead of communist? Let us see how this bizarre young man led millions of Chinese into abandoning their traditional faith for the cause of Christ.

Hung was born in Kwangtung province on January 1, 1814. His people were Hakkas, who had migrated from northern China in order to escape Mongolian conquerors. Although the Hakkas clashed frequently with the local Punti, they especially disliked the ruling dynasty of Manchus, who had come down out of Manchuria in 1644 and ruled China ever since.

The fourth of five children, Hung was a leader in childhood games. Quick tempered, he would beat children who opposed him. Since he had a good memory and knew the classics well, everyone predicted a big future for him. At the age of 13 he took first place in local examinations. Three years later he took the national examinations at Canton, and failed them.

Government examinations were the key to entry into the civil service and thus into entrance into the gentry class. Since there were relatively few openings in government administration each year, the examinations were rigid and only about 12 out of 1,000 passed. Hung was not very discouraged, therefore; he took a job as a teacher.

In 1836 Hung again failed the national examinations. But two significant things happened to him that year. He met the great Confucian scholar, Chu Tz'u-ch'i, who imbued him with the great need for social reform. And he first encountered Christianity. Two missionaries, preaching to a crowd, answered his questions and predicted he would attain "the highest rank." They gave him a set of Christian pamphlets written by a Chinese minister, Liang Fa. Hung put the pamphlets on his shelf and went back to teaching.

In the spring of 1837 Hung failed the examination in Canton for the third time. This time the effect was catastrophic. He was so ill that he had to be carried home. He raved in delirium for several days. His family feared for his sanity and for his life.

Hung started having visions. In one vision he is being operated on, with his heart and other organs being replaced by new shiny red organs. A venerable Man with a golden beard, He who has made the earth, laments human ingratitude and worship of demons — He gives Hung a sword, telling him to exterminate the demons. A middle-aged man, whom Hung calls his Elder Brother, instructs Hung on how to live and promises to help him find and slay evil spirits.

Perplexed, the family called in an exorcist, but Hung chased him away. Hung told his father that the venerable Man had said that all men would turn to him (Hung), and that all treasures would flow to him. Later Hung felt sure that the venerable Man was God, and the Elder Brother was Christ.

The visions changed Hung. He felt that he was now a divinely-appointed king. He walked upright, with a new dignity. He wrote poems eulogizing himself as the ruler of all China. He changed his name from Jen-k'un (which he had assumed at his marriage) to Hsiu-ch'üan, which he interpreted to mean "the people's king." He said God had assigned this name to him.

A man with a mission, Hung began asserting authority in his home district. He criticized the national government for tolerating opium smoking. When asked about his illness, he said his delirious thrashing was due to his struggle against the devils who opposed God. Hung felt divinely appointed to defeat the demons, who increasingly came to be equated with the Manchus. He later said that in heaven he saw Confucius berated and beaten for having led people astray from God. Thus was his unconscious getting revenge for his failure in the Confucian-oriented examinations.

Hung's China was a country ready for change. The Manchus faced problems on every side. Floods had cut down on the cultivated land area, while the population had doubled, to 400,000,000 in seventy years. European powers were breaking up the Chinese trading monopoly. Opium smuggling was rampant, and since the traffic was illicit, Chinese currency was exported with no balancing import products to stave the deficit.

In 1839 war broke out with England over the opium trade. The British demanded open ports, so that when $9,000,000 of opium was seized and dumped by Chinese inspectors, England sent its ships to seize Canton, Shanghai, and other ports. By the Treaty of Nanking in 1842 China granted foreign nations access to five ports and ceded Hongkong to the British. A treaty with the United States in 1844 gave Americans extra-territorial rights, meaning that they would be tried in their own courts, rather than Chinese, when charged with offenses in treaty ports. That same year the French government obtained permission for Catholic missionaries to penetrate China's interior, rather than being confined to the Canton area. In 1845 similar privileges were extended to Protestant missionaries.

The loss of face in submitting to foreign nations was not the only burden that the Manchus had to bear. For over fifty years internal rebellions had been a problem. The White Lotus Society outbreak in 1796 had impoverished the provinces of Hupei, Szechuan, and Shensi. In 1813 the Heavenly Reason Society had tried to capture Peking. In the 1830's an anti-Manchu secret society known as the Triads was causing trouble, particularly in Fukien province. Later another rebellious group, the Nien-fei, began to capture cities in Shantung province.

The Manchus had long been resented as outsiders by the other Chinese. The Manchus caused the non-Manchu men to wear their hair in queues as a mark of submission. Not trusting the native Chinese, the Manchus assigned one of their own kind to supervise each Chinese official. To preserve Manchu identity, separate examinations existed for them. Examinations open to the Chinese required not only a knowledge of the classics but an expression of loyalty to the Manchu dynasty.

Unable to solve the economic problems, the Manchus raised taxes and paid local warlords to collect the taxes. To raise funds, high government jobs were sold to the highest bidder. Since their army could not keep the peace, they permitted local leaders to raise their own forces to fight off the ubiquitous pirate bands.

It is not surprising, then, that Hung found open ears when he preached a doctrine of rebellion against the Manchus. The time was ripe for a change.

In the spring of 1843 Hung failed the national examinations again. This time, leaving Canton by boat, he wrote a poem showing his determination to lead a revolution against the Manchus.

That summer his cousin Li Ching-fang reminded him of the Christian pamphlets on his shelf. Upon re-reading them Hung was firmly convinced that God had selected him to reform and liberate his country. The two cousins baptized each other, and a Chinese version of Christianity was born.

The new faith, based on the pamphlets, reflected Liang Fa's version of Christianity. The pamphlets attacked superstition and idolatry but virtually ignored such topics as the Fatherhood of God, the life of Jesus, the parables, the Trinity, and the Lord's Supper. An angry and vengeful god of the Old Testament predominated over the loving Father and Son of the New Testament.

The nine pamphlets of roughly fifty pages each contained biblical quotations and paraphrase, short sermons, and stories illustrating biblical teachings. Bible passages were taken from the translation into Chinese made by the missionary Robert Morrison. The dilemma he and other translators faced was whether to use a common dialect, and thus be better understood, or use a classical dialect, and thus gain the respect of the scholars. His effort at a compromise pleased neither group.

Passages of scripture that seemed ambiguous to Hung either charmed him by their mysticism or inspired him to give his own fanciful interpretations. Several general principles predominated, however. All people should worship the one true (Christian) God. God-fearing people lived a strict moral life. Since Liang Fa attacked the Big Three of Chinese culture (Buddhism, Confucianism, Taoism), so did Hung, who said, "Too much patience and humility do not suit our present times, for therewith it would be impossible to manage this perverted generation."

Since Hung and his followers met Christianity through fundamentalist Protestantism, there is little stress on the social gospel in the Taiping movement. Even fundamentalists would not accept Taiping Christianity as orthodox, however, for several reasons. First, Hung retained some normal Chinese traditional elements. Second, he employed selectivity in accepting some but rejecting other facets of Christian doctrine. Third, he placed much greater stress on the Old Testament than on the New Testament.

Hung's religious approach was thus a synthesis of Chinese and Christian elements. He announced that he was setting up T'aip'ing T'ien-kuo, "the Heavenly Kingdom of Great Peace." This, Hung said, is the Kingdom of Heaven that Christ speaks of in the New Testament. But it is also the name of the last, and the most utopian, of the three ages mentioned in the Kung Yang interpretation of the famous Ch'un Ch'iu, one of the Five Classics of China.

The Taiping goal, the establishment of God's kingdom on earth, would set up a society with justice and equality for all people. What made it unique was its attack upon the complete social system. Previous Chinese rebellions aimed at political takeover and even occasionally economic reform, but never before had a leader had the audacity to set aside Chinese traditions and customs in favor of a new, foreign religion and its mores. Franz Michael calls the Taiping rebellion "as violent and complete a social revolution against an existing order as was ever attempted. It can serve as a case study of revolution."

But its very ambitious scope also predetermined its failure. By attacking Confucian ideals as it did, it alienated the gentry, those products of the Confucian society. And it was the aroused gentry, given power by the Manchus, who ultimately overthrew the Taipings. The Manchus, in their own right, never could have done the job.

After being dismissed as teachers, Hung and Feng set out in April 1844 to preach the gospel. After traveling through Kwangtung province they settled with Hung's relatives, the Wangs, in Kuei-hsien, a rich district in the southeastern section of Kwangsi province. But Hung realized that this area was too accessible to outsiders to be a good base for building a revolution, so he and Feng began to look for a more sheltered area.

A son of the Wangs was unjustly imprisoned. Hung's strong plea to the authorities resulted in his release. Overjoyed, the entire Wang family was converted to Hung's cause.

Other converts came from Chinese aboriginals like the Miao, the Yao, and the Lolo, who had never been fully assimilated into Chinese culture. Poor farmers, oppressed by high taxes, were lured by the Taiping promise of land reform. By the time Hung returned to Kwangtung in September 1844 there were approximately 100 converts to the new cause.

Feng stayed in Kwangsi, where he organized the first Taiping group, called the God Worshippers Society. He found a secluded spot north of Kuei-hsien in an area called Thistle Mountain. This became the Taiping stronghold during the years of organization.

The God Worshippers were soon armed, defending Hakkas against raids by Punti and by roving bandit gangs. Arms were easily acquired, since the Manchus had helped communities secure arms during the battle against the British. Also, the Manchus recognized the right of many secret societies to arm themselves against pirate raids. Initially the central government interpreted growing Taiping power as another instance of a secret society serving as a protective force against lawless groups. It was several years before the Manchus realized the true nature of the Taiping threat.

While Feng was organizing the God Worshippers in Kwangsi, Hung returned home to prepare himself for the future. Since he seemed more moderate in his conduct, he was again given a teacher's job. He spent two years in solitude — reading, writing, and planning. In his theology can be seen the influence of Liang Fa's pamphlets.

Since his mental frame was Confucian, certain Chinese elements persist in Hung's Christianity. He starts with the brotherhood of man under the Fatherhood of God. To maintain human dignity above the animal level, humans must rigorously abstain from evil thoughts and deeds. Their guiding principle should be magnanimity. If this is practiced at all levels, an ideal society can be achieved, and all people will live in peace and prosperity (Taiping). In erecting a synthesis of Eastern and Western moral codes, Hung described his goal: "We will serve together one common heavenly Father, and together honor the doctrines of one common heavenly Brother, the Savior of the world. This has been the wish of my heart since the time when my soul was taken up to heaven," he added, referring to his 1837 visions.

In early 1847 Hung spent several months visiting an American missionary in Canton. Reverend Issachar J. Roberts, a Southern Baptist, gave Hung the only formal instruction he received in Christian doctrine. Hung learned much from Roberts — how to conduct worship services, how best to battle idolatry. For the first time he read the entire Bible. Everything he learned strengthened his belief in the message of his visions and in the urgency of his God-given mission.

In August 1847 Hung rejoined Feng at Thistle Mountain. The 3,000 God Worshippers were grateful to see their spiritual leader, as Feng had always referred to Hung. One woman said that during a serious illness ten years previously she had been taken into heaven and told that in 1847 a great man from the east would show them how to worship God, and that they should obey him. Hung fit well the description, and his leadership was enhanced.

The Thistle Mountain area was ideally suited as a revolutionary base. The eighteen mountains were heavily forested and scantily populated. Many of the residents were Hakkas. Few travelers ever came down the two primitive roads.

Soon the movement was spreading through the southern parts of the provinces of Kwangsi and Kwangtung. Hung and Feng carefully selected leaders of local branches. Always the rallying cry was "Worship God!" The ethical code was the Ten Commandments, translated into Chinese poetry by Hung. Additional rules were added, outlawing drinking, smoking, gambling, and brawling. Transgressors faced severe punishment. A number of foreign observers compared the God Worshippers to the American Puritans. Later, as they proved lusty warriors, they were more often likened to Oliver Cromwell's rigidly disciplined Roundheads.

In late 1847 Feng was arrested for destroying idols. Loyal God Worshippers raised money to bribe the officials to secure his release. This money was called "The Charcoal Collection," because it came from the mountaineers' small income from charcoal burning.

Although released from prison, Feng was banished to his home in eastern Kwangtung. While traveling there with two armed guards he converted the guards into becoming God Worshippers. Hung accompanied Feng home. That winter they spent studying the Bible and making plans for their coming revolt. When Hung's father died, he received a Christian burial, and Hung abstained from the traditional Chinese mourning practices.

Hung's first wife died in childbirth, after bearing two daughters. His second wife bore him a son in 1849. The son, T'ien-kuei, later became Hung's heir and was called the Young Monarch.

During the absence of Hung and Feng from Thistle Mountain a leadership crisis occurred. Who was to lead the God Worshippers? The resolution of the crisis, which seemed innocent enough at the time, had ominous repercussions for the success of the revolt.

In April 1848 a leader of charcoal burners named Yang Hsiu-ch'ing asserted control. He said that during a two-month illness, when he had been deaf and dumb, he had been seized by the Holy Ghost, who had been sent by God to give Yang instructions on what their group should do. Since no one had a clear concept of the Holy Ghost, Yang was believed, his instructions were followed, and he became one of the main leaders of the movement.

Another leader also emerged at this time. A local farmer, Hsiao Ch'ao-kuei, said that he had had trances in which Christ gave him directions for the God Worshippers to follow. He too was believed. In a sense he and Yang spoke on higher authority than Hung, for to their followers Hung was simply Christ's younger brother, whereas Yang spoke on the authority of God and the Holy Ghost, and Hsiao spoke on the authority of Christ Himself.

When Hung and Feng returned to Thistle Mountain in the summer of 1849 they found Yang and Hsiao in charge. Hung promptly averted any rift by declaring that both Yang and Hsiao did indeed speak on divine authority, but that now there would be no more spokesmen for God in their camp. Although a possible schism was temporarily averted, Hung may have later regretted this important concession.

How could the God Worshippers have grown to over 10,000 in a few years? Emperor Tao-kuang's administration was stifling reports concerning existing problems. Since he insisted that all districts report positive achievements, nothing negative, like an incipient revolt, would be reported. The governor of Kwangsi province had a similar policy. In addition, he forbade local officials to kill bandits. Over thirty bandit gangs, ranging in size from 1,000 to 20,000 members, scoured the province. For self-protection, God Worshippers took up arms against the bandits. Neutral persons admired the bravery and honesty of this new religious group, and, appalled at the laxity and bribery in the government, soon joined the rebels. Defeated bandit gangs also often joined the God Worshippers.

Natural calamities helped. When pestilence and famine hit Kwangsi in 1849, Hung said it was God's wrath upon infidels — only His worshippers would be saved. When wealthy granary owners raised the price of rice exorbitantly during the famine, the government did nothing. Disgusted, many villagers joined the new religious group in protest.

As the God Worshippers grew bolder in their actions, government repression mounted, creating martyrs for the rising cause. Two of their group were tortured to death in jail. Hung used their deaths to warn his followers of what might happen to them, unless they adamantly supported God and him.

Hung and the other leaders made plans to mobilize all their forces in the Thistle Mountain area. In preparation for the outbreak of hostilities they had printed many military manuals and religious conduct pamphlets. The story of Hung's visions was told over and over — Hung was seen as "the true Lord" of the age. Now the rallying cry became, "Worship God, support the true Lord, and fight for the new Kingdom!"

Since a number of wealthy families had now joined the movement, there was no shortage of food or money. Needing weapons, they forged their own from scrap iron. To cover the sound of their forges, they had a large flock of geese whose constant honking disguised the metal clanking.

In May 1850 Yang, having trouble mobilizing his troops, again fell ill. For months he lay in bed, again deaf and dumb. His close followers gave him up for dead.

In June Hung moved his family to Kwangsi province, to be safe from reprisal during the coming uprising. In July all 20,000 God Worshippers met, to plan their campaign. When bandit members saw the rigid codes of conduct demanded, most left. One of them, the female bandit leader Su San, remained to become a top Taiping army leader.

In September the forces led by Hung and Feng seemed to be hopelessly surrounded by government troops. Yang suddenly made an immediate recovery from his illness, broke through the official troops, and rescued Hung and Feng. This bold move gave Yang an unprecedented following. He not only became the chief military leader from this point on, but he also added a new religious dimension to his charisma. After his recovery Yang said he had been given his illness as a punishment for mankind's sins, including Hung's reluctance to mobilize their forces for battle.

From now on Yang was known as "Redeemer from Illness," since he seemed to have had a miraculous recovery. Sick people in their camp were henceforth referred to him to be cured of their maladies.

The mobilization area was the village of Chin-t'ien, an isolated spot in the Thistle Mountain region. One reason it was chosen was that the wealthy Wei clan lived there. They had turned their home over to the arms makers, and their fortunes into the Holy Treasury of the God Worshippers. People joining the movement sold all personal property and donated the proceeds to the Holy Treasury. In return, all food, shelter, and clothing were provided by the movement.

Women and children lived in the Females' Camp. Men could visit their wives once a week under strict chaperonage. The ideas behind segregation of the sexes were to prevent the usual immorality of wartime conditions, to keep the men strong for battle, to provide security for women whether their men lived or died, and to use the women as a kind of hostage to prevent the men from defecting from the cause.

Hung now set up a leadership called "Seven Sworn Brothers." Arranged in rank according to age they were (1) Jesus Christ (2) Hung (3) Feng (4) Yang (5) Hsiao (6) Wei Ch'ang-hui, a wealthy landowner (7) Shih Ta-k'ai, a young Hakka who, like Hung, had failed the government examinations.

The goal of the movement was to overthrow the Manchu dynasty and set up Christ's Heavenly Kingdom on earth. The phrase "Kill the imps!" meant to kill anyone supporting the Manchus. To disguise their effort, no mention of the term "army" was used. Flags and uniforms of the God Worshippers bore the mysterious label: "T'ai-p'ing."

Hearing of the mobilization, the Manchu government ordered troops sent to quell the disturbance. Fortunate for the Taipings, two of the three able leaders selected by the government died on their way to assume command. Hung assured the Taipings that God was going to lead them to victory. This seemed to be true when the Taipings, aided by 10,000 new recruits, drove the government forces away from Chin-t'ien in a battle late in 1850.

On January 11, 1850, Hung assembled the God Worshippers for a series of solemn ceremonies marking the formal beginning of the rebellion. Ascending a throne he took on the title of Heavenly King. His son was given the title of Young Monarch, avoiding the term Crown Prince, which was a name the Taipings reserved for Christ. As his first proclamation Hung designated the new kingdom as T'ai-p'ing T'ien-kuo, the Heavenly Kingdom of Great Peace. The new dynasty was called The Heavenly Dynasty, and the current year was designated the year 1 under a new calendar.

Five rules were given to the 30,000 Taiping troops:

1. Absolute obedience to the Heavenly Commandments and to military orders.
2. Rigid segregation of sexes.

3. Conduct which would not offend civilians.
4. Loyalty to the common cause (meaning no private fortunes) and to harmonious relations with one another.
5. Total dedication to the success of the Taiping cause.

People wondered whether it would be possible for the Triad Society to merge with the Taipings. Although both the Triad Society and the Taipings worked to overthrow the Manchus, they could not merge their forces. Hung said that unlike the Triads, who wanted to restore the Ming dynasty, the Taipings were setting up a new dynasty. The Triads, he said, worship the devil but Taipings worship the true God. Because God and Christ are on our side, he said, a few of us equal a multitude of them.

In general appearance, the two rebel groups looked alike. The soldiers of both groups were unshaven and wore red turbans. The government name for the Taipings was "Long-haired Bandits."

As the Taipings began to capture towns in Kwangsi the provincial governor, in a tribute to their fighting valor, said, "A tiger is breaking out of its cage." Feeling they were under God's special protection the Taipings swept aside Chinese superstitions about lucky days for starting a battle. "To one who obeys God every day is a lucky day," they said.

Hung constantly stressed spiritual matters, even in battle. Taiping soldiers practiced their religion daily. There were morning and evening worship services, grace before meals, prayer before battle, and special Sunday services. Jen Yu-wen feels that "this was the real secret of their strength—a secret known to the Imperialists but dismissed as a kind of witchcraft."

Most Taipings believed deeply in the new religion. Success or loss, they felt, depended on how scrupulously they obeyed the Taiping code of conduct. A loss meant there were too many backsliders in that unit. A victory meant that everyone was following God's orders, as relayed through the Taiping leaders.

In August 1851 Hung established the Taiping hierarchy. He was in overall command, with five armies led as follows: Hsiao and Shih led the two advance armies, Wei and Feng led the two rear armies, and Yang had command of the central army, in which Hung himself traveled.

For military organization the Taipings followed the classical Chou-li system ascribed to the Duke of Chou, founder of the Chou dynasty. This system intermingled military and civil government. The men were farmer-soldiers—farmers in peace time, soldiers during war time. Their leaders were civil governors in peace time and military commanders in war.

In a key battle in September 1851 the Taipings successfully used firecrackers as a diversionary tactic to capture the key city of Yung-an. They spent the winter there, preparing battle plans.

Yang capably used spies to enhance his leadership. His spies located a traitor in the Taiping camp. Yang said God had informed him about the traitor. When the traitor confessed, Yang grew increasingly powerful.

Perhaps reflecting this growth, Hung in December 1851 issued a new edict, in which he downgraded himself. He stated that the only true God is the Heavenly Father. It was wrong for Hung to be called "Supreme," he confessed, because only God is supreme. As Hung descended from his pedestal, Yang doubled his efforts to build himself a throne.

Although the government had 400,000 troops to besiege Yung-an in April 1852, the Taipings, with 45,000 men, were able to pierce the government lines because of their greater zeal, discipline, and determination. The Taiping army pressed relentlessly northward, capturing villages and gaining new recruits.

A major setback occurred in June 1852 at Ch'üan-chou. Here a successful governmental ambush killed 10,000 Taipings, one-fifth of their total force. Worse perhaps from Hung's standpoint was the death of his comrade, Feng, who had originally built the God Worshippers Society. Now Hung lacked Feng's support as Yang, step by step, made himself ever more powerful.

In an effort to reward and placate his chief commanders, Hung gave them the title of Wang (King). The five (including Feng's replacement) were called the East, West, South, North, and Central Kings. Two of the Kings, Yang and Hsiao, issued three fiery recruiting proclamations in 1852, charging the Manchu "devils" with the following crimes:

1.  Forcing Chinese to wear queues.
2.  Changing Chinese dress habits.
3.  Intermarriage with Chinese.
4.  Debauchery of Chinese women.
5.  Replacement of traditional laws.
6.  Replacing native language with Mandarin.
7.  No relief for flood and famine victims.
8.  Corrupt officials who accept bribes.
9.  Killing off all opposition.

These proclamations, issued in the name of God and Christ, urged the people to throw off their superstitious beliefs and accept Christianity. Within two months there were 20,000 new recruits, raising the Taiping army to its highest total, 70,000 troops.

Unfortunately standards had been lowered to get these recruits, and from now on it could no longer be expected that the conduct of Taiping soldiers would be exemplary. Soon their army was guilty of the same excesses that characterize most armies. But many years later people in Kwangsi remembered favorably the "kind and righteous" army that fought bravely but always treated the people well.

In September 1852 Hsiao was killed in battle at Ch'ang-sha. Yang was thus deprived of his most loyal supporter. But he took over Hsiao's troops, and by excellent military generalship, continued to win victories for the Taiping cause.

As they moved northward, the Taipings captured vessels needed for transport on the Yangtze River. At Yo-chou they won 5,000 ships, and the capture of Hankow brought 10,000 more. This enabled them to move people and supplies rapidly on Tung-ting Lake and on the Yangtze River.

Aided by their new transport, the Taipings proceeded down to Wu-chang, which they captured in February 1853. For the first time atrocity was attributed to the Taipings here, but it must be remembered that it is an old Chinese custom for losers of a battle to commit suicide. Some records say there were 100,000 suicides in Wu-chang. After the initial slaughter of government forces by Taipings, a rigid code of military and moral discipline was again enforced.

Realizing that their force of 100,000 would be insufficient to conquer all of China, the Taipings conscripted all adults, male and female, who had not left Wu-chang. The men were put into the army, the women into the Females' Camp.

In Wu-chang the Taipings inaugurated a series of institutes, which from now on they set up in each city they conquered. Separate institutes were set up for the sick, the disabled, the civilian women, the aged, the children, and the literati.

Quite possibly the Taipings now made their greatest error in military strategy. Instead of proceeding northward and capturing the capital city of Peking, which they might well have been able to do, they turned eastward toward Nanking. Their plan was to continue to augment their forces until they had an overwhelming superiority over the government troops. But this delay not only gave the Emperor an opportunity to reinforce his armies. It also subjected the puritanical Taipings to the rich sensuous life of the eastern region. It was a temptation that proved to be too appetizing — and it was fatal in its consequences.

When the Taipings left Wu-chang for Hanking, the Imperialist Army, accusing the occupants of collaboration with the Taipings, ravaged the city. The massive Taiping contingent of 500,000 persons set off for Nanking by road and river. By now the countryside thought they were invincible, and laid down arms before them. Through Anhwei province they received all sorts of gifts, and volunteers enlisting in their ranks raised their army to a new total strength of 750,000.

Nanking, the capital of Kiangsu province, lies on the southeast bank of the Yangtze River. In 1853 it was surrounded by a thick high wall thirty miles long. The wall had ten gates and over 15,000 battlements. Yang's battle plan worked well in capturing the city. Deceit plus force brought the Taipings success.

One night Imperialist forces saw several hundred soldier silhouettes. When they fired a line of paper effigies fell; the Imperial forces had been located. For days "Buddhist monks" infiltrated until finally 3,000 Taipings were inside the walls, where they could direct the time and place to attack. The Taiping miners did their customary work — they dug tunnels under the walls and ignited charges; Taiping soldiers poured through the breach.

After a 13-day siege Nanking fell to the Taipings. All Manchus they could find they killed. At least 30,000 Manchus were executed after the battle ended. It was the only massacre of its kind performed by the Taipings.

On March 29 came the triumphal entry of the Heavenly King, Hung. While over 100,000 soldiers lined the river bank, a parade came by, with Hung in a sedan chair, wearing a rich yellow robe emblazoned with nine dragons. They renamed the city T'ien-ching, the Heavenly Capital.

Their forces now numbered over 1,000,000. The capture of Nanking gave the Taipings six times as much silver as was in the imperial treasury at Peking. In addition, they captured large stores of rice. It seemed merely a matter of time before Hung would achieve his goal of driving the Manchus out of power and setting up the Heavenly Kingdom he had long contemplated.

Once order was restored, strict moral discipline was installed, especially concerning rape and adultery. Offenders were beheaded. Opium smokers were also put to death. Westerners praised the Taipings for their orderliness. They seemed to be a different race, said one observer. Their doxologies, hymns, and public prayers seemed to indicate that they were indeed relying upon divine guidance. Speaking of Hung, an editorial writer for the *North China Herald* in 1854 showed typical foreign hope for the movement: "We regard him as the instrument in the hands of God for accelerating, perhaps by ages, the civilization and the Christianization of the Chinese."

The Institute for Women in Nanking had 145,000 women in it in 1853, including 5,000 officers. The women organized and supervised all the work done by institute members. Some women complained that the hardy Hakka officers expected too much work from the others, many of whom had bound feet. A severe rice shortage forced the institute to close in 1855.

The Taipings continued their iconoclastic crusade, destroying idols, temples, and monasteries, whether Taoist, Buddhist, or Confucian. Priceless religious treasures were lost, including the famous Porcelain Tower constructed in the early Ming dynasty. A special commission was set up to revise the Confucian classics, eliminating all passages relating to idolatry or superstition.

As the Taiping Heavenly Capital, Nanking was rebuilt. Hung lived in the Grand Palace of Glory and Light. In its formal garden was a boat carved from granite, the only relic today of Taiping rule in Nanking. In the center of the square stood the Heavenly Terrace, a place reserved for the worship of God. Soldiers were segregated from civilians, who lived on the outskirts of the city.

Great attention was given to defense. Ditches were built, walls were strengthened, and outpost guard forces were posted. Despite three lengthy sieges by Imperialist troops, Taiping forces held Nanking for eleven years, until the entire collapse of the Taiping movement.

Now that he had the time and the tranquility, Hung spent much time codifying and clarifying his religious position. It is not remarkable that Chinese concepts permeated his Christianity. The resulting amalgam was bound to be offensive to many orthodox Christians.

Three factors affected Hung's version of Christianity — what was available, what was understood, and what was acceptable. All three factors made for limitations and modifications.

What was available to Hung, besides the pamphlets of Liang Fa, was the Gützlaff translation of the Bible. The Dutch missionary Karl Gützlaff was the most active Bible translator at the time. In 1844 he had organized the Chinese Union, which distributed Christian materials throughout China. Hung became familiar with this translation while working with Reverend Issachar Roberts in 1847. The Chinese were getting Anglo-Saxon versions of Jewish traditions and events. Chinese readers are used to many explanatory notes, which were lacking in this Bible.

It is clear that Hung did not understand many Christian concepts. Particularly was he confused by the idea of Holy Ghost, which appeared in Liang's pamphlets as "Holy God's Wind." Since Yang said that the Holy Ghost had visited him, Hung gave him the title of "Wind Master." Yang was also called "Holy Comforter," since he had often comforted Hung.

God the Father was accepted in the Old Testament monotheistic version, in which He corresponded to Shang-ti, the Chinese version of God prior to Buddhist innovations. Reflecting the Chinese belief in the family, there is a Heavenly Family system, which includes a Heavenly Mother. Jesus, the Heavenly Elder Brother, has a wife but no children.

Hung accepted Christ as Savior, but since the Chinese observe filial respect, the Son is never quite equal to the Father. Hung generally avoided calling Jesus the only Son, since he felt he was a Younger Brother of Jesus ever since his visions of 1837.

The doctrine of the Holy Trinity really puzzled Hung. How could three be one? Having worked so hard to convert China to monotheism, and thus free it from superstitious concepts of the demon world, he was not about to flirt with polytheism. He finally admitted, "Of the three persons, Father and Son are of one blood-vein in kinship." Hung permitted Christian rituals which mentioned the Trinity but he never came close to understanding the concept.

Taipings felt that God was intervening in their behalf. *The Book of Heavenly Decrees and Imperial Edicts* published in Nanking lists seven such divine interventions between 1848 and 1852. Once He showed His power through miracles, once He gave directions for prophecy, and three times He supported Hung's orders. He also ordered a Taiping leader killed for ordering a retreat, and He exposed a Manchu plot against the Taipings.

Taiping doctrine stressed the Ten Commandments, as amended by Hung. To "Thou shalt not steal" was added "Be content with your station in life." To "Thou shalt not covet thy neighbor's house" Hung added "Also, do not gamble." To "Thou shalt not bear false witness," was added "Avoid scandal-mongering and garrulousness." Most impressive of all was Hung's addition to "Thou shalt not commit adultery." The addition included observing strict sex segregation and avoiding amorous glances, lustful thoughts, singing libidinous songs, and smoking tobacco and opium.

Where Jesus had prayed "Deliver us from evil," Hung used "Deliver us from evil spirits." Taipings observed the Sabbath (a custom foreign to the Chinese), with a doxology chanted to the deafening accompaniment of cymbals and firecrackers. They apparently did not observe the Lord's Supper. Instead of the cross as a symbol they used twin dragons, the dragon being a traditional Chinese symbol for beneficence, power, and intelligence.

Hung stressed the Old Testament concept of Jehovah as the God of battle rather than the redemptive love and forgiveness of Christ. Thus, following Liang, he could conceive of fairness but scarcely of charity and certainly not loving one's enemy. In terms of ethics his system was far more Christianized Confucianism than it was Confucianized Christianity.

The Taiping goal, never fully realized, was to establish a church for every 26 families. Sunday attendance would be mandatory. Since their plan of social organization was totalitarian, the sergeant conducted Sabbath services and presided over weddings and funerals. The Taipings had no priesthood nor plan for educating religious professionals. Everyone was given religious instruction. During the week children attended a religious school, which was under the sergeant's supervision. The curriculum was primarily the Bible and Taiping documents. Because of the constant warfare, the sergeant was actually seldom at home to perform these functions.

One of the factors leading to the downfall of the Taiping movement was the polygamy practiced by Hung and other leaders. Chinese classics sanctioned the taking of plural wives or concubines, but only by emperors, nobles, and scholars. Hung had read about polygamy in the Old Testament, and found nothing specifically prohibiting it in the New Testament. So, as Taiping successes mounted, so did the number of his wives. After founding the kingdom at Chin-t'ien, he had 16 wives; at Yung-an he had 36, and at Nanking he had 88. Lesser numbers of wives were permitted other dignitaries: the East and West Kings were allowed 11, the other Kings 6, top-level officials 3, and middle-level officials 2. All others had to strictly observe monogamy.

Possibly as a Christian influence, women had equal status with men. Thus, Hung's wives were not concubines. In fact, because of Hung's status as Younger Brother, his wives were considered to be daughters-in-law of God. Since each wife was considered to be in a true marriage, adultery, a major Taiping sin, was never a question.

Hung's palace was extraordinary in that it employed no eunuchs. Eunuch intrigue has overthrown many a dynasty. No males, save for those in Hung's family, were allowed in the palace, where over 1,000 women served in various roles. Hung insisted on their moral education; he wrote a book of 500 poems and aphorisms for their edification. Every day each woman read one poem plus one chapter of the Bible.

The Christian stress on human dignity overcame the traditional low social status of Chinese women. At a time when most Western women were denied many rights, including the ballot, the Taipings gave women a higher status than that given women in most Christian countries. The Taipings outlawed footbinding, concubinage, and wife purchase. Traditional exclusion of women in the family was broken down. Taipings addressed each other as brother and sister. The same six grades of nobility given to men were given to women. Women were allowed to progress up the administrative ladder.

Just as polygamy got Joseph Smith into trouble among his Mormon compatriots, so did Hung's harem present a problem to him. Late in 1853 Yang used his trances to humiliate Hung. Finding out from his own harem women that Hung had been mistreating *his* harem women, Yang said he had a vision in which God ordered that Hung be beaten for having mistreated his female entourage. Yang ordered Hung to never again mistreat his women. Yang further reported that God had given instructions that only he, Yang, would have the power to make decisions concerning capital punishment. Hung submitted to Yang's authority, although he was spared the beating.

From this point on, Yang became the most powerful Taiping leader. As one sign, his harem grew larger than Hung's. Many of Yang's women protested against their mistreatment and several plotted to kill him, but his spy system identified the plotters and squelched the plot.

Hung realized, however, a long-sought objective in 1853 — he drew up an examination system that he felt remedied the defects of the system he had so often failed. Taiping examinations were open to everyone, although there is no record of women having taken them. Scholars were given all sorts of comforts, such as free transportation, excellent meals, and special privileges. The themes for the poems and essays which constituted the tests were taken from official Taiping literature.

The Confucian classics were among the books banned from publication by the Taipings. In the period 1852–1862 Hung supervised the publication of 44 Taiping books. These include histories, poems, and essays on Taiping topics, as well as Chinese editions of books of the Bible and various books dealing with religious instruction, government decrees, and military regulations. No other aspiring Chinese leaders had ever undertaken such an ambitious publishing program.

Yang's forte was military leadership. He was good at organizing and executing military campaigns. His directions were clear and well planned. Without him the Taiping movement would not have gone as far as it did. Each commander had his staff, of which Yang's staff of 7,200 aides was the largest.

Since the Chou pattern of organization integrated political structures with military, Yang, as the overall military leader, also served as the political head. Land reform, which was never carried out, promised to divide land equally among all Taipings, including women. Local officials were to be elected by the people, an innovation for China. Unfortunately the top-level efficiency did not permeate down to the lower levels of government, and lacking the competent gentry-scholars, Taiping local administration was not very efficient.

A further complication was the Taiping attitude towards the peasant. Whenever a Taiping official was punished, he was reduced to the level of the peasant. There was by no means any glorification of China's most abundant group, the poor farmers. This prevented the Taiping movement from getting mass acceptance. It also provides delicious irony when Marxists call this movement proletarian, ignoring not only its demeaning posture toward peasants but also its very real religious base.

The capture of Nanking brought the Taiping revolt to the attention of Western nations. Official Taiping documents, translated by Christian missionaries, began to appear in the *North China Herald* in Shanghai from 1853 on. Since the Manchu government had reneged on its promise to open China to foreign trade, British, French, and American forces fought the Imperial government throughout the 1850's. The Taipings, being nominally a Christian movement, could have benefited greatly had they joined the Western powers in opposing the Manchus.

But Taiping leaders were ill-equipped for international diplomacy. They knew little of the outside world, having had virtually no contact with foreigners. They spoke no foreign language, and they did not understand political protocol. When Western representatives visited them in Nanking, Taiping leaders irritated them by acts of ignorance, arrogance, and religiosity. Thus they failed to receive help which might have turned the tide.

When Sir George Bonham, governor of Hong King, visited Nanking in 1853, his ship was fired upon by Taiping forces. Bonham assured Hung that England would remain neutral during the rebellion. Bonham was told that since the British had traveled far to show their allegiance to the Heavenly Dynasty, they had the Heavenly King's permission to help the Holy Soldiers exterminate the Imperialist imps. Enraged, Bonham threatened the use of British force unless all agreements were observed in the five treaty ports. Bonham felt that the so-called Christianity was a cover-shield being used by Taipings to gain political and military goals. The British, busy with the Balkan problems that led to the Crimean War, did observe neutrality for the next eight years.

The American minister to China, Robert McLane, was shocked upon his visit to Nanking in 1854. He was told that in return for American recognition of the universal sovereignty of the Heavenly Dynasty, Americans would be granted permission to pay annual tribute to the Heavenly Court. The irate McLane reported to his government that it would be in America's interest to help keep the Manchus in power.

The French representative, fearing that the Protestant Taipings would harass their Catholic missions in China, received assurances that the missions would be unharmed. But when Bonham's son was also given a shoddy reception in July 1854, the Western powers stayed away from Nanking for nearly five years.

The overall military plan developed by Yang divided all Taiping forces into three armies:

1. The central army defended the capital at Nanking.
2. A northern army was to capture Peking and then take the north-western provinces of Shensi, Shansi, and Kansu.
3. A western army was to conquer the western provinces along the Yangtze River, and link up with the northern army in Szech-uan. The combined armies were then to subdue the remaining provinces.

In retrospect, it seems that they made several strategic errors. By permitting Imperialist armies to besiege Nanking, they were constantly weakening their attacking forces in order to defend their capital. A single expeditionary force sent northward could perhaps have been strong enough to capture Peking. Further, they should have reinforced the Triads, who had captured Shanghai but then lost it. Shanghai, a major port, could have brought them badly needed supplies.

The northern army had great early success. People welcomed them as liberators, giving them food and supplies. So deep was the desire to overthrow the Manchus that sometimes, as at Ho-chou, townspeople opened city gates from the inside to greet the invading Taipings.

The Taipings, however, made a great error at Ts'ang-chou, where they slaughtered 10,000 civilians after hostilities had ceased. It was hard to envision the newcomers as harbingers of a heavenly kingdom of love and peace after that.

The farthest northern penetration, to within three miles of Tientsin, was achieved on October 30, 1853. Taiping forces were now within 70 miles of their goal, the capital city of Peking.

Imperialist forces, often outnumbered by the Taipings, used a strategy known as "sitting warfare." Frequently they would permit the Taipings to take a town, and then besiege it and cut off its supplies. When the Taipings were sufficiently weak, Imperialist soliders could recapture the city.

In the suburbs of Tientsin northern Taiping forces made their last stand. A relief force sent out from Nanking to help them never reached them. Hopelessly surrounded, they surrendered in March 1855. Their leaders were summarily executed. They had traveled over 2,000 miles simply to be wiped out completely as a rebel force.

The western army had far greater success. For ten years they ranged the Yangtze River area, capturing towns and provinces, losing them, then recapturing them. Their great opponent was Tseng Kuo-fan, who, unlike Hung, had passed the government examinations and had received seven promotions in eight years. As a great scholar, he had caught the Emperor's attention and been asked to lead an army against the Taipings. Tseng felt it was important to defend traditional Chinese culture against the heretical Western-inspired religious threat. Like Hung, Tseng stressed moral virtues in soldiers. His regulations forbade opium, rape, gambling, and even bizarre clothing. Carefully he chose officers who were brave, honest, educated, and loyal. In ten years of fighting the Taipings not a single officer of his Hsiang Army defected to the enemy.

In his original battle proclamation Tseng outlined the case against the Taipings:

1. These "bandit dogs" had committed many atrocities.
2. They were destroying the social order recommended by China's ancient sages.
3. They had enraged China's gods by their attack upon idols.
4. As Confucius recommended, loyal Chinese would support their emperor when he was under attack.

Thus did Tseng appeal to many Chinese people—those harmed by the Taipings, scholars who defended the status quo, the superstitious common people who feared the vengeance of wrathful gods, and all loyal Chinese. Since Tseng's forces never numbered over 120,000, he had to rely on better training and careful strategy for victory.

The turning point of the western campaign occurred at the Taiping defeat at Yüeh-chou in Hunan province in July 1854. Here the Taipings lost over half of their boat fleet, and thus control of the Yangtze River. Then when they failed to stem Tseng's advance at T'ien-chia-chen in December 1854, their ultimate fate was sealed. Shih Ta-k'ai led Taipings to a third capture of Wu-chang in April 1855, but when Tseng retook the city in December 1856 the Taipings were forced to fight a long losing defensive battle out of Nanking.

A significant factor in the Taiping collapse was the loss of leadership in Nanking. Yang was more concerned with seizing total Taiping command than in giving his armies the personal guidance and support they needed. Leading a religious crusade, he lacked spiritual depth. He had the most power but knew not how to use it. Unlike his adversary Hung, he could not provide a cohesive ideology. In desperation, he reversed the policy on male/female separation in 1855 and permitted marriages. He collaborated with the Nien, a large rebellious force in northern China. By this means he was able to take some pressure off the long Imperialist siege of Nanking. Also, the return of Shih's forces from the western front helped lift the siege in June 1856.

Opposition to Yang began to mount within the Taiping ranks. The army losses showed that he had no supernatural military power. His commanders and troops resented that he gave them no rest. His fellow kings resented Yang's bullying tactics, including his treatment of Hung.

In the fall of 1856 a civil war broke out among Taiping leaders, a war that eventually meant the end of the movement. What set it off was Yang's effort to seize all power from Hung. First Yang got Hung to put him over all the other Taiping kings. He then persuaded Hung to confine himself to religious and literary affairs, ceding all political and military authority. He humiliated the other kings, chiefly by cruel acts toward their families.

Then Yang made his final move. With all other army leaders off on military expeditions, he told Hung that, as spokesman for God, he (Yang) was to receive the royal title "Ten Thousand Years" for his great work in defeating Manchus. This title was reserved for the monarch. Hung asked what, then, would be his title? "One Hundred Million Years!" replied Yang facetiously. Hung now realized that Yang meant to kill him. To stall for time to develop a counter-plan, Hung said he would grant Yang's request on Yang's birthday in the following month.

A king formerly loyal to Yang confirmed the assassination plot to Hung. Hung called his top leaders back to Nanking to overthrow Yang. Two of them, Wei Ch'ang-hui and Ch'in Jih-kang, plotted and carried out Yang's murder. They also killed all of Yang's family and guard that they could locate.

To further trap Yang's followers, Hung announced that Wei and Ch'in would be publicly beaten at a banquet attended by all persons loyal to Yang. On September 4, 1856, about 5,000 of Yang's followers attended the banquet. Upon signal the troops of Wei and Ch'in fell upon them and killed young and old, male and female. The troops then went on a rampage, killing all of Yang's soldiers that they could find. Soon there were 20,000 dead Taiping bodies.

Returning to Nanking, Shih protested the excessive slaughter, though not the killing of Yang. Wei now tried to kill Shih, but he escaped over the city wall in a basket. Wei did, however, kill Shih's family and many of his followers.

Shih now vowed vengeance upon Wei and Ch'in. He raised an army of 100,000 and besieged Nanking, threatening to destroy the city, if necessary, to get Wei and Ch'in. To prevent shelling from its heights, just outside the city wall, the famous Porcelain Tower was dynamited at Wei's command. Hung's forces now turned against Wei and Ch'in within the city and captured them. Wei and Ch'in were beheaded and their heads sent, in a box of brine, to Shih at Ning-kuo. Hung invited Shih to take over as the chief military commander. By now the self-slaughter of Taipings had reached 30,000.

Demoralized, lacking leaders, and having no economic base for supplies, the Taiping movement now had no chance for ultimate success. It was only a question of where and when the final surrender would occur.

Shih entered Nanking triumphantly in November 1856, and began the laborious job of rebuilding the army. Although he was only 26, Shih had a good record as a military leader and as a civil administrator. His justice and efficiency had earned him the respect even of the people he had conquered. His only defect as a Taiping leader was the absence of religious feeling in him.

Shih soon perceived that his biggest problem would be to control Hung's two older brothers. They had lost their kingships during the wholesale governmental reorganization. Jealous of Shih's rise, they subtly opposed him and even plotted to kill him. Aware of this, Shih left Nanking, never to return. Hung knew he could not survive without Shih, and so he tried to get him to return, even offering him Yang's former title of "Holy God's Wind"—but to no avail. Shih organized a large personal army and set off on an autonomous westward expedition, completely uncoordinated with the Taiping master plan for destroying the Manchus.

The Taiping civil war had been more than costly—it had been fatal. But the movement had been so successful and so powerful that it took the Imperial government another decade to wholly stamp it out.

The blood bath in Nanking left everyone frightened and depressed. Perhaps because Yang's following had been so intense, official Taiping publications treated Yang as a fallen hero, and Wei and Ch'in as villains who received their due rewards.

When the British and French attacked the Manchu government from 1857 to 1860 for not carrying out trade agreements, the Taipings, had they not suffered such internal loss, might have been able to seize Peking. The Western powers by now considered the Taiping threat to be virtually over, and so they concentrated on putting pressure on the Imperialist government. No doubt the Taipings would have been wiped out earlier had the Western powers not fought the Manchus.

Just when Hung's spirits were in a state of depression bordering on despair, new hope arrived for him. In April 1859 his distant cousin, Hung Jen-kan, arrived in Nanking. Jen-kan knew Christianity better than did Hung, having worked as a catechist of the China Inland Mission. One of the first modern Chinese nationalists, he knew not only China but the outside Christian world. He realized that if the Taiping movement were to remove its superfluous excrescences it would more likely attract support from Christian nations.

Jen-kan did everything humanly possible to revive a fading movement. Hung made him second in command, a king with the title of "Nine Thousand Years." Unlike the most recent Taiping leaders, he never neglected the vital role of religion in the movement. He published many prayers and religious essays, exhorting Taipings to follow God's will in their lives. Unlike Hung, he stressed the loving God of the New Testament. He ordered a stone slab, 9 feet by 11 feet, erected with the Beatitudes inscribed on it, for his palace courtyard. Realizing that many Chinese still revered the classics, he had them restored, making sure, however, that there was no worship of traditional Chinese gods. He encouraged visits by Western missionaries to Nanking. Had he been the top Taiping leader in

1853, he may have been able to rally Chinese forces, with Western support, to overthrow the Manchus.

Jen-kan was greatly impressed by the United States, "the most righteous and wealthy country of all," because of its democratic processes. He drew up a list of Taiping goals, accepted by Hung, which if implemented would have westernized China fifty years before both Japan and Sun Yat-sen's China became modernized. Among innovations he proposed were the strengthening of civil liberties, prison reform, a national health program, construction of roads and railroads, and religious reform, with a presbyterian form of church administration.

Although he could not rid Hung of his xenophobia and megalomania, Jen-kan did straighten out some of Hung's misconceptions concerning Christianity. He restored the Holy Trinity concept, he explained Paul's teachings, and he emphasized the importance of Christ's agape. The most gifted of all Taiping writers, he based his call for the overthrow of the Manchu government on the distinction Confucius made between Chinese and barbarians. Like Hung, he reformed the examination system to make it more humane for all candidates. In 1860 he devised a successful defense of Nanking, which had now been under siege for seven years.

The top Taiping military commander was now Li Hsiu-ch'eng. Li's troops took Changchow and Soochow in 1860, and had Shanghai surrounded on three sides. Because the Western forces were fighting the Manchus in the Second Opium War, Li counted on them for help in winning Shanghai. A number of Western missionaries tried to persuade the Western powers to at least be neutral, if they could not support the Taipings. While awaiting a reply from the British government, hundreds of Taiping soldiers were killed by British troops. The Yankee adventurer, Frederick Ward, led a group of international renegades against the Taipings. Frustrated, Li withdrew from Shanghai in order to rebuild his forces.

In December 1861 Li captured Hangchow and Ningpo. The Taipings now had control of Chekiang and Kiangsu, two of China's richest and most densely populated provinces.

Meanwhile the circle around Nanking was growing ever tighter. Anking, an important gateway to Nanking, fell to Imperialist troops in September 1861 after a British blockade of the Yangtze kept supplies and reinforcements from reaching the beleagured city.

Against the advice of Jen-kan, Li tried again to capture Shanghai in 1862. Defending their property and interests, the British helped repel the Taiping attack, as did Ward and his "Ever Victorious Army." In June Li's forces were winning when he was recalled to help defend Hung in Nanking. His reduced army was finally compelled to surrender at Shanghai in October. The Taipings nearly succeeded in regaining control of the Yangtze River. A northern force seized its objectives, but the southern commander withdrew from the battle plan and failed to reinforce the northern army, which was consequently destroyed in May 1862.

In March 1863 a British major, Charles Gordon, took command of the Ever Victorious Army, which had 5,000 men and a strong artillery section. Though not always victorious, Gordon's forces generally beat the Taipings. Since Gordon treated prisoners humanely, some Taipings defected to his army.

Another British subject, Augustus Lindley, befriended the Taipings. He organized a force headed by foreign officers, and used a steamship for attack purposes. Lindley's troops were easily repulsed, and Gordon took Soochow in December, 1863. When the Manchu commander beheaded eight Taiping generals during the surrender ceremony, Gordon became so enraged that he threatened to join the Taipings and win back for them all the territory that his army had seized from them. Eventually Gordon was placated and was instrumental in helping sever the Taiping supply line from Chekiang to Nanking.

The former Taiping leader Shih relieved some of the pressure on Nanking by fighting Manchu troops for several years after he left the movement. Since he had trouble feeding his large army of 300,000, most of his troops deserted him. With only a handful of men he retreated into mountain hideouts. Finally, persuaded by the promise of a pardon, he surrendered to Imperialists on June 13, 1863. After making his confessional statements, he was sliced to death on August 6.

Early in 1863 Tseng could see the complete defeat facing his antagonists, the Taipings. He described how they had changed. In the early days, he said, they followed principles. They prevented rape and looting, and brought peace to the people they conquered. But as they lost their religious discipline they reverted to pillage and unnecessary violence. They no longer build strong defenses. They no longer go to rescue wounded comrades. They now fight among themselves for power. Victory will soon be ours, said Tseng. And he was right. In one battle, outnumbered twenty to one, he still beat the Taipings. Aided by British and French cannon and boats, Tseng was able to blockade the Yangtze and isolate Nanking.

In the final days, Hung refused to evacuate the Heavenly Capital. To give in to the imps would be deserting the holy decree of God and Christ. When his people were starving, he said, "Let them live on grass or weeds, as the Israelites lived on manna in the desert." He confined himself to his palace, praying for God to save his kingdom. On June 1, 1864, after a 20-day illness perhaps brought on by poison, he died. He had been on the Taiping throne for 13½ years. His son succeeded him on the throne.

On July 19, 1864, Nanking fell, and over 100,000 Taipings were killed. Tseng wanted to stamp out every trace of Taiping ideology. Buildings were burned, and there was much looting. After the war, one hundred of Tseng's generals had huge fortunes.

Hung's two brothers were executed, but the Young Monarch and Jenkan escaped. They were captured and executed in November, the Young Monarch being only 16 years old.

There were still about 300,000 Taiping troops in Fukien province, and four large Taiping armies in Kiangsi. Wang Hai-yang, the last Taiping commander, maintained a force in Kwangtung until February 1866, by which time virtually all Taiping forces had been destroyed. Some Taipings north of the Yangtze merged with the Nien and survived until their defeat in July 1871.

What had the rebellion cost China? There were over 20,000,000 dead from the fighting, starvation, and floods, with countless more wounded. Over 600 cities had been captured by the Taipings, and since they opposed traditional Chinese culture, irreparable damage was done to buildings, art treasures, libraries, and other objects.

The Manchu dynasty never fully regained control of China. To survive, it had granted concessions to foreigners and had given warlords permission to raise independent armies. The gentry, without whose support the Taipings could never have been crushed, now had new power. Above all, the revolt had demonstrated that millions of Chinese were so disillusioned with their current mode of life that they were prepared to abandon their traditional culture to follow a new, even Western, ideology in the hope that a better social order would result.

Why did the Taiping Rebellion fail? Many reasons can be given. Chief of all has to be the loss of its original religious motivation. While the early God Worshippers expressed their religious zeal, they were almost universally successful. They felt that death in battle brought them face to face with God and Christ, their ultimate goal—so what was there to fear in bodily death?

Leadership was an equally crucial factor. Hung gave the movement its religious ideals, based upon his imperfect understanding of Christianity. But Hung was not a good civil or military administrator. Had his religious visions been experienced by his able cousin Jen-kan, the outcome could have been wholly different.

Yang was the best Taiping military commander, but he lacked the ethical and spiritual depth needed to head a movement of this sort. A combination of Feng's religious grasp with Shih's administrative and military prowess could have given the movement the dynamic it needed to succeed.

Most early Taipings were southerners, who found the northern climate too severe for them. Furthermore, when the Manchus called upon Mongolian reinforcement, the Taipings lacked the trained cavalry to oppose them.

Economic factors contributed to the demise of the Taipings. They never were free enough from battle to establish their land reform program, or to build a sound economic base for supplying their needs. Blockades kept them from enduring the long Manchu sieges.

Are the Western powers to blame for the Taiping defeat? Probably not. Had the Taipings beaten the Manchus those powers would have done their usual about-face and supported the new regime. Initially the West looked with favor on the prospect of a huge conversion to Christianity, but after their rebuffs in Nanking in 1853 and 1854 they fell back into neutrality. They actively opposed the Taipings from 1860 onward because they felt it to be in their economic interest to do so.

External factors were not what beat the Taipings. Idealistic as their movement was, based upon Christian values and beliefs, the Taiping leaders were all too human, in the last analysis. Hung became so comfortable with his harem in Nanking that he lost his concentration on military and political objectives. Their friend Lindley warned the Taipings that a revolution is lost when the forward surge of momentum is surrendered because of temporary success and luxury.

Yang's effort to displace Hung was the beginning of the end. The resulting civil war was catastrophic to the Taipings. As things grew ever more desperate, Hung began handing out titles of nobility in a vain effort to purchase by materialistic standards what had been lost through religious apostasy. When the movement was young and virile, Hung had five kings who reported to him. As the movement collapsed, kingships were easily acquired. Hung appointed 17 new kings in 1861 and over 100 in 1862. But mercenary kings proved to be a poor substitute for dedicated peasants.

A final tribute must be paid to the Taipings' chief adversary, Tseng Kuo-fan. Not trained in military affairs, Tseng nonetheless converted his genuine administrative talent into a spirited defense of Confucian China. Though often outnumbered he was rarely outwitted, and he patiently bore down upon the Christian rebels until he had defeated them.

To thoroughly extirpate all Taiping influence, the Manchu government destroyed all its records and artifacts. Most extant documents were those preserved by Europeans. A few Taiping leaders escaped abroad, and continued to agitate for the revolution, which came in 1911, after their death.

Sun Yat-sen, a Christian, liked to be called "Hung Hsiu-ch'üan the Second" as a young man, for like Hung, he dreamed of destroying the Manchu dynasty. During the revolution he later led, Sun and his officers often told Taiping stories to inspire their troops. Sun's supreme statement of policy, The Three People's Principles, derives from Taiping doctrine. Sun's troops won their final victory over Imperialist forces at Wu-chang on October 10, 1911, and Sun became provisional president of the new Republic of China in 1912.

Despite his many weaknesses, Hung has had many who consider him to be of signal posture as a religious leader. C. P. Fitzgerald goes so far as to call Hung "the most outstanding Christian prophet known to history." Holger Cahill tends to agree: "Hung tried to retain the cardinal principles of Chinese life and thought within the structure of his Christianity. In doing this he showed a clearer understanding of historical Christianity than the missionaries who criticized him. It may well be that Hung was the true prophet of Christianity in China."

Had Hung's movement succeeded, would modern China be Christian rather than communist? Perhaps. Robert E. Speer says, "It is doubtful whether in all her history another such opportunity as this has been presented to the Christian Church." W. A. P. Martin agrees. By the Taiping defeat, he says, "an opportunity was lost such as does not occur twice in a thousand years."

Little could the mayor of Kuan-lu-pu have predicted that the religious-minded teacher he exiled in 1844 for breaking Confucian idols would ever prove to be so momentous a figure in Chinese history.

# 9
## A World Religion Is Born

The prophecies of two great religions converged in 1844. When Mirza Ali Muhammed proclaimed himself Bab-ud-din ("Gate of the Faith") in Persia that year, he fulfilled major prophecies of both the Christian and the Moslem faiths.

Daniel predicted that in 2300 prophetic days the sanctuary would be cleansed and "the time of the end shall be the vision" (Daniel 8:17). If one adds 2300 years to 456 B.C., the year that Artaxerxes decreed the rebuilding of Jerusalem, one arrives at A.D. 1844. Followers of the Bab, as Mirza Ali Muhammed came to be called, feel that his announcement of his manifestation fulfilled Daniel's prophetic vision.

When Daniel said that the time of the end shall be "a time, times, and a half" (Daniel 12:7), this total of 3½ prophetic years, or 1260 calendar years, is the exact time span from the hegira of Mohammed in A.D. 622 until 1844, using the Islamic method of reckoning years.

Also in 1844 the Ottoman Empire passed the Edict of Toleration, permitting Jews to return to their homeland after twelve centuries of exclusion. Babis, as followers of the Bab were called, interpreted this as the fulfillment of "the times of the Gentiles" mentioned in Luke 21:24. John had said in Revelation 11:2-3 that for 1260 prophetic days the Gentiles would tread Jerusalem under foot. Babis noted that 1260 years elapsed from Mohammed's hegira until the Bab's proclamation.

The Persian branch of Islam, the Shiites, were eagerly awaiting the second coming of the Mahdi, the twelfth Imam or Divine Guide. This young Imam had vanished mysteriously, but his expected return would usher in a new age in world history, the Shiites believed. When the Bab announced himself as the gateway of the new faith for a new world, it was precisely 1000 years after the Mahdi had become the final Imam of the Shiite faith.

It is little wonder then that the Mulla Muhammed Husayn sat enthralled at the feet of the Bab that fateful night of May 23, 1844. Their meeting began an hour before sunset. All night long the Mulla put forth challenging questions. He was amazed at the brilliant answers given by the Bab. Surely such inspiration, Husayn felt, could only come from the man who was indeed the Qa'im, the promised one described in the Koran.

The call to prayer by the muezzin at daybreak awakened Husayn from his state of religious ecstasy. "This revelation," he said, "benumbed my faculties. I was blinded by its dazzling splendor." He and several of his friends became immediate followers of the Bab.

The Bab's proclamation stated that he had been selected to be God's mouthpiece, as promised by ancient prophets. He announced the coming of a new age in world history, an age of peace and justice. He said that a person greater than he would appear as God's Manifestation for the new age. He warned the Shah and other political leaders that they should lay aside their earthly dominions and "advocate God's cause in lands both East and West." He cautioned that failure to heed God's voice would lead to unequaled destruction and ruin on a world-wide scale.

The religion he founded is considered by some to be one of mankind's hopes for survival in the atomic age. Leo Tolstoy said that while we spent our lives futilely trying to unravel the mysteries of the universe, a prisoner of the Turkish government—Baha-u-llah, the one whose coming the Bab heralded—already had the key. Queen Marie of Rumania said of this new faith, called Baha'i, "It is Christ's message taken up anew." In 1920 H. G. Wells, the agnostic, wrote, "Out of the trouble and tragedy of these times there may emerge a religious revival of a simplicity and a scope to draw together men of alien races into one common and sustained way of living."

Baha'is say that their way of life, heralded by the Bab's proclamation in 1844, is God's solution to the warfare, discrimination, and exploitation that has always been the human lot but which in an age of advanced technology could lead to the suicide of the human race. They ask us to look at the founders of this faith, at its continuity with world religious traditions, and at its teachings for the modern world.

Mirza Ali Muhammed was born in Shiraz, Iran, on October 20, 1819. He was a Siyyid, a descendant of Mohammed. When his father died young, Mirza was reared by a maternal uncle. After traditional elementary education Mirza assisted his uncle, who was a wool merchant. At 17 he moved to Bushihr, a port on the Persian Gulf. He was a devout and studious youth, noted for his good looks and his ethical character. In 1842 he married and had one son, who died in 1844.

Mirza was influenced by Siyyid Kazim, the leader of the Shaykhi sect of the Shiite branch of Islam. Mohammed, the founder of Islam, had descended from Abraham through Abraham's eldest son, Ishmael. Thus the Moslem claim to the Holy Land is as authentic as the Jewish claim through Abraham's second son, Isaac.

As is well known, Mohammed accepted Abraham as having found the One True God, Moses as having established the religious and civil law, and Jesus as having brought the new doctrine of divine love. Mohammed, who called himself the last of the prophets, named his faith "Islam," meaning complete submission to God.

Abdul-Baha, son of Baha-u-llah, founder of Baha'i. (Courtesy Culver Pictures.)

In Genesis 17:20 God says He will bless Ishmael and "multiply him exceedingly; twelve princes shall he beget, and I will make him a great nation." Moslems feel that the great nation referred to is Arabia. The Shiite branch of Islam feels that the twelve princes were the Twelve Imams, or Divine Guides, beginning with Mohammed's son-in-law, Ali.

In his early teaching Mohammed asserted that he was merely affirming the main tenets of the Jewish and Christian faiths, to which he was deeply indebted for his religious views. In time, however, he came to believe that they had both strayed from their own scriptural sources, and that, under God's inspiration, he had been chosen to re-establish God's sovereignty over mankind. He accepted much of Christianity, such as Christ's virgin birth, His miracles, and His resurrection, but he steadfastly denied that Christ was God's son, feeling that therein lay the road backwards towards polytheism.

In his religio-political synthesis Mohammed's job was to show how a nation can be governed under God. To do this he taught that the good citizen must surrender some of his local loyalty to family, tribe, and city in favor of the broader loyalty to a nation under God. The Koran spells out guidelines for persons having trouble finding a clear path through the maze of conflicting loyalties.

Because of his background, Mohammed showed special concern for the rights of Jews and Christians. He taught that the lives, property, and laws of both Jews and Christians are under God's special protection and thus should be respected. He was particularly considerate of Christians, saying that they were the nearest to Moslems of all who lived outside the faith. He told Moslems to accept Christ and His gospel. He said that if a Moslem married a Christian woman he must respect her religion. If Christians build a church, Moslems should help them. Since Christians survived under government protection in Moslem lands, he felt that it was fair that they pay a small annual tax. The charter granted by Mohammed to the monks of the monastery of Saint Catherine, near Mount Sinai, has been preserved. In it Mohammed granted Christians privileges they did not have even under Christian sovereigns.

When Mohammed died, a struggle ensued over leadership. The majority of his followers supported his father-in-law, Abu Bakr, a member of the powerful Ummayyad family. This branch of Islam is known as the Sunni branch, meaning the majority.

The Shiite (meaning "separatist") branch of Islam said that God, not the people, must select Mohammed's successors. They argue that Mohammed's cousin and son-in-law Ali was the rightful heir to his leadership, and was the first Imam. The Iranians have always prized the Imams highly, not only for religious reasons but also because they descended from the ancient Persian royal family of Sasan. The Iranians, who believed in the divine right of kings, resented and resisted the more democratic religious and political beliefs of the Arabs who had conquered them.

In fact, the Shiites argue that Ali and the ten Imams who followed him were all killed by the Sunnis. The Twelfth Imam, Muhammad, son of Hasan el-Askari, disappeared as a child at his father's death in A.D. 873. Shiites believe that he is still alive, living in the mysterious city of Jabulqa. They constantly think of his messianic return at the end of time, when he will "fill the earth with justice after it has been filled with iniquity."

Various sects have arisen among the Shiites. One such sect, the Shaykhis, followed Shaykh Ahmad al-Ahsa'i, who died in 1826. He taught that there must always be a Perfect Shiite, a person who would maintain spiritual communication with the Hidden Imam. He himself was so considered, as was his successor, Siyyid Kazim of Resht, the man who influenced the Bab.

The Shaykhis taught that because 1000 years had elapsed since he became Imam, the Hidden Imam (or Mahdi) was about to reveal himself. When Kazim died in 1843 a split occurred over leadership. One group, who continued to be called Shaykhis, followed Hajji Karim Khan of Kirman. Another larger faction followed Mirza Ali Muhammed of Shiraz, the Bab, and hence became known as the Babis.

Shiites argue that mistreatment of Christians and Jews, contrary to the will of Mohammed, began and continued under the Sunnis. The Shaykhis, and later the Babis, are considered to be unorthodox Shiites because of their belief that all major prophets and imams are actually Manifestations of God. This distinction became important when one of the Babis, Baha-u-llah, after the death of the Bab, announced himself as a Manifestation of God, the One foretold by the Bab.

Iran in the early nineteenth century was a decadent nation. Its rulers tended to be cruel, corrupt, or feeble. Although there was much so-called religion, there was little love of man for man. If a non-Moslem's wet garments happened to touch a Moslem on a rainy day, the Moslem was considered to be defiled and might kill the non-Moslem. When Moslems received coins in payment from non-Moslems, the coins had to be washed before being pocketed. The rancor among Moslem sects was severe. The traditional Zoroastrians lived apart, refusing to associate with followers of other faiths. It was into this hotbed of straight-laced sectarianism that the ecumenical approach of the Bab made its appeal.

The Bab's first convert, Muhammed Husayn, was a man of great learning and influence. Soon other Shaykhis joined the movement. The first eighteen followers, who believed that the Bab brought a new revelation from God, were called "Letters of the Living."

The Bab sent his disciples to various parts of Iran and Turkestan to spread the news of his advent. As he instructed them he recalled the words that Jesus had used in sending out His disciples. The Bab reminded them of the triumph of Abraham over Nimrod, Moses over Pharoah, and Mohammed over the tribes of Arabia.

In October 1844, while on a pilgrimage to Mecca, the Bab was questioned by the ulama, religious scholars charged with keeping the purity of the Shiite faith. After belief in God and in Mohammed as His prophet, Shiites are expected to show loyalty to the Hidden Imam. "He who dies without recognizing the Imam dies an unbeliever," runs a Shiite saying.

Finding the Bab deficient in a knowledge of Arabic and of religious studies, the ulama forced him to publicly recant and to be beaten. Recantation is not too difficult for Shiites, since they practice taqiya, the prudent concealment of true belief under adverse circumstances.

The Bab made a few converts in Mecca but was rejected by the Sharif of Mecca. When he returned to his home in Bushihr he found that some of his followers in Shiraz were being persecuted.

In early 1845 a Babi, the Mulla Sadiq-i-Khurasani, in the call to prayer in a mosque in Shiraz, added, "I testify that Ali Muhammed is the Gate of God." He and two other Babis were led into the public square, where their beards were burned and their noses pierced with a halter. After being led in disgrace through the city, they were banished from the city.

Meanwhile the Bab continued to attract attention in Bushihr. His followers liked his eloquent delivery, the inspired wisdom of his teaching, and his zeal as a civil and religious reformer. Orthodox Islam was not about to tolerate his uncomfortable message, however. The ulama denounced him and persuaded the governor of the province of Fars to suppress the new heresy. The Bab was again formally examined, found guilty, and placed in house arrest under the supervision of his uncle in Shiraz.

As the Bab continued to write and preach, he and his followers continued to be persecuted. He spent most of his final five years in prison. Although he was able to write and to meet with his followers, he was not physically present at the bloody battles fought between Babis and government troops.

Aware of the commotion being caused by Babis, the Shah sent a leading Moslem scholar, Yahyay-i-Darabi, to investigate the Bab. In the course of three interviews Darabi became a convert. He was so deeply impressed by the Bab's teachings and knowledge of the Koran that he became a fanatical Babi and later died a martyr's death.

Another learned convert was Mirza Ahmad-i-Azghandi, who had compiled over 12,000 prophecies concerning the return of the Mahdi. He felt that the Bab was the promised herald of the new age.

In September 1846 the Bab attracted large followings in Isfahan because of his doctrine and his medical cures. He was imprisoned, but the governor of Isfahan proved to be friendly to him, permitting him to carry on his ministry from prison.

When the governor died in 1847, however, the Bab was transferred to prisons in the mountains of Azerbaijan, where he spent his final three years. Here he wrote most of the 19-volume *Bayan* (meaning Exposition), which includes his chief teachings. He advocated brotherly love and woman's equality with man. He forbade begging and use of intoxicating beverages. Government's job was to assist the poor and provide all citizens with a good basic education. Stress in the schools was to be upon useful and practical arts.

The number nineteen came to have special significance, because of the nineteen Letters of the Living. Also, the numerical value of the Arabic word "Wahid" (meaning One, or God) is nineteen. Thus, the Babi calendar has 19 months of 19 days each (with several holy days added). Babi groups were to be governed by a leadership consisting of 19 persons. The Moslem month of fasting, Ramadan, was reduced to a Bayan month of 19 days.

All Babis were encouraged to be married by puberty. Only two wives were permitted to men, compared to the four sanctioned by the Koran. Special kindness should be shown to women and children. Men and women could freely associate with one another, unlike the Moslem practice.

The Bab's dispensation altered many Moslem traditions concerning prayer, fasting, marriage, divorce, and inheritance. It described the coming of a new world order, the Kingdom of God on earth. The Bab addressed many messages to contemporary political leaders, criticizing them for misgovernment and asking them to recognize the "new day of the Lord."

New charges were pressed against him by the ulama in Tabriz. Here he announced himself as the Mahdi, the long-awaited Imam. He meant by this that he was the new prophet for a new age in world history. Each revelation was more perfect than its predecessor, he said, and the one who would succeed him, "He Whom God Will Manifest," would be far greater than himself. In fact, he said, one verse revealed by the new Manifestation would be worth more than 1000 *Bayans*.

It was important for everyone to accept the new Manifestation, the Bab insisted. Otherwise the same confusion and discord would prevail as when the Jews rejected the new Manifestation, Christ; or when the Christians rejected the new Manifestation, Mohammed; or when the Moslems rejected the new Manifestation, the Bab.

When he was criticized for using poor grammar, the Bab cited similar usage in the Koran. He told Moslems that if it took God's help for the illiterate Mohammed to write the Koran, how much more had God been present to guide a young Iranian writing a long work in the foreign Arabic.

The government now took renewed interest in putting down the Babi heresy, since traditionally whenever a person announces himself as the returned Mahdi, a political rebellion breaks out in Iran. Babis cried, "The Lord of the age has come!" Those eager for reform, who often constitute a majority of the people, tend to follow the new leader, unless squelched by the government. Under pressure, the Bab continued to announce that he was a Gate of God, a Major Manifestation of God. He was sent to prison in a fortress at Maku, where he was a mild and obedient prisoner. Outside, however, violence had broken out in clashes between Babis and government forces.

In 1848 armed outbreak occurred between Babis and soldiers in Maz-anderan. By the time the revolt was quelled there were over 1500 Babis and 500 soldiers dead.

Guerrilla warfare continued in the mountains of Mazanderan. For eleven months a small band of Babis held off government troops. The Mulla Husayn, the Bab's first convert, wore a green turban and carried a black standard, symbols that would precede the coming of God's vice-regent to earth, according to the Koran. After leading a series of successful charges, Husayn was shot to death when his horse's hooves became entan-gled in a tent rope.

Also in 1848 an important conference of Babis took place in Badasht. The purpose of the meeting was to weigh the consequences of the revolu-tionary *Bayan*, and to find ways to free the Bab from prison. An ardent Babi, Mirza Husayn Ali, here received the title Baha, which was later ex-panded to Baha-u-llah ("Splendor of God").

A dramatic event then occurred. The poetess Tahirih, the only one of the Letters never to have met the Bab personally, appeared on a platform unveiled, as a symbol of the new age in which women would be granted equality with men. Most Babis were shocked to see her unveiled face. One slashed his throat. The learned Quddus, another of the Letters, seemed so stunned by her brazen behavior that his hand was on the hilt of his sword as she descended from the platform.

At this point Baha intervened on Tahirih's behalf, pointing out that the Bab's teachings were truly revolutionary, and old ways must be set aside in order to prepare for the new age. His counsel prevailed, and Tahirih went unharmed. The chief decision of the conference was that the Bab was a new prophet. Like Mohammed, he was the founder of a new faith.

According to Shiite tradition, the Mahdi would appear in the latter days to overthrow all infidels and inaugurate a new era of peace and happi-ness. He would raise the dead and lead armies to victories. Since these signs had not occurred, traditional Shiites rejected the Bab with the vigorous scorn that the Jews had shown Jesus. The Babis, on the other hand, inter-preted many of the prophecies figuratively. They saw the Bab raising to spiritual life those dead through ignorance and sin. The conquest they en-visioned was over human hearts rather than over human possessions.

The Bab now announced himself as "The Primal Point," a title ap-plied to Mohammed by his followers. By confirming himself as the founder of a new religion, the Bab incurred the implacable hostility of most ortho-dox Moslems.

The Bab announced adoption of a new Bayan calendar, starting with 1844. He advised Babis to follow the Blessed One, whom God would soon make manifest. As clues he mentioned two significant years, the year 9 (1853) and the year 19 (1863).

For years the Shah's government had been using the Bab as a pawn to help keep the ulama in check, for they had shown an increasing tendency to try to get involved in political decisions. Hamid Algar says that the Babis served as a punching bag between the government and the ulama, "exposing them to blows each side was aiming at the other."

The latest pronouncements by the Bab brought the government out of its position of neutrality. Persecution increased. At Nayriz the woman relatives of slaughtered Babis were forced to ride through rows of disembodied heads mounted on stakes, to identify their sons, husbands, brothers, and fathers. In Zanjan over 3,000 Babis lost their lives in a heroic but futile defense of a fortress.

But the tortures and deaths seemed not to stem the rising Babi tide. After all, the Shiite tradition stated that in the final days there would be great persecution and cruelty.

In a final determined effort to wipe out this heretical sect, the Amir-Nizam ordered the execution of the Bab. Fearing a public outbreak he transferred the execution from Teheran to Tabriz. When the governor of Azerbaijan refused to carry out the sentence, the Amir-Nizam had his own brother carry it out. The Bab was never given a hearing or told the charges against him.

The execution took place on July 9, 1850. The Bab told his followers to recant his doctrines to save their lives, which most of them did. One ardent Babi, Aqa Muhammed Ali, refused to recant and was executed with his leader.

Colonel Sam Khan, the Christian commander of an Armenian regiment assigned to the execution, tried to be released from his assignment. The Bab told him, "Follow your instructions, and if your intention be sincere, the Almighty is surely able to relieve you of your perplexity."

At 10:00 A.M. the two prisoners were hung by ropes under their arms to a scaffold. The firing squad of 750 soldiers opened fire. When the smoke cleared, the prisoners had vanished! The bullets had cut the ropes, they had dropped to the ground unhurt, and were visiting with a friend in a nearby building.

At noon they were again suspended on the ropes. Colonel Khan and his regiment refused to participate, so another firing squad was called in. This time the aim was better, and the two men died.

If the Moslems thought they had destroyed the new faith, they were mistaken. The martyrdom of the Bab led his followers into deeper religious commitment. The bodies of the two martyrs were recovered by stealth and are now interred on the slopes of Mount Carmel, near the resting place of Baha-u-llah.

Today Baha'is point to swift retribution that overtook the Bab's slayers. Within two years both the Amir-Nizam and his brother were dead. An earthquake killed 250 of the firing squad, and the other 500 were killed in a mutiny several years later. Baha'is relate the great earthquake in Shiraz in 1852 to the one mentioned by John in Revelation 11:13.

Baha'is, who accept Christ as the Savior of mankind, like to point out similarities between Christ and the Bab: both had brief turbulent ministries that culminated in sudden arrest, scourging, ignominious suspension before a hostile crowd, and execution; both boldly challenged religious conventions in the name of God; both founded new religions that made numerous converts within a short time.

For the Baha'i the time of the Bab marks the end of the Age of Promise and the begining of the Age of Fulfillment. His death signals to his followers the end of the Adamic Cycle, which started at the earth's creation, and the start of the Baha'i Cycle, destined to last the next 5,000 centuries.

Persons from many countries acclaimed the Bab for having laid the basis for the unity of mankind based upon the oneness of the prophets. "He sacrificed himself for mankind," wrote Count Joseph Gobineau, first Western historian of the movement. A distinguished English clergyman called him "the Jesus of the age — a prophet, and more than a prophet." The Master of Balliol College at Oxford called his movement "the most important religious movement since the foundation of Christianity." The czar asked the Russian consul in Tabriz to investigate fully this remarkable religion. Sarah Bernhardt asked Catulle Mendes to write a tragedy based on the Bab. In 1903 a Russian poetess wrote a play called *The Bab* which aroused the sympathy of Tolstoy. "The passion of Jesus Christ, and indeed His whole public ministry, alone offer a parallel to the mission and death of the Bab," said Shoghi Effendi, a great-grandson of Baha-u-llah.

Before his death the Bab had selected as his successor Mirza Yahya, half-brother of Baha-u-llah. Impressed by Yahya's loyalty and zeal, including letters sent to him in prison, the Bab gave Yahya the title of Subh-i-Ezel ("Dawn of Eternity"), gave him rings and other personal possessions, and authorized him to make additions to the *Bayan*.

Most Babis accepted Yahya as the Bab's successor, including Baha-u-llah, who was thirteen years older than the 19-year-old Yahya. Because of his relative youth, Yahya's education was under the supervision of his older brother. In addition, Baha-u-llah tended to act as regent, assuming many of the administrative functions of the religious head. In time intense rivalry developed between the two half-brothers over the leadership role.

In 1852 a fanatical Babi, acting without orders from above, tried to avenge the Bab's murder by assassinating the Shah. The young man, Sadiq, shot the Shah in the arm while the Shah was on his morning ride.

Governmental retaliation was swift. All known Babis were arrested. Sadiq was immediately executed, and twenty-eight other Babi leaders were tortured to death in Teheran. Among those killed were the poetess Tahirih and Siyyid Husayn, secretary to the Bab.

As a lesson to stamp out this heretical sect the Shah gave each prisoner to a different group, to see which one could devise the most heinous torture technique. The ulama, the government officials, and even students participated in the competition. Ernst Renan in *The Apostles* called the massacre "a day perhaps unparalleled in the history of the world."

Tahirih was strangled with her own silken handkerchief. Her final words were "You can kill me as soon as you like, but you cannot stop the emancipation of women." The English clergyman Dr. T. K. Cheyne said that her harvest was fruitful: "This noble woman has the credit of opening the catalog of social reforms in Persia."

The Hajji Sulayman Khan walked to death with nine lighted candles burning in holes made in his body. Even devout Moslems marveled at his self-control as he approached his fate, which was to be sawn in half on the gallows.

The courage and devotion shown by these martyrs in Teheran did much to build the Babi following. Gobineau says that these factors probably did more to win converts than had all the previous attempts to proselytize.

Yahya escaped to Baghdad. Bahu-u-llah was imprisoned in Teheran for four months. While in prison he received what he believed was a revelation from the Holy Spirit. He described his vision. A maiden appeared to him in a dream saying, "Grieve not for that which hath befallen thee. Ere long God will raise up men who will aid thee." Pointing at his head she said, "By God! This is the Best Beloved of the worlds, and yet ye comprehend not. This is the Beauty of God amongst you." Whenever he remained quiet, the voice of the Holy Spirit would arouse him, and God would appear, accompanied by the angel Gabriel. "And the Spirit of Glory stirred within my bosom, bidding me arise and break my silence," said Baha-u-llah. He nonetheless kept his revelation secret for another decade.

Aided by intervention by the Russian Minister, Baha-u-llah was released from prison but banished from Iran. Prince Dolgorouki, the Russian Minister, offered him asylum in Russia but he preferred to go to Baghdad. Baha'is compare his hasty retreat from Iran to the flight of the Holy Family into Egypt, Mohammed's hegira from Mecca to Medina, and the banishment of Abraham from Ur to the Promised Land. His family accompanied Baha-u-llah through the snowbound mountains of western Iran to Baghdad, the capital of what was then the Turkish province of Iraq.

Baha-u-llah did not remain long in Baghdad. Fear of violence at the hands of Yahya's followers, plus a desire to avoid controversy among the faithful, led him to live in the mountainous wilderness of Kurdestan for two years. Sometimes he lived in caves, sometimes in rude stone houses. Much of his time he devoted to writing poems describing his love of God. Soon he began to attract the attention of the herdsmen. To demonstrate his versatility as a poet he wrote a poem of 2,000 lines in the same meter and rhyme as that used in a favorite Arabic ode. This poem continued to receive acclaim among his Arabic followers. Soon he was accepted by the herdsmen as a sage and a prophet.

He returned to Baghdad in March 1856 to find the Babis in severe internal strife. No fewer than twenty-five Babis had announced themselves as the Promised One foretold by the Bab. Civil war had resulted in several deaths, including that of the Bab's cousin. Most of the Letters were now dead. Many Babis recanted and returned to Islam. The crisis appears to have been one of poor leadership.

Baha-u-llah's return to Baghdad inspired the Babis with new faith. Kurds, Iraqis, and Persians flooded him with questions and were so pleased with the answers that many converts were made, particularly among the educated classes. Many Persian Babis returned to the faith, including four cousins and an uncle of the Bab. Even many of the twenty-five persons who had announced themselves to be the Promised One now started following Baha-u-llah.

Baha-u-llah interpreted the Bab's teachings, many of which had been forgotten, obscured, or twisted. Baha-u-llah stressed non-violence, obedience to authority, separation of religion from politics, and emphasis on such virtues as godliness, kindness, honesty, chastity, justice, patience, and submission to God's will. There seemed to emanate from Baha-u-llah such a deep feeling of love of God and love of man that soon his followers were imbued with it. Observers noted the changed conduct of those who were closest to their leader.

What sort of person was this Mirza Husayn Ali who came to be called Baha-u-llah, or God's Splendor? He had been born in Teheran in 1817, eldest son of a wealthy government official. Educated at home, he early showed great wisdom and knowledge. By the time he was thirteen, mullas consulted him for religious opinions and advice. Because of his personal charm and charisma he was well liked by all who knew him. At the age of 22, upon the death of his father, he took up the responsibility of managing the family's affairs, including the supervision of his younger sisters and brothers.

Although he never met the Bab, he accepted the latter's revelation. The Bab wrote him a letter containing 360 derivations of the root "Baha." After the Bab's execution, Baha-u-llah arranged for his body to be rescued and buried later in a shrine near Acre.

Baha-u-llah wrote many poems and books of religious devotion. One such work was *The Hidden Words*, supposedly the message addressed by Gabriel to Fatimih upon the death of her illustrious father, Mohammed. He also wrote *The Seven Valleys*, which describes the seven stages of the soul as it seeks oneness with God. This latter work has been compared to the spiritual struggle and ecstasy described by St. John of the Cross in his *Dark Night of the Soul*.

One of Baha-u-llah's most important works appeared in 1862 as the result of what he described as a two-day vision from God. This work, the *Kitab-i-Iqan* ("the Book of Certitude") was written to fulfill the Bab's prophecy that the Promised One would complete the unfinished *Bayan*. For Baha'is it sets forth God's grand plan of redemption, and it is surpassed only by Baha-u-llah's most sacred writing, the *Kitab-i-Aqdas* ("the Book of God").

Baha'is feel that the Book of Certitude breaks the seals of the book referred to by Daniel, disclosing the meaning of "the words destined to remain closed up until the time of the end." This book, they say, sweeps away the age-old barriers that have separated the leading world religions, showing their essential oneness and laying the foundation for a world community built upon faith in God. The main teachings of this book are:

1. There is one God.
2. Divine revelation is an unbroken continuity.
3. God's prophets carry a unified, universal message.
4. Most clergy are blind to spiritual reality.
5. The mystical and symbolical passages of the *Bible* and the *Koran* underscore this fundamental unity of religion.
6. The Bab's revelation is inspired by God and necessary for mankind.
7. The purity and innocence of the Virgin Mary should be obvious to all.
8. The spiritual sovereignty of the Imam Husayn cannot be denied.
9. Proper interpretation of such religious terms as "Return," "Resurrection," "Seal of the Prophets," and "Day of Judgment" further bolsters this view of the oneness of mankind's religion.
10. The coming City of God will be magnificent beyond description.

The Babi presence in Baghdad was a source of discomfort to orthodox Islam, for Shiites on their pilgrimage to Mecca often were converted to the new faith by the Babis. Furthermore, Baha-u-llah's growth in prestige loomed as a challenge to the ulama. Accordingly, they tried to get him or his followers to commit violence, to have a pretext for arrest, but the Babis obeyed Baha-u-llah's injunction: "It is better that you should be killed than that you should kill."

Finally the ulama insisted that Baha-u-llah should perform a miracle to demonstrate his divine authority. Baha-u-llah agreed, subject to two conditions: the ulama must state in writing what miracle they wanted done, and they must agree to become Babis if he performed successfully. Since the ulama rejected the conditions, the test was never made. Moslem authorities finally succeeded in removing Baha-u-llah and his followers to Constantinople, on the grounds that his proximity to Iran was a threat to disorder.

On April 22, 1863, the Babis prepared to leave Baghdad on their four-month journey to Constantinople. This day is now celebrated by Baha'is as the first day of the Ridvan Festival. The Garden of Ridvan is located across the Tigris River from Baghdad. It was here that Baha-u-llah declared his sacred mission to his followers.

He told them of his anointment by the Holy Spirit in 1853 as the Promised One. The ancient prophecies were being fulfilled, he said. Christ had indeed returned: "The Lord of the Kingdom, Jesus Christ returned in the glory of the Father, was about to ascend His throne and assume the scepter of a world-embracing, indestructible sovereignty."

The 1290 prophetic days fixed as the duration of the abomination of desolation in Daniel 12:11 had elapsed, since it had been 1290 years from the proclamation of the prophethood of Mohammed to the announcement by Baha-u-llah. The hundred lunar years prophesied by Daniel had begun. The 19 years predicted by the Bab in the *Bayan* had been completed. In Revelation 11:14 John, speaking of two successive revelations, had said, "The second woe is past, and behold the third woe cometh quickly." The revelation of Baha-u-llah came quickly after that of the Bab, and both revelations produced woe and suffering for believers.

Baha-u-llah was proclaimed by his followers as the long-awaited rebirth of the Spirit of God for the new age. To Israel, thus, he is the long-expected Messiah; to Christianity, the returned Christ; to Shiite Islam, the Imam Husayn; to Sunni Islam, the Spirit of God (Jesus Christ); to Zoroastrianism, the Shah-Bahram; to Hindus, a reincarnation of Krishna; to Buddhists, the fifth Buddha.

Baha-u-llah traced his lineage back to Abraham, Zoroaster, Jesse, and Ali, son-in-law of Mohammed. He described a string of covenants passed on from one prophet to another. Abraham, who had established the oneness of God in a polytheistic age, passed God's covenant to Moses. Moses had established the civil and religious law, and passed the covenant to Christ. Christ brought God's love and peace to the world, and passed the covenant to Mohammed. Mohammed's covenant of complete submission to God and Buddha's similar covenant of renunciation of worldly things were passed on to the Bab, who predicted the coming of God's Promised One for the new age. The Bab's covenant was passed on to Baha-u-llah, who now pronounced the unity of the world family under God. The unifying concern through the chain of covenants was belief in the brotherhood of man under the Fatherhood of God.

The reason for God's progressive revelation through prophets is explained. At the end of each spiritual cycle, only form without spirit remains. Empty ritual carries no inner meaning, so God sends a new Manifestation to renew His Spirit for each age. In the time of Christ the Mosaic law had degenerated into outward forms, so God sent His Spirit to remind man of his mission. In time, Christianity became an outward form, meaningful only to priests, and so God sent His Prophet Mohammed to remind man of God's predominance. But in time Islam became mainly outward form, losing the inner awareness of God's presence, and so now Baha-u-llah had been sent with God's message for this age.

Each prophet sent by God renews the old covenant with Abraham, and adds a new Manifestation of God's nature to assist in meeting man's new problems. Thus Christ renews the law of Moses, but adds divine love. Mohammed renews the law and divine love but adds utter submission to God. Baha-u-llah renews the law, divine love, and submission, but adds the assurance of God's protective Fatherhood over His entire family.

For Baha'is, as the Babis who accepted Baha-u-llah were now called, the day of April 22, 1863, is called "The Day of God" and is considered to be the greatest day in human history, for on it God's forgiveness was extended to all of creation.

After a short stay in Constantinople most Babis, including those who followed Baha-u-llah and those who followed his half-brother Yahya, were sent to Adrianople, where they remained four and a half years.

Yahya refused to accept his half-brother as "He Whom God Will Manifest," the one promised by the Bab. A vicious battle ensued between the two brothers. Each brother accused the other of making an effort to poison his rival. The differences between the two were now very apparent. Yahya was not a forceful leader nor an inspired ideologue. His sect of Babis, called the Ezelis, never grew into much prominence. Baha-u-llah, on the other hand, recognizing the need for broader appeal, revised the Bab's teachings so as to appeal to followers of most of the world's great religions. In addition, he took a somewhat more conciliatory attitude towards the Shah, realizing that iron-clad opposition within Iran could keep the new faith from the nourishment it needed at its roots if it were ever to have multifold branches abroad.

While at Adrianople Baha-u-llah addressed a number of tablets, or messages, to world leaders, making clear his goal to establish the Kingdom of God throughout the earth. In his tables he proclaimed his mission as the Spirit of Christ reborn in the new age, and he challenged the leaders to show their true faith in God by being responsible trustees for their people. He reminded the rulers that they derived their power from God, and that He expected them to rule with justice and mercy. He assured them that unless they followed God's direction, every manner of calamity would befall their countries.

He commended Queen Victoria for ending the slave trade, and asked for help in establishing a common faith in God for all the world. He called upon the pope and all Christians to recognize that God's promised day had now come—the prophecies of Isaiah and of Christ had now been fulfilled. He thanked Czar Alexander II for the kindness of the Russian intervention on his behalf, and he asked the Czar to tell the world the importance of the great Manifestation God had made for the modern world.

He sent two tablets to Napoleon III, requesting that the emperor first purify his soul and then govern in accordance with God's laws. He urged cooperation in the unification of the human race. If man's rulers continue to ignore God, he predicted, "the time for the destruction of the world and its people hath arrived." If leaders continued to ignore his words, he warned, "a most great convulsion will appear."

Baha'is point to the fact that by not heeding his warnings, the rulers paid dear penalties. Within a year Napoleon III was overthrown, and the pope lost his temporal power. The Czar was assassinated a few years later, and the empire built so assiduously by Queen Victoria has now been virtually dissolved.

In 1869 Baha-u-llah sent a tablet to the Shah by a personal messenger. Not only was his request for a chance to confront his accusers denied, but for managing to gain personal access to the Shah, the messenger was pressed to death between hot bricks.

Disgusted by the constant warfare between the two half-brothers, the Turkish government finally separated the two factions in 1868.

Yahya and his party of 30 were sent to Cyprus, where he lived his final years in seclusion. His following diminished in numbers and in authority.

Baha-u-llah and a party of 66 were sent to Acre in Palestine, where he remained until his death in 1892. For two years they lived in filthy army barracks, surrounded by dysentery, malaria, and other diseases.

Acre was a penal colony to which Turkey sent all sorts of transgressors. At first Baha-u-llah was not allowed to see anyone but family members. Many of his followers were imprisoned. The townspeople were hostile to the new faith and its adherents. Baha-u-llah was confined to a small house for seven years, where he continued his prayer, study, and writing, Ultimately governmental restrictions were lifted and he was permitted to rent large houses which amply provided for his entourage.

With time's passage conditions at Acre improved. The Baha'is' devotion to love of God and love of man led to the conversion of a number of townspeople. The Mufti of Acre, originally very hostile, became a Baha'i. The governor of the province sent his son to Baha-u-llah for religious instruction. The greater freedom now granted the Baha'is allowed them to send missionaries abroad.

An increasing broadening of religious outlook occurred as a result of the Baha'i missionary thrust. Countries as distant as India were for the first time exposed to the divine origins of Judaism as a result of Baha'i missionaries. Simultaneously, converts to Baha'i from Jewish, Buddhist, and Zoroastrian backgrounds for the first time accepted the divine authenticity of Christianity and Islam. By creating a larger more comprehensive religious umbrella of faith, Baha-u-llah had given religionists in an area of constant religious turmoil a way to retain their own approaches to God while still respecting, and even accepting, other approaches than their own. After all the atrocities committed in His name, Baha'is felt that God might have rejoiced to see loyalty to Him taking precedence over petty creeds and rituals.

Baha'is developed property on Mount Carmel, which Isaiah had called "the mountain of the Lord, to which all nations shall flow." They also purchased property on the Sea of Galilee, for the building of "noble and imposing structures dedicated to the worship and service of the one true God." Assured of the good will of a sympathetic government, they planned the first Baha'i temple to be built in Ishqabad in Russian Turkestan.

Baha-u-llah grew increasingly optimistic over future prospects. "These fruitless strifes, these ruinous wars shall pass away," he said, "and the Most Great Peace shall come." He gave all credit to God, saying that "the Almighty hath transformed this prison-house into the most exalted Paradise." His son, Abdul-Baha, who had been born the night of the Bab's revelation, agreed with his father: "His enemies intended that his imprisonment should completely destroy the blessed Cause, but this prison was in reality of the greatest assistance and became the means of its development."

In Iran, however, Baha'is continued to be persecuted. Baha-u-llah's pacifistic message of "Kill not" was reaping a grim harvest against the rabid Moslem persecutors. Many Baha'is chose to die rather than to use violence in self-defense. Like the early Christian martyrs, these Baha'i martyrs also brought great dignity to their cause.

Lord Curzon, viceroy of India, estimated that there were one million Baha'is in Iran by 1890. He felt that this new faith might someday supplant Islam in that country. He refuted charges of communism levied against them, saying that their alms-giving and sharing of common goods was that practiced by the New Testament church. The unwarranted charges of immorality levied against them grew, he felt, out of their insistence upon equal treatment of women, "which in the Oriental mind is scarcely dissociable from profligacy of conduct."

The writings of Baha-u-llah at Acre were numerous. Besides the tablets to rulers, he also wrote many works containing statements and explanations of his dispensation. His central doctrine is the oneness of the human race under God. "We verily," he said, "have come to unite and weld together all that dwell on earth." Unity, he believed, is "the goal that excelleth every goal."

In his tablets to Christians, he identified himself as a Manifestation of the Father spoken of by Isaiah, the Comforter promised by Christ, and the Spirit of Truth who will guide moderns into total truth. In writing to Moslems he challenged them to no longer desecrate the Koran by using cruelty but instead to practice the justice and brotherhood which it prescribes. To the Jews he announced that "from Zion hath appeared that which was hidden" and that "from Jerusalem is heard the voice of God, the One, the Omniscient."

The charter of his new world order is contained in his most holy book, the *Kitab-i-aqdas*. In this work Baha-u-llah outlines the ordinances upon which the future world order must be built, and describes the institutions needed to achieve this ambitious goal. Localities are to be governed by Houses of Justice, and nations by National Houses of Justice. He explains their functions and sources of revenues. World order is to be achieved by adherence to an International House of Justice, which is empowered to adjudicate international disputes and to prevent war by having the support of invincible armies on its sides.

This work admonishes all believers in God to practice concord with all other believers in God, to guard against fanaticism and contention, and to practice such virtues as chastity, truthfulness, and justice. Other items discussed are prayer, fasting, inheritance, priesthood (which Baha-u-llah abolishes), prohibition of slavery, prohibition of gambling and of use of drugs and intoxicating beverages, and obedience to government. Now Baha-u-llah prescribes monogamy and permits divorce only in exceptional circumstances. Great stress is placed upon education. Specific punishment is prescribed for persons guilty of adultery, arson, murder, and theft.

The peace which he prescribes is the peace of God: "All of you are the fruit of one Tree and the leaves of one Branch. If one of the companions vexeth any one, it is as though he had vexed God Himself. O people of God, do not concern yourself with yourselves; take thought for the reformation of the world and the purification of its peoples."

Political ideals espoused by Baha-u-llah include reduction of armaments, use of collective security organizations, a world parliament (called the International House of Justice), constitutional government which merges the ideals of republicanism with the majesty of kingship, and use of wise men as governmental advisors. Newspapers must be unprejudiced and fair-minded, and can remain free only as long as they exercise their freedom responsibly.

"The world," said Baha-u-llah, "is but one country, and mankind its citizens. The whole earth is in a state of pregnancy." Patriotism to a specific nation is inadequate as a directing force in human society because of its parochialism. To love one's country too often means to hate a rivaling country, he says. To love the human race and to serve all of humanity are the worthiest goals for humans. Religion is for him "an impregnable stronghold for the protection and welfare of the peoples of the world." It is "the chief instrument for the establishment of order in the world."

But what of religion that has caused wars, discrimination, and untold human misery? To Baha-u-llah this is a matter of definition. Religion in the etymological sense of binding together man to man and man to God is the only true religion. That which fosters separatism, discord, and exclusiveness is irreligion. Schools, he feels, should teach religion in order to further the love of God and of humanity but not the irreligion which promotes prejudice and fanaticism.

He was aware of the growing secularism in the world. "The vitality of men's belief in God is dying out in every land," he lamented. Continued neglect of God could only lead to "convulsions of such severity as to cause the limbs of mankind to quake."

At his death in 1892 Baha-u-llah could point to many evidences of the "Divine Chastisement" he had foretold in his tablets to world leaders. The Shah who had exiled him and sentenced the Bab to death had been assassinated, and soon the entire Qajar dynasty was to be overthrown. The wars of 1877–78 had emancipated eleven million people from the Sultan's rule, and the Ottoman Empire, like the Hapsburg dynasty, was about to crumble and fall. Napoleon III had been exiled, and the Romanov dynasty was near its collapse in Russia. Baha'is could say that if these rulers had heeded their leader's admonition to serve God and put the cause of His peace foremost, they might have been able to save their respective regimes.

George Townshend, former canon of St. Patrick's Cathedral in Dublin, wrote in the introduction to his book, *Christ and Baha-u-llah*: "Facts are given in this book to prove that the Kingdom of God, as foretold in the Bible with a thousand details, has at last come with those details all fulfilled." One of the signs Townshend mentioned was the final blessing Moses gave his people before he died (Deuteronomy 33:2): "The Lord came from Sinai and rose up from Seir; he shined forth from Mount Paran and he came with ten thousand of saints." Townshend identifies Moses with Sinai, Christ with Seir, Mohammed with Mount Paran, and the Baha'is with the ten thousand saints. Just as Mohammed taught how a nation could be governed under God, he says, so did Baha-u-llah teach how the world must be so governed.

For Baha'is the problem is simple — there is only one race, the human race; there is only one nation, the planet Earth; and there is only one religion, the religion of God. Whereas most prophets speak of a reign of peace and righteousness after the Last Judgment, Baha-u-llah tells of peace and unity achievable here and now.

He analyzed the chief causes of war and how to overcome them. One leading cause has always been religious prejudice — each sect says that it alone has the true religion. A synthesis of world religions, which accepts the authenticity of each approach but then shows that it is related to kindred authentic approaches, is the best way to convert religious hatred into religious love.

Another cause of war is racial prejudice. Since there is really only one race, there is no basis for any ethnic group to manufacture false superiority feelings. The Divine Parent would show no preferences among His children, so neither should members of the human family. Intermarriage among all groups is abolishing the superficial differences based upon skin pigmentation.

Ethnocentricity, or the assumption that one's nation is the best, has always fanned the fires of war. One must learn to love one's neighbor as oneself. "Let not a man glory in this, that he loves his country; let him rather glory in this, that he loves his kind," said Baha-u-llah.

Territorial ambition, or greed and lust for power, has been a major factor leading toward war. "Whose land is it?" asks Baha-u-llah. "It is God's." And He would not have a few of His children control land at the expense of His other children. All goods are a stewardship, for which we are responsible to God. Those who have much will share with those who have little, when the Holy Spirit seizes their hearts.

The many languages in the world create a babel of confusion and misunderstanding, said Baha-u-llah. One language should be taught in schools all over the world, so that better communication among peoples can be achieved.

Baha-u-llah saw no quarrel between science and religion, since all truth is one. Although he stressed the importance of education and cleanliness in healing sickness, his approach to healing is holistic—mind, body, and spirit are conceived of as a unity in which health or disease areas spread throughout the entire organism. To him the most potent healing influence is the power of the Holy Spirit, examples of which are seen in the miracles performed by Christ.

By Christ's sacrificial death, "a fresh capacity was infused into all created things." The rapid growths in knowledge and government "are but manifestations of the quickening power released by His transcendent Spirit. Through His power, born of Almighty God, the eyes of the blind were opened, and the soul of the sinner sanctified. He it is Who purified the world. Blessed is the man who hath turned towards Him," said Baha-u-llah.

He taught that man's purpose in living is to know God and to enjoy Him forever. To love God means to love all of creation, for everything is of God. By obeying God's laws, as revealed in the holy books of the world's religions, you will free yourself from the tyranny of materialism and God's inner peace will take possession of your spirit. You will not try to force your ideas upon others, since you now respect the sanctity of their personalities as God-given. You will vigorously uphold civil rights for all persons in all places, on similar grounds. By being true, humble, and just, you achieve your greatest self-realization, which is a oneness of your personality with God. Prayer can help you achieve this atonement, but really all of your life should be one dedicated prayer.

Baha-u-llah realized how urgently there needed to be a meeting of East and West, since the strength of each bolstered the weakness of the other. Western technology and governmental progress would fructify the East by helping raise standards of living and participation in governmental processes. The art and religion of the East can keep the West from becoming sterile and too materialistic. Each not only can benefit from the other but probably cannot long survive without the other.

Discord has marked the transfer of Baha'i authority whenever the leader dies. Just as the Bab's death led to a struggle between Baha-u-llah and his half-brother Yahya, so did the death of Baha-u-llah lead to a struggle between two of his sons. Baha-u-llah's will made it clear that one son, Abbas Efendi (also called Abdul-Baha, meaning "the servant of Baha") should succeed him. As he took over, however, Abdul-Baha assumed that he would be the sole authorized interpreter of the Word of God, and thus that he spoke with the authority of God.

His brother, Mirza Muhammed Ali, was designated to succeed Abdul-Baha upon his death. Meanwhile Mirza disputed heatedly his brother's claim to being God's channel, pointing out that their father had closed revelation for at least a millennium in the *Kitab-i-Aqdas*: "Whosoever lays claim to a revelation direct from God before the completion of a millennium is assuredly a liar and a calumniator."

For four years the conflict raged between the two brothers. Mirza won over to his side his two other brothers, Baha-u-llah's two surviving wives, and a number of other Baha'i leaders. His faction was called the Unitarians. Abdul-Baha responded by excommunicating all who followed his brother.

Because of the intra-family strife the Turkish government in 1901 once again confined both factions to the Acre vicinity. Much of their lives had already been lived under governmental restriction, and now once again they lost their freedom to travel. When the Turkish Revolution came in 1908, however, all political and religious prisoners were set free, and so both sides were free to travel again.

Asked to define what a Baha'i was, Abdul-Baha replied, "To be a Baha'i simply means to love all the world, to love humanity and try to serve it, and to work for universal peace and universal brotherhood." He said that one could be a Baha'i without ever having heard of Baha-u-llah. "When Christians act according to the teachings of Christ, they are called Baha'is," he said. "And when Buddhists act according to the teachings of Buddha, they are called Baha'is." Abdul-Baha thus further expanded the already ecumenical theological outlook of his father.

As early as 1893 Abdul-Baha paid special attention to the United States as being God's chosen country. At the Parliament of Religions held at the World's Fair in Chicago that year his words were read: "The American people are indeed worthy of being the first to build the Tabernacle of the Most Great Peace and proclaim the oneness of mankind. Your mission," he told Americans, "is unspeakably glorious. Should success crown your enterprise, America will assuredly evolve into a center from which waves of spiritual power will emanate, and the throne of the Kingdom of God will in the plenitude of its majesty and glory be firmly established." He later wrote that "the continent of America is in the eyes of the one true God the land wherein the splendors of His light shall be revealed, where the mysteries of His faith shall be unveiled. This American democracy may be the first nation to proclaim the unity of mankind."

In 1899 an American, May Bolles, established in Paris the first Baha'i center in Europe. American newspapers gave the movement considerable attention. On August 12, 1900, a headline in the *New York Herald* ran: "These Believe that Christ has Returned to Earth." The article said that tens of thousands of people now believed that Baha-u-llah was the returned Christ, and that hundreds of people recall having met him and talked to him.

In 1902 a Baha'i Publishing Society was formed in Chicago. Also in that city a periodical *The Baha'i News* (later called *The Star of the West*) began to appear. Many Baha'i works were translated into English. Baha'i centers were opened in many American cities. Americans began travelling around the world to spread the faith. In 1908 a site for the erection of a Baha'i temple was purchased in Wilmette, a suburb of Chicago.

An article in the *New York Times* for July 2, 1911, was headed: "Bahaism, Founded in Martyrdom, Taking Root Here." The article said that between 10,000 and 30,000 persons had been martyred for the faith in Iran from 1848 to 1852. It gave the current number of Baha'is at 10 million, probably an inflated figure.

As soon as he was permitted to, Abdul-Baha travelled widely in an effort to spread Baha'i doctrine. He concentrated his efforts in Europe and America. In 1911 he visited Egypt, France, and England. The following year he dedicated the ground for the temple in Wilmette, saying, "This temple of God in Chicago will be to the spiritual body of the world what the inrush of the spirit is to the physical body of man." The temple was completed and dedicated in 1953.

The first Baha'i temple was begun at Ishqabad, Russia, in 1902. Construction was supervised by a cousin of the Bab. Baha'i temples are nonagons, with an entry door for persons from each of the world's nine major religions. The holy books are the scriptures of these religions, including of course the writings of Baha-u-llah. In conjunction with each temple are planned a number of buildings, such as a school for orphans, a hospital for the indigent, a home for the disabled, a hospice, and in some cases a college.

Perhaps because he was focusing his attention upon a Christian portion of the world, Abdul-Baha gave special consideration to the importance of Christ and His Spirit in addressing the current world situation. Most of us imperfectly reflect the sun of God's divinity implanted within us, said Abdul-Baha, but "the Reality of Christ was a clear and polished mirror of the greatest purity and fineness. The Holy Spirit is the Bounty of God which becomes visible and evident in the Reality of Christ. The Sonship station is the heart of Christ, and the Holy Spirit is the station of the spirit of Christ."

In Christ's sacrificial death Abdul-Baha found two meanings: on the one hand, it promotes a Cause to educate the world and to enlighten all mankind; on the other hand, Christ, like a seed, was destroyed so that the Tree of Life might flourish. "The position of Christ was that of absolute perfection," he said. "He made His divine perfections shine like the sun on all believing souls. Every one who partakes of this bounty and receives these perfections will find eternal life." He accepted Christ's pre-existence as described in John 17:5, saying that "the Reality of Christ, who is the Word of God, with regard to essence, attributes, and glory, certainly precedes creation."

Human beings, said Abdul-Baha, have two natures: "The physical nature is inherited from Adam, and the spiritual nature is inherited from the Reality of the Word of God, which is the spirituality of Christ. Christ sacrificed Himself so that men might be freed from the imperfections of the physical nature, and might become possessed of the virtues of the spiritual nature. The Reality of Christ does not descend from Adam; no, it is born of the Holy Spirit."

Like many other religious teachers, Abdul-Baha condoned the use of violence only to prevent further violence: "The tent of existence is upheld upon the pillar of justice and not upon forgiveness. For example, if the governments of Europe had not withstood the notorious Attila, he would not have left a single living man. The words of Christ refer to the conduct of two individuals towards each other. If at this moment a wild Arab were to enter this place with a drawn sword, wishing to assault, wound, and kill you, most assuredly I would prevent him. If I abandoned you to the Arab, that would not be justice but injustice. But if he injure me personally, I would forgive him."

Because of the rapid growth of science, Abdul-Baha devoted considerable attention to its relation to religion. He traced the history of the atom through mineral, vegetable, and animal kingdoms, showing that its changes are directed by a power beyond itself. This same Power, God, he said, directed the progress of humanity towards its goal—God's Kingdom on earth. He found, thus, not only a oneness of mankind but a oneness of all of God's creation.

Although Abdul-Baha accepted evolution, particularly in a spiritual sense, he was unwilling to accept the struggle for existence as an adequate explanation of man's moral development. Man's narrow struggle for existence was only leading to ever more disastrous wars. The big job facing humanity was to develop within human souls the capacity to receive the Holy Spirit and to obey divine law, thereby escaping the degrading struggle for existence, which is beastly and ungodly. Neither in man's nature, "nor in the conflict of races, nor in the clash of nations, nor in the rancor of creeds," is the struggle for existence a valid law, he insisted.

His dietary advice echoes that of the Seventh-day Adventist leader, Ellen White: "When the science of medicine reaches perfection, treatment will be given by foods, aliments, fragrant fruits, vegetables, and by various waters, hot and cold."

Abdul-Baha taught that the greatest values in life are knowledge of God, love of God, and goodwill towards mankind. He cited the example of Galen, the non-Christian physician who praised the Christians because of their good actions, which he could see were based on those three greatest values.

The great variability among humans Abdul-Baha felt was an asset, since it could lead to remarkable creativity. But when this diversity is not guided by the three greatest values, it can lead to selfishness, hatred, warfare, and chaos. Thus, he taught, humanity needs a unifying force which will keep man loyal to his entire species, and not just to his family, tribe, or nation. The three greatest values keep human divisiveness from becoming suicidal, unifying the species into the whole contemplated by God.

Abdul-Baha differentiated between valid and invalid visions from God. Certain imaginary visions are merely the hallucinations of one person, and lead nowhere. Genuine visions which are divinely inspired lead to fruitful results, and to that extent are verifiable by others.

When asked why Baha-u-llah was said to have 24 holy souls supporting him, compared to the usual 12 (Jacob had 12 sons; Moses had 12
tribes; Christ had 12 disciples; Mohammed had 12 Imams), Abdul-Baha replied that the Everlasting Kingdom of Love and Peace is arriving, the time
toward which all creation points. He referred to the 24 elders mentioned in
Revelation 4:4.

In illustrating the era of Great Peace described in Isaiah 11:6, when
the wolf will dwell with the lamb, Abdul-Baha said that the Baha'i faith was
achieving precisely this peace, for in it the Moslem can dwell with the Jew,
the Christian with the Hindu, and the Buddhist with the Parsee.

He believed that the 1335 days referred to in the last two verses of
the book of Daniel were to be computed from Mohammed's hegira in the
year 622. Adding the two figures he prophesied that by 1957 a Lesser Peace
would be achieved on earth. The Most Great Peace spoken of by Baha-u-llah
would continue to evade man as long as he put his trust in armaments rather
than in God.

Shortly before his death, Abdul-Baha warned world leaders that if
they continued to ignore God's laws, they would be deprived of His gifts,
and chaos would ensue. He quoted his father: "The hour is approaching
when its flame will devour the cities, when the Tongue of Grandeur will
proclaim: 'The Kingdom is God's, the Almighty, the All-Praised!' "

By his death in 1921 Abdul-Baha had united virtually all Baha'is
under his leadership. Like his father, he was gifted with extraordinary
charm and charisma. Even at the age of 76 he made converts by his toler-
ance, kindness, and diplomacy. He loved to gather at his table representatives of all races, nations, and creeds, exemplifying in his life what he taught
in his theology.

In 1918, when Haifa fell into British hands, he was made a knight of
the British empire, for his work for peace, for relief of famine, and for providing leadership for his people. The man born in 1844, the night of the
Bab's revelation, had worked unceasingly to bring into reality the Bab's
vision of God's Kingdom on earth.

The usual discord prevailed in selecting a successor to Abdul-Baha,
whose will specified that in the absence of any sons, his grandson Shoghi
Effendi was to succeed him. The trouble was that Baha-u-llah's will had
specified that the successor to Abdul-Baha was to be his brother, Mirza
Muhammed Ali. Mirza, though still alive, did little to contest the designation of Shoghi Effendi as Guardian of the Faith. So effectively had Abdul-
Baha unified the majority of Baha'is into his cause that Mirza's followers
were few by now.

The problem Shoghi Effendi faced was an old one, an inner family
quarrel. He was 25, a student at Balliol College, Oxford, when he became
Guardian of the Faith. This was a new undefined title, and the quarrel arose
over what it meant. Shoghi Effendi interpreted it to mean that, to keep the
faith pure, he had an absolute mandate to rule on all Baha'i matters. Loyal

Baha'is, including family members, could be excommunicated if they failed to follow his rulings. Eventually all the remaining members of Abdul-Baha's family were excommunicated for challenging Shoghi Effendi's authority. The list of purged was then extended to include Shoghi Effendi's parents, brothers, and sisters. The abstract love of God once again seemed so much more simple to practice than the practical love of man.

By now the Baha'i faith was mature enough to have dissenters within the cause. Baha'is who wrote books attacking Shoghi Effendi included Mirza Ahmad Sohrab, Mirza Subhi, and Ayati (also called Avareh). Most protests centered around the fact that Shoghi Effendi was too autocratic.

Shoghi Effendi felt that his chief role, besides keeping the faith pure, was to organize the structure of the movement from the local assembly up to the International House of Justice. A local Baha'i assembly can consist of nine or more members. They are linked together into national organizations, with a governing body of nine members elected by the local assemblies. National assemblies were set up in England, India, and Germany in 1923, Egypt in 1924, United States in 1925, Iraq in 1931, and Australia and Iran in 1934. By now there are national assemblies in over sixty nations.

An interesting feature is that representatives to Baha'i assemblies are unanswerable to those who elected them. The reason for this is that their guiding principles are those given by Baha-u-llah (as interpreted by the Guardian of the Faith), and thus grass-roots participation in formulation of policy is discouraged. Shoghi Effendi, whose blood lines ran back to both the Bab and Baha-u-llah, felt that the Guardian was God's vicar, and that no one should oppose God. He insisted that his rule was not autocratic, however, since upon "the international elected representatives of the followers of Baha-u-llah has been conferred the exclusive right of legislating on matters not expressly revealed in the Baha'i writings."

"We stand on the threshold of an age whose convulsions proclaim alike the death-pangs of the old order and the birth-pangs of the new," Shoghi Effendi said. He called his age the Iron Age, a formative period for developing the institutions to lead mankind into the long-awaited Golden Age, "the establishment of a world civilization and the formal inauguration of the Kingdom of the Father upon earth as promised by Jesus Christ Himself."

Ultimately Baha'i spiritual assemblies are expected to evolve into the Houses of Justice described by Baha-u-llah. Representatives from national assemblies are elected to serve on the International Spiritual Assembly. In 1929 Shoghi Effendi called for a world community of nations with the power to outlaw war, and for a world parliament with representatives elected from all nations. World law and order would be achieved under the spiritual guidance of Baha-u-llah and the other major world religious prophets. A world executive body, backed up by an international military force, would enforce the decisions of the world parliament. In recent years Baha'is have submitted their proposal for a world parliament to the United

Nations. The proposal suggests means for outlawing war and sets up a supreme tribunal to adjudicate international disputes.

The Baha'i faith employs much number symbolism, the two key numbers being nine and nineteen. A Baha'i temple has many of these symbolic features built into it. The Wilmette Temple, for example, has a circle of eighteen steps (representing the Letters of the Living) surrounding the exterior. The steps lead to a door, which stands for the Bab. It is called "The Temple of Light," since it symbolically lets in light from all sides. Dean Rexford Newcomb of the University of Illinois College of Fine and Applied Arts said of it: "This Temple of Light opens upon the terrain of human experience nine great doorways which beckon men and women from every race and clime, of every faith and conviction, to enter here into a recognition of that kinship and brotherhood without which the modern world will be able to make little further progress."

Horace Holley, an American who died in 1960, was of great assistance to Shoghi Effendi. Holley drew up the model for Baha'i national assemblies, and served as secretary of the United States national assembly from 1924 until 1955. He wrote many articles and pamphlets and edited the yearbook *Baha'i World* as well as the collection entitled *Baha'i Scriptures*.

In 1937 Shoghi Effendi married a Canadian Baha'i, Mary Maxwell. Mary was a daughter of May Bolles, a Canadian who had visited Abdul-Baha in Acre in 1898 and had become an enthusiastic Baha'i.

At his death in 1957 Shoghi Effendi could not say that the Lesser Peace predicted by that year by Abdul-Baha had come to pass. On the contrary, one of his final statements was the familiar warning that because world leaders refused to follow God's teachings, it seemed as if it would take a final major world catastrophe to drive home once and for all the inevitable need for the people of the world to form themselves into a common family under God the Father. A revolution in modern transportation, technology, and warfare had made all the world one community, he felt. To endure, this must be an orderly community under God.

The death of Shoghi Effendi again raised problems of succession, for he had no children and left no will designating a successor. Confused, church leaders chose nine Hands, persons to serve as an executive committee but with no power to interpret scripture. The Hands based their authority on the will of Baha-u-llah, which stated that the Universal House of Justice would ultimately be the head of the Baha'i faith.

One Hand, however, demurred. Charles Mason Remey, an American architect, proclaimed himself to be the new Guardian of the Faith, on the ground that Shoghi Effendi had appointed him president of the first International Baha'i Council, an organization that Shoghi Effendi had expected to evolve into the Universal House of Justice. Lawsuits, ultimately lost by Remey, ensued between him and the orthodox Baha'is. Excommunicated, Remey died at the age of 99 in Florence, Italy, in 1974. The Hands continue to function as the highest authority in the Baha'i faith.

Baha'is feel that such fundamental changes have occurred in the modern world that old ethical systems and antiquated religious practices are no longer relevant. Just as scientific laws are universal, so, they argue, are the spiritual insights of the Bab and Baha-u-llah. "World problems are without precedent," but "no vital results are now forthcoming from the customs and institutions of the past." The spiritual insights of the age-old prophets have been twisted by human misinterpretation. "The essential realities which the prophets labored so hard to establish in human hearts and minds have now well nigh vanished."

Baha'is argue that Baha-u-llah has restored the love of Christ in its original form as the great antidote to modern problems. Abdul-Baha declared that it was the spread of Christianity into Europe and Asia that helped the peoples of the world realize that the Jews are in a special sense God's chosen people. "Through the supreme power of the Word of God," Abdul-Baha wrote, "Christ united most of the nations of the east and the west. He led them beneath the overshadowing tent of the oneness of humanity. Through His spirit of conciliation the Roman, Greek, Chaldean, and Egyptian were blended in a composite civilization. This wonderful power and extraordinary efficacy of the Word prove conclusively the validity of His Holiness Christ."

As an example of how Baha'is apply their doctrine of progressive revelation to solve modern problems, Abdul-Baha gave his approach to the age-long controversies over the Holy Land. He pointed out that Christians accept the chief Jewish prophet, Moses, and that Moslems accept both Moses and Jesus. "Could it be said that the acceptance of Moses by the Christians and Moslems has been detrimental to those people?" he asked. "On the contrary," he replies, "it has been beneficial to them, proving that they have been fair-minded and just. What harm could result to the Jewish people then if they in return should accept His Holiness Christ and acknowledge the validity of the prophethood of his Holiness Mohammed? By this acceptance and praiseworthy attitude the enmity and hatred which have afflicted mankind so many centuries would be dispelled, fanaticism and bloodshed pass away, and the world be blessed by unity and agreement. Then there will be no more warfare and bloodshed in the Promised Land." Antiquated religious codes will only lead to further strife, he believed. "If we remain fettered by human dogmas, day by day mankind will be degraded, warfare and strife will increase, and satanic forces converge toward the destruction of the human race."

To those who considered Baha'i goals too idealistic, Abdul-Baha pointed out that modern Baha'is generally live in peace and fellowship, despite their differences in race, creed, and national background. Humanity, he said, is like a bird with two wings, one male and one female. If either wing is too weak or too strong, the bird's flight is impaired. Women in positions of authority, he felt, would hasten the replacement of the use of violence as a problem solver with compassion and understanding.

Given the nature of modern weapons, peace is an absolute necessity for the survival of mankind. What once might have been thought of as a Utopian dream has become a hard-headed reality if our species is to endure.

Although there are only several million Baha'is in the world today, they have a disproportionate influence because their appeal is primarily to thoughtful persons. Thus although there may be no more than 50,000 Baha'is in modern Iran, many of them are wealthy factory owners, high government officials, or members of professions like doctors, lawyers, and teachers. In most countries, including the United States, many black people have joined this faith because of its stress on racial brotherhood.

Even adverse critics concede that the Baha'i movement has led to much human progress. Baha'is in many countries have been leaders in modern medicine and education. Despite the occasional quarrels at high levels, Baha'is have been notable for living together with a remarkable spirit of love surrounding them. Their reluctance to propagate their faith openly helps account for their relatively few numbers. Their stress on faith in God, love of mankind, and world peace makes them a world religion that will continue to attract followers as humanity seeks to find a way to survive its own cunning of destructive ingenuity.

George Townshend, the one-time Canon of St. Patrick's Cathedral in Dublin, says: "The Baha'i message has kindled once more on earth the ancient fire of faith that Jesus kindled long ago, the fire of spontaneous love for God and man, a love that changes all life. To them who have recognized Christ's voice again in this age has been given in renewed freshness and beauty the vision of the Kingdom of God as Jesus and the Book of Revelation gave it."

# 10

## *The Impact of 1844 upon the Present*

After looking at a number of significant religious events of 1844 and their subsequent development, one asks what can be learned for application in the present world. Valuable lessons come out of each specific event.

William Miller is a prime example of a godly man who tried to impress his interpretations of the Bible upon a world that was looking for salvation. Whenever one knows the Bible well, as he did, and is sufficiently obdurate in holding to one's sense of inspiration, one will find followers. To try to predict the precise date of Christ's second coming, however, is almost sure to set up frustrating expectations.

Nevertheless much good came out of Miller's life. His stress upon the Bible led to great moral and spiritual growth among his contemporaries. Ellen White and other adventist leaders founded a movement that has borne much good fruit. Schools, colleges, medical institutions, and healthful dietary programs are among the benefits to society that grew out of the adventist movement that centered on 1844.

Joseph Smith, like William Miller, deplored the chaos produced by hundreds of competing denominations, each one professing to be the one true road to God. Ironically, Smith ended up like Ellen White — the prophet of another such religious organization.

Persons who deplore the babel of multifold religious groups each asserting its own type of superior spiritual insight frequently end up adding one more group to the list. A sociologist of religion, like Peter Berger, can explain this on the basis of individual and group needs for in-group superiority. Virtually all religion contains some amount of this invidious emotion.

One cannot ignore the many positive contributions made by Joseph Smith's followers. In a society coming apart at the seams with alcoholism and other drug abuse, crime and delinquency, broken families, and other materialistic decadence, the Mormons are a strong island of decency and morality. As one college counselor said, "I can always spot a Mormon. His or her outward attractiveness radiates an inner peace and strength which has to be envied and admired."

Margaret Fuller would like to be alive today. Her fervent protest for treating women with dignity and justice grew into a humane concern for all the underprivileged and oppressed. Recent gains in civil liberties by women and minority groups would gladden her heart. Her insistence that fair treatment to all must be grounded upon an economic base sounds surprisingly modern. She will continue to inspire all those who feel that every human being, as a child of God, deserves to be treated with respect and esteem. Computers, created by man, can never rival the computers' creator, who was created by God.

Samuel F. B. Morse has been called "the American Leonardo." He was so versatile that when his milieu found no room for a gifted portrait painter, he could adapt his creativity into the form preferred by his society and produce one of the most important scientific inventions of the century. Gifted though he was, Morse said that he could do nothing without God's help. One admires his basic humility just as one is repelled at the bigoted application of his religious values to the consideration of fellow Americans who were Catholic or black. Morse was misled by what he considered to be a literal interpretation of the Bible. Countless mischief has been done by those who staunchly insist that their literal interpretations of scripture are God's only true word. Unless love of man accompanies love of God, religion will continue to produce deaths in Ireland, the Holy Land, and Iran, among other places. When Jesus was asked which commandment was greatest of all, he cited two — love of God and love of one's neighbor.

When John Henry Newman made the agonizing switch from the Anglican Church to the Roman Catholic Church, he did it because he felt the change was necessary in order to save his soul. Few members of his new church would today agree with such a radical statement. Although Newman had a parochial religious perspective, he had a painfully active conscience and a thoroughly logical brain. His *Apologia* is so soul-searching that a reader of any religious persuasion can benefit from reading it. Moreover, despite the special pleading of his book on the development of church doctrine, that book contains a number of tests of religious validation that are both psychologically penetrating and universally applicable. Newman's synthesis of the aristocratic and democratic parameters of religion are far from being outdated in the modern world.

In many ways, Nokolai Gogol was a pathetic human being. Ridiculed for his bizarre physical appearance, he developed a deep inferiority complex which exhibited itself in overweening vanity and egotism. He scarcely ever had a close friend, and he never experienced a love relationship. These things should be impossible for a person who is truly deeply immersed in fellowship with God, as Gogol alleged he was. The person who says he loves God but hates his brother is a liar, John says in his first epistle. Religious fanaticism is always a danger in a society, and one of its most recognizable features is its insistence that one can treat one's fellow humans in a sub-human fashion even while worshipping the supernatural God who created all things.

Gogol nevertheless made some important contributions. His unerring wit unmasks ubiquitous governmental fraud and deceit. His deep democratic sympathies, revealed in his very literary style and language, undercut tyranny and bullying wherever they are practiced. And his unconscious appreciation of the dignified spirit of man will always be a timely warning in a world of overpopulation, mechanization, and materialistic standards of excellence.

One wonders why the Taiping Rebellion is so little known to the western world. Chinese historical sources on the nineteenth century were long closed to the West, and Red China has had little interest in giving publicity to a rebellion based upon non-Chinese religious values. But several important messages grow out of a study of the movement.

It was to be expected that the form of Christianity that was spread by Hung Hsiu-ch'üan would be a hybrid of Christian and native Chinese elements. Christianity, like any great religion, takes different forms in different cultures. Unless some roots are native to the culture, the result will be a transplant which dies in the foreign soil.

Yet the attempted hybrid was strange indeed. Here was one Chinese man's version of an anglicized version of a Semitic religious movement. Such inaccuracies, a product of translation and cross-cultural problems, occur as calling the Holy Spirit "Holy God's Wind." Little wonder that the transplant never survived the shock.

Moreover, Hung's exposure to Christianity was one that put virtually the whole emphasis upon saving the soul. The social gospel was ignored, and thus Hung's doctrine was too weak to prevent eventual mistreatment and even torture and killing of opponents — all in the name of conversion to Christianity. This, of course, has happened in places other than China. It is likely to happen whenever a religious movement loses sight of the second dimension — that love of man must inevitably proceed out of love of God.

The Taiping Rebellion failed when Hung and his followers became so absorbed in their material comforts at the Heavenly Palace in Nanking that they forgot to pursue their original goal of building Christ's Kingdom throughout China. Multiple wives and concubines, personal envy, and civil strife made the Taipings too weak to overthrow the Manchu dynasty.

The error made by the Christian West in helping defeat the Taipings can be attributed to ignorance and greed. Western representatives, who were either government officials or businessmen, felt that it was either more expedient or more profitable to put down the Taipings and maintain a weak Manchu government that could easily be manipulated. Christianity thus lost its golden opportunity for what might now be a billion converts.

Of all the interesting religious developments of the year 1844, one of the most intriguing was the beginning of the Baha'i world faith. Starting as a reform of a branch of Shiite Islam, this movement grew into one of the few truly worldwide religions. By accepting the major prophets of the chief world religions, it constitutes a synthesis that is pregnant with possibilities in a world which must recognize itself as a global community if mankind is to survive the threat of nuclear holocaust. A world that fails to codify and enforce world law will probably die as its lawlessness seizes the twin demons of terrorism and nuclear destruction. Fortunately for Baha'i, it appeared on the world scene with a worldwide scope of scriptural and prophetic acceptance. Unlike most religions, it is willing to say, "Yes, yes" where usually the reaction to other faiths is "No, no."

Baha'i has had its share of internal quarrels and splits, the kind that occur in all religious movements. It is so much easier to say "Love thy neighbor" than it is to love one's neighbor. Like all religions, Baha'i has its special preferences and dislikes, which become more apparent as one grows more familiar with the details of its religious position. Nevertheless, because of its synthesis of Jewish, Christian, Moslem, and other elements, Baha'i will continue to warrant careful study as the concept of world community becomes ever more a survival necessity.

A few overall considerations remain. Was 1844 in some special sense truly a "year of the Lord?" One can find significant religious developments in almost every year. Perhaps something setting 1844 apart was the fact that in this case these developments are still bearing fruit a century and a half later.

Are there times when God, sensing human stupidity and misguided knowledge that can prove devastating, reveals Himself to a world needing salvation? Carl Jung postulated a theory of synchronicity, stating that acausal but meaningful coincidences do occur. He tied this theory in with his explanation of the process of mental and spiritual health known as individuation, and united both concepts in his elucidation of the collective unconscious, a vast reservoir of racial memory grounded in man's origin in the spirit of God. Further work needs to be done before Jung's concept can gain universal acceptance.

Another question arises. Granted the demonstrable socially desirable consequences of many of the religious movements of 1844, what happens when they interface with one another? Alas, the usual result is the typical religious ethnocentricity — my view is orthodoxy, your view is heresy. Relatively little sophistication has taken place through the years in the field of religious encounter. Few persons have the love of Ruth for Naomi: "Thy people will be my people, and thy God my God." We need to explore the whole matter of religious interface. How can we live with persons of another religious outlook so as to love them, respect them and their right to their own religious expression, and still not give up our own deep faith in God and Christ? Is there even some way that by loving and respecting them we more truly worship the God who made both of us?

A final necessity is a Spiritual Bill of Rights. Just as we have laboriously hammered out bills of rights concerning political activity, property and legal rights, and civil liberties, so we are overdue for postulating a Spiritual Bill of Rights, recognizing each person's right to conceive of God and worship Him in his own way, as long as other kinds of rights are not violated in the process.

The new bill of rights should have as its goal the intensification of humans' love for God and fellow humans. Basic to its provisions would be respect for the spiritual dignity and sanctity of every human personality as a child of God. Statements of rights should be broad enough to permit amendments to be added as the need arises. The religious movements of 1844 will not be in vain if they can deepen all of us in our faith in God and our love of Him and of our fellow human beings.

# Suggested Readings

## Chapter 1

Bode, Carl, ed. *American Life in the 1840's*. New York: Doubleday & Company, 1967. Panorama of the daily life of the average citizen.

Clark, Jerome L. *1844*. 3 volumes. Nashville: Southern Publishing Association, 1968. Comprehensive study of religious, social, and political events centered on 1844.

Cross, Whitney R. *The Burned-Over District*. Ithaca: Cornell University Press, 1950. History of religious enthusiasm in western New York State from 1800 to 1850.

Harrison, John F. C. *The Second Coming: Popular Millenarianism, 1780–1850*. New Brunswick: Rutgers University Press, 1979. Study relating millennial thinking to challenge to authority in many fields.

Lindsey, Hal. *The Late Great Planet Earth*. Grand Rapids: Zondervan Publishing House, 1970. Best-seller that uses Bible prophecies to predict Christ's imminent return.

Nye, Russel Blaine. *Society and Culture in America, 1830–1860*. New York: Harper & Row, 1974. Well-documented study of the development of key American ideas and institutions.

Tuveson, Ernest C. *Redeemer Nation: The Idea of America's Millennial Role*. Chicago: University of Chicago Press, 1968. Broad survey of millennialism in America.

Tyler, Alice Felt. *Freedom's Ferment: Phases of American Social History to 1860*. Minneapolis: University of Minnesota Press, 1944. Comprehensive picture of American reform movements of the period.

## Chapter 2

Algermissen, Konrad. *Christian Sects*. New York: Hawthorn Books, 1962. Useful compilation on minor sects, but not always objective.

Bliss, Sylvester. *Memoirs of William Miller*. Boston: Joshua Himes, 1853. Reminiscences of highlights in the life of the adventist leader.

Clark, Jerome L. *1844*. Volume I: Religious Movements. Nashville: Southern Publishing Association, 1968. Study of the year from a Seventh-day Adventist viewpoint.

Damsteegt, P. Gerard. *Foundations of the Seventh-day Adventist Message and Mission*. Grand Rapids: Wm. B. Eerdmans Publishing Company, 1977. Comprehensive summary of major Seventh-day Adventist doctrines.

251

Kirban, Salem. *Guide to Survival*. Wheaton: Tyndale House Publishers, 1968. Specific predictions about the coming end of the world, based upon Bible prophecy.

Lindsey, Hal. *There's a New World Coming*. Santa Ana: Vision House Publishers, 1973. Detailed picture of the imminent millennium that comes after the destruction of the present world.

Nichol, Francis D. *The Midnight Cry*. Washington, D.C.: Review and Herald Publishing Association, 1944. Interesting history of the Seventh-day Adventist movement.

White, James. *Sketches of the Christian Life & Public Labors of William Miller*. New York: AMS Press, 1970. Early biography by another adventist leader.

## Chapter 3

Briggs, Kenneth A. "Mormon Church at 150: Thriving on Traditionalism," *The New York Times*, March 30, 1980, Section 1, pp. 1 ff. Objective account of some of the tensions in modern Mormonism.

Brodie, Fawn M. *No Man Knows My History: The Life of Joseph Smith*. New York: Knopf, 1971. Interesting account, well documented, with valuable appendices, bibliography, and index.

Clark, Jerome L. *1844*. Volume I. Religious Movements. Nashville: Southern Publishing Association, 1968. Study of the year from a Seventh-day Adventist viewpoint.

Crowther, Duane S. *Prophecy — Key to the Future*. Salt Lake City: Bookcraft, 1962. Mormon prophecy, particularly as it relates to the coming end of the world.

Hill, Donna. *Joseph Smith: The First Mormon*. New York: Doubleday & Company, 1977. Readable, comprehensive, and objective biography.

Mullen, Robert. *The Latter-day Saints: The Mormons Yesterday and Today*. New York: Doubleday & Company, 1966. Mormon history, particularly good on recent developments.

Richards, LeGrand. *A Marvelous Work and a Wonder*. Salt Lake City: Deseret Book Company, 1970. Clear presentation of Mormon doctrine.

Stegner, Wallace. *The Gathering of Zion*. New York: McGraw-Hill, 1964. Detailed description of the early Mormon years.

## Chapter 4

Blanchard, Paula. *Margaret Fuller: From Transcendentalism to Revolution*. New York: Delacorte Press, 1978. Biography especially valuable for showing Fuller's relationship to Emerson.

Brooks, Van Wyck. *The Flowering of New England, 1815–1865*. New York: World Publishing Company, 1946. Rich picture of Fuller's milieu.

Brown, Arthur W. *Margaret Fuller*. New York: Twayne Publishers, 1964. Biography that traces the growth of Fuller's ideas and social consciousness.

Chevigny, Bell Gale. *The Woman and the Myth: Margaret Fuller's Life and Writings*. New York: The Feminist Press, 1976. Biography stressing Fuller's role as a feminist leader.

Chipperfield, Faith. *In Quest of Love*. New York: Coward-McCann, 1957. Interesting biography, with bibliography and index.

Deiss, Joseph Jay. *The Roman Years of Margaret Fuller.* New York: Thomas Y. Crowell Company, 1969. Full account of Fuller's work with the Italian republic.

Stern, Madeleine B. *The Life of Margaret Fuller.* New York: Haskell House, 1968. Comprehensive and objective biography.

Wade, Mason. *Margaret Fuller.* New York: The Viking Press, 1940. Sympathetic biography, with a useful summary by Fuller of her *Woman in the 19th Century.*

## Chapter 5

Billington, Ray Allen. *The Protestant Crusade, 1800–1860: A Study of the Origins of American Nativism.* New York: Times Books, 1976. Excellent account of the background of anti-Catholic thought.

Larkin, Oliver. *Samuel F. B. Morse and American Democratic Art.* Boston: Little, Brown & Company, 1954. Morse as an artist, showing his contribution to a growing movement.

Mabee, Carleton. *The American Leonardo: The Life of Samuel F. B. Morse.* New York: Knopf, 1957. Comprehensive, readable, and objective biography.

*Morse Exhibition of Arts and Science.* New York: National Academy of Design, 1950. Tribute to Morse, with illustrations of his paintings, pictures of his inventions, and a brief account of his work as an artist and inventor.

Nye, Russel Blaine. *Society and Culture in America, 1830–1860.* New York: Harper & Row, 1974. Well-documented study of the development of key American ideas and institutions.

Prime, Samuel I. *The Life of Samuel F. B. Morse.* New York: Arno Press, 1974. Reprint of D. Appleton 1875 edition. Authentic biography by one of Morse's friends.

*Samuel F. B. Morse: His Letters and Journals.* 2 volumes. Edited by Edward Lind Morse. New York: Kraus, 1972. Reprint of Houghton Mifflin 1914 edition. Valuable primary-source material, edited by Morse's son.

Thompson, Robert L. *Wiring a Continent.* Princeton: Princeton University Press, 1947. History of the American telegraph industry up to 1866.

## Chapter 6

Campbell, William D. *Approaching the Venture of Faith.* Washington, D.C.: Catholic University of America, 1964. Dissertation studying Newman's Anglican period.

Coulson, John. *Newman and the Common Tradition.* Oxford: Clarendon Press, 1970. Careful study of Newman's views of the role of the laity in church affairs.

Dessain, Charles S. *John Henry Newman.* London: Thomas Nelson, 1966. Readable biography which stresses Newman's contribution to Catholicism.

Lapati, Americo D. *John Henry Newman.* New York: Twayne Publishers, 1972. Study particularly useful on the Oxford Movement and Newman's early career.

Moody, John. *John Henry Newman.* New York: Sheed and Ward, 1945. Biography largely valuable for Newman's work within the Roman Catholic Church.

Newman, John Henry. *Apologia Pro Vita Sua.* Edited by David J. DeLaura. New York: W. W. Norton & Company, 1968. Good recent edition, with notes, criticism, and background material.

Shane, Leslie. *Studies in Sublime Failure.* Freeport, N.Y.: Book for Libraries Press,

1970. Reprint of 1932 edition published by Ernest Benn. Brief but fair appraisal of Newman's struggles within the Anglican and the Roman Catholic Churches.

Walgrave, Jan Hendrik. *Newman the Theologian.* Translated from the French by A. V. Littledale. New York: Sheed and Ward, 1960. Detailed analysis of the development of Newman's theological position.


## Chapter 7

Erlich, Victor. *Gogol.* New Haven: Yale University Press, 1969. Biography chiefly valuable in tracing Gogol's early development.

Gogol, Nikolai. *Selected Passages from Correspondence with Friends.* Nashville: Vanderbilt University Press, 1969. Personal account revealing Gogol's tortuous spiritual struggle.

Karlinsky, Simon. *The Sexual Labyrinth of Nikolai Gogol.* Cambridge: Harvard University Press, 1976. Interpretation of Gogol as a homosexual, based largely on circumstantial evidence.

Lavrin, Janko. *Nikolai Gogol: A Centenary Survey.* New York: Macmillan, 1952. Brief readable biography covering the essential facts.

Magarshack, David. *Gogol: A Life.* New York: The Grove Press, 1957. Objective and comprehensive biography.

Mirsky, D. M. *A History of Russian Literature.* New York: Knopf, 1949. Useful background material on Gogol and his period.

Nabokov, Vladimir. *Nikolai Gogol.* Norfolk, Conn.: New Directions, 1961. Impressionistic account, amusing and entertaining, but not always objective.

Troyat, Henri. *Divided Soul: The Life of Gogol.* Translated from the French by Nancy Amphoux. New York: Doubleday & Company, 1973. Interesting psychological study of the complexities of Gogol's personality.


## Chapter 8

Anderson, Flavia. *The Rebel Emperor.* New York: Doubleday & Company, 1959. Interesting biography of Hung Hsiu-chüan.

Boardman, Eugene P. *Christian Influence upon the Ideology of the Taiping Rebellion, 1851–1864.* Madison: University of Wisconsin Press, 1952. Good study of the Christian and non-Christian elements of Taiping ideology.

Cheng, James C. *Chinese Sources for the Taiping Rebellion, 1850–1864.* Oxford: Oxford University Press, 1963. Reprint of edition by Hong Kong University Press. Brief but valuable history based on Chinese sources.

Gregory, John S. *Great Britain and the Taipings.* London: Routledge & Kegan Paul, 1969. Careful study which describes British policy as vacillating and ill-informed rather than deliberately hostile.

Jen Yu-wen. *The Taiping Revolutionary Movement.* New Haven: Yale University Press, 1973. Exhaustive history covering virtually every facet.

Michael, Franz. *The Taiping Rebellion.* Seattle: University of Washington Press, 1966. Analytical study showing the comprehensiveness of the revolution.

Shih, Vincent Y. C. *The Taiping Ideology: Its Sources, Interpretations, and Influences.* Seattle: University of Washington Press, 1967. Study of the ideological background that produced the Taiping movement.

Teng, Ssu-yu. *The Taiping Rebellion and the Western Powers.* Oxford: Clarendon Press, 1971. Comprehensive survey based on many Chinese sources.

## Chapter 9

Abdul-Baha. *Some Answered Questions*. Translated from the Persian by Laura Clifford Barney. Wilmette: Baha'i Publishing Trust, 1957. Baha'i doctrine applied to many current social and religious issues.

Algar, Hamid. *Religion and State in Iran, 1785–1906*. Berkeley: University of California Press, 1969. Scholarly study of the relationship between church and state in Iran.

*Baha'i World Faith*. Selected Writings of Baha-u-llah and Abdul-Baha. Wilmette: Baha'i Publishing Trust, 1971. Useful compilation of some of the major Baha'i statements.

Baha-u-llah. *The Book of Certitude*. Translated from the Persian by Shoghi Effendi. Wilmette: Baha'i Publishing Committee, 1931. Baha'i prophecy, with useful glossary, notes, and index.

Effendi, Shoghi. *God Passes By*. Wilmette: Baha'i Publishing Trust, 1965. History and application of Baha'i doctrine, from the Guardian of the Faith.

Esslemont, John E. *Baha-u-llah and the New Era*. Wilmette: Baha'i Publishing Committee, 1948. Comprehensive and readable description of the Baha'i faith, with index.

Miller, William McElwee. *What is the Baha'i Faith?* Grand Rapids: Wm. E. Eerdmans Publishing Company, 1977. Critical analysis of basic Baha'i concepts by a Christian missionary who served 43 years in Iran.

Townshend, George. *Christ and Baha-u-llah*. London: George Ronald, 1957. Assertion by the former Canon of St. Patrick's Cathedral, Dublin, that Christ's Kingdom has been revealed through Baha-u-llah.

## Chapter 10

Abdul-Baha. *Some Answered Questions*. Translated from the Persian by Laura Clifford Barney. Wilmette: Baha'i Publishing Trust, 1957. Baha'i doctrine applied to many current social and religious issues.

Berger, Peter L. *The Heretical Imperative: Contemporary Possibilities of Religious Affirmation*. New York: Doubleday & Company, 1979. Thoughtful presentation of religion as an answer to the failures of modernity.

Crowther, Duane S. *Prophecy— Key to the Future*. Salt Lake City: Bookcraft, 1962. Mormon prophecy, particularly as it relates to the coming end of the world.

Jung, Carl G. *Man and His Symbols*. New York: Dell, 1964. Good introduction to Jung's psychology, with discussion of individuation, synchronicity, and the collective unconscious.

Lindsey, Hal. *The 1980's: Countdown to Armageddon*. King of Prussia, Pa.: Westgate Press, 1980. Bible prophecy used to foretell Christ's imminent second coming.

Northrop, F. S. C. *The Meeting of East and West*. New York: Macmillan, 1958. Recommendations for fruitful encounter between the theoretic component of the West and the esthetic component of the East.

Slater, Robert Lawson. *World Religions and World Community*. New York: Columbia University Press, 1963. Study of the problems of interface among the world's leading religions.

White, Ellen G. *The Great Controversy between Christ and Satan*. Phoenix: Inspiration Books, 1967. Seventh-day Adventist prophecy concerning the coming end of the world.

# Index